THE LIFE & TIMES OF AN MK

MISSION CANDIDATE AID SERIES

THE LIFE &
TIMES OF AN
MK

C. John Buffam

William Carey Library
Pasadena, California 91104

William Carey Library
P.O. Box 40129
Pasadena, CA 91104

Printed in the United States of America

Library of Congress Cataloging in Publication Data

Buffam, C. John.
   The life and times of an MK.

   Bibliography: p.
   1. Children of missionaries, I. Title.
BV2094.5. B84   1985   649'.1'0882   84-27482
ISBN 0-87808-198-4

For three special MKs

Anne Bethel, David John, and Sharon Grace

CONTENTS

FOREWORD

The author and I were classmates in seminary. We then became missionaries, he in India, I in Mexico. As a parent of three children born in Mexico, spending their early years among the Mazatec people, educated first in Mexico and then in the United States and now as adults serving the Lord, I identify with John in much of what he has written in *The Life & Times of an MK.* At many points he expresses my own views and the experiences he describes I could document from those of my own family. To me this gives credibility to what he writes, and I am sure he speaks for many more missionary parents. Even more importantly, by quoting liberally from the testimonies of missionary children he lets them speak for themselves.

In my opinion the people who will profit most by reading this book are the people at home in our churches. Many of them have an unrealistic idea of missionaries, either putting them on a pedestal or considering them weirdos. But missionaries are people like themselves, simply serving God in quite diverse and changing environments. Meeting the growing needs common to children everywhere may therefore call for different solutions in the case of MKs.

This book, while not attempting to give all the answers, will introduce the reader to the variety of situations, some relevant factors to be considered, and the range of choices for missionary parents at critical periods in the growth and development of their children. It is not meant to be a missionary thriller, but the person who reads it thoughtfully, thinking of the missionary families he or she knows, ought to be able to pray more intelligently, converse more perceptively, and think about and act toward missionary children more understandingly than otherwise. And that will make both the writing and the reading of this book well worth the effort.

George M. Cowan
President Emeritus
Wycliffe Bible Translators

PREFACE

This study is designed to present an overview of the major phases in the missionary child's life from infancy to adulthood. In addition, the contemporary environment in which he moves and matures is to some extent identified. When in later adolescence the MK in the family homeland is confronted with vital issues and choices, we try to determine how his overseas background fits him for life in today's changing world.

The writer trusts that the volume will find a useful place, as a sort of manual or handbook, in homes of missions-hearted Christians and prospective missionaries, as well as in the missionary home and the parsonage. While the study is popularly oriented, not minutely documented, we've attempted to check the subject matter against an abundance of relevant material. Nevertheless substantial difference of opinion exists on not a few themes discussed and we don't claim to have the last word on these; we can write only what we see or think we see.

Hindsight has resulted in our having early bobbles and blunders in parenting stand out in bold relief. In line with C.S. Lewis's chiding of those "whose imagination far exceeds their obedience," our acknowledgment of ineptness should nip in the bud any illusion that we're super-parents. We'd like to have another time around as parents of young children!

Not that any one of our three adult children was, or is now, wilful or undisciplined. They've had their problems, but we're thankful that each is respectful and articulate. (What a heaven-sent blessing is the resilience of most children to parental lapses!) One daughter is a computer programmer in Boston, a son is a lawyer with an investment company in New York City, and a second daughter and husband are halfway through their third term of missionary service in Thailand.

We've learned, however, that missionaries' children don't blossom naturally into models of saintliness; also that what we as parents don't learn in time *can* hurt us and our offspring. Still, thousands of

older missionary parents would testify to God's faithfulness and to
the joy their children have brought them. Our heavenly Father
wonderfully unmesses the mess and blesses the messer.

Some missionary writing, overly idealistic, fosters misconceptions
regarding missionaries' children. We parents, too, may on occasion
betray ourselves as being similarly pollyannish—until our own
brood begins to express its Adamic stock. (This writer and parent, as
the reader will see, hasn't been entirely delivered from this frailty!)

Be that as it may, there's plenty of gold in these MKs. They don't fit
any stereotype—they break the mold, being as different as
snowflakes—yet certain distinguishable patterns emerge among
them. Accordingly we plan to follow this interesting person through
sunshine and shadow as he matures physically, mentally,
emotionally, spiritually, and socially.

In a chronicle of this nature the MK himself should have a
platform to share his observations—what he prefers, accepts, resists,
fears, and dreams of. We haven't made use of a questionnaire—not
all MKs appreciate being made the object of projects—but about 25
MKs, mostly young adults, have favored us with personal
statements. These quotes should bring a down-to-earth dimension to
the study, though they don't necessarily present our own position.
Personnel of ten major mission boards have reviewed the manuscript
and added their suggestions.

Moreover, we're grateful for permission granted by mission
societies to use certain MK testimonies appearing in their
periodicals. It seems best to keep most of these statements
anonymous with respect to source, but each is indicated by an
asterisk(*). A listing of periodicals proving useful, along with
abbreviations used in the study, are to be found on page 205. Please
note that each paragraph in groupings of testimonies represents a
separate affirmation.

The editorial "we" employed throughout refers to the writer alone,
though not invariably; the study has been a family project, with our
daughter Anne as chief editor. The quiet influence and prayerful
support of my "favorite" wife Eunice have warmed and encouraged
me from the beginning.

C. JOHN BUFFAM

Adamsville, Rhode Island
February 1, 1985

INTRODUCTION

Nowadays only the very, very wise person can make a definitive statement, on either a secular or Christian theme, without being taken to task concerning its complete credibility; some hail it while others assail it. Of course ringing the changes of pros and cons on any concept is salutary so long as argument is carried on considerately in the interest of clarity and truth.

To bring the present enquiry into focus: If one's use of a particular word or phrase offends good manners, it would be puerile to insist on its usage. There are two specific expressions on the carpet at this juncture, both used repeatedly in the study.

The first problem rests with the term *missionary*. We frequently read and hear that every believer is a missionary, whether as a witness for Christ he crosses a street or an ocean. Some missiologists acknowledge the validity of this definition; others prefer or at least accept the limited connotation—one assigned to service across geographic and cultural borders.

Though clearly every born-again person is constituted a *witness* by virtue of his position in Christ, it's been explained that this designation may indicate more what the believer *does* than what he *is*. Consequently "missionary" may be less meaningful when applied to Christians in general than to others with a normal, distinct ministry in foreign lands. So we employ "missionary" in this sense. Nonetheless we insist that "Jerusalem and Judea" and "the ends of the earth" in Acts 1:8 are equally important as fields of witness.

The other expression in the dock is the diminutive *MK*, "missionary kid" or more precisely "missionaries' kid." A highly respected educator who has counseled missionaries and their adult offspring reports that the latter "voiced varying degrees of negative feelings . . . at the manner in which the North American churches supporting their parents treat them as 'MKs' . . . packaged entities presumably typed, classified and catalogued."[1]

Our personal enquiry into the sentiment of missionary children has brought a contrary response. Most of those questioned are college graduates, yet very few evinced more than gentle displeasure at being occasionally called MKs. Two statements only, one by a Harvard student, the other by a missionary lady serving with LAM:

> In my opinion, MK is a badge of honor and I am proud to be different and to have a distinctive title. I would miss it in a study such as yours. I suspect it acquires negative associations when churches treat MKs on furlough as zoo animals or expect super spirituality from them.

> I never minded being called an "MK." On the contrary, I liked it. My sister and I used to call everyone else just "OKs" (ordinary kids)! My mother and father were also MKs, and in their generation they had used "mish kids," but we always thought that sounded kind of silly—MK was somehow more sophisticated or something.

We're not implying that "MK" should replace "missionary child"—a usage that might likewise be construed as stereotypical if applied en masse to the offspring of missionaries; and some adolescents and adults might not relish being called children. But surely no responsible writer on missions would rubberstamp these young people in terms of personal qualities or characteristics. Each is unique, with pluses and minuses.

Our language doesn't have a fully acceptable alternative for "missionary child" that incorporates masculinity and femininity so unobtrusively as "MK" does. Granted, the expression leaves something to be desired, but perhaps "missionary child" suffers even more from negative connotations.

Finally, the term "MK" seems to carry a single concept, having almost lost its double-constituent meaning in missionary circles. The idea of "kid" is all but submerged, not being consciously conveyed when the term is popularly used (the use of "MK girls" is becoming quite common). Its brief, readily understood character is applicable to young and old and doesn't stress the missionary and childhood elements to the repression of adult individuality as "missionary child" seems to do.

1
HIS PARENTS
Dreamers & Doers

"Unless the Lord builds the house, its builders labor in vain" (Psalm 127:1).

MISSIONARY IDEAL

Unclouded skies? Once upon a time there was a youngish missionary couple in a perfect foreign setting. Wonderfully prepared for each other, their union was blessed with several exemplary children. At this point we find their offspring, hungry and expectant, seated animatedly with Mom and Dad around the supper table. All bow quietly and reverently as Dad offers thanksgiving for the Lord's bounty, whereupon each of the children voices the Amen. Then as Mom fills the plates with nourishing food, everyone becomes absorbed in the matter at hand, secure and happy in family unity. Expressing the sentiments of all, the littlest child pours forth with "Oh, oh, isn't this the nicest place! Mommie loves Daddy, an' Daddy loves Mommie, an' everybody loves everybody!"

This euphoric scene depicts a typical missionary family on the field, doesn't it? Not a cloud in the bright, friendly skies. Well, no, it's unrealistic; scratch that fantasy. But it's nice to dwell for a moment on the scene portrayed, such as might be envisioned by a young husband and wife before they reach the field and before the first child arrives. An extract from a newspaper editorial strikes a similar chord:

> If "family" has many verbal definitions, its visual definition is singular. Say the word to many Americans and the response will be the silent summoning up of one vital image: the group Norman Rockwell used to paint gathered around the Thanksgiving table. Today it is still the family of dreams. . . . Those who try to paint the American family today have to work with multiple images and, skill aside, they'll have a hard time erasing that old one.[2]

Divine therapy. Even for missionaries with their feet solidly planted on terra firma there's a rational ring to this blissful scene; it's

1

not entirely dream business. Almost every parent and many MKs recall such times with warm sentiment. The day may have brought its toll of frustration for Dad and Mom, with major problems still unresolved; the children may have displayed annoying attitudes in sibling relationships—yet in these sunset hours, gathered as a family with cheerful spirits, all sense the sweet savor of togetherness. Kipling capsulizes the mood of such moments in the form of a prayer: "Teach us delight in simple things,/And mirth that has no bitter springs."

Precious experiences of this nature, providing a therapy missing from the medical handbook, constitute the heritage of Christians the world over. For missionary families, far removed from their homeland and kinfolk, there's an extra measure of divine refreshing. And for Mom and Dad it's just another evidence of God's seal on their union and His guidance into foreign ministry.

MISSIONARY PARENTS

Charting the course. Sociologists stress that a healthy marital status represents the most vital single element in the development of a good home environment—emotionally stable, relaxed, communicating. As frequently noted by writers, enduring values are more often caught than taught. In this respect, most stateside friends from their casual acquaintance with overseas workers would conclude that with rare exceptions missionary parents are mutually committed. While this evaluation must be qualified, doubtless a creditable majority of parents are securely pledged to each other, though not always effervescent in outward display of affection. (Yet children benefit from seeing their parents share fond embraces; it assures them of unwavering parental love.)

Having prayed together for years, meditated on the Word, studied each other's nature, and worked as a team in and outside the home, most couples learn the gentle art of forgiving and forgetting. They strive to live out their faith in conjugal relationships, building each other up at all times. Despite the rigors of much foreign living—a debilitating climate, unsanitary living conditions, sickness of family members, burden of gospel testimony—shared love and work mature them both in the brasstacks situations of daily life.

Have we overstated things? Certainly some missionary mothers and fathers lack the mellow glow of indepth love for each other. Christian counselors who conduct seminars for missionaries report an incidence of marital conflict; one account terms the problem "conspicuous." Patently the revolutionary impairment of family life in the West hasn't left the missionary community unaffected. Inevitably the children are caught in the crossfire.

The emotional strain that counselors deal with, touching mainly the wife, may not be directly related to incompatibility with her spouse. With clear convictions and keen enthusiasm, she may lack the outlets he enjoys for letting off steam. Usually more sensitive and highly strung than her husband, Mom suffers from depression and frustration, feeling at times more like a totaled woman than the Total Woman.

Possibly no other area of missionary life so dramatically reveals our humanness than practical adjustment to our partners. Each individual introduces his or her weaknesses as well as strengths into a host of daily circumstances, some of which are unknown to couples in developed countries. In a boarding school essay, a CAM student writes: "Missionaries come in all varieties of humanness and constantly defy stereotypes. At times they have problems with themselves and with each other."

The husband who is able to identify patiently with nationals in their spiritual needs may yet fail to maintain openhearted communication with his life partner. Aggressively committed to the work and giving it his time and energy, he returns home as to a refuge from the demands of the day; a "Phantom Father," as one writer terms him—emotionally removed from his wife and children. Meanwhile Mom begins to wonder where she fits into the missionary picture.

Prospective parents. Normally young marrieds on the mission field aren't rank amateurs in the parental role despite not having begun their family. They won't have an Rx for faultless parenting, but the prospect of raising Christ-honoring offspring will have had no small part in their prayer and planning. The low status assigned to child-rearing in the West by the women's movement won't affect this young couple's conviction: rearing a family with its fragile, mysterious bonds adds up to one of life's supreme fulfillments. All this regardless of the fact that parents envision the likelihood of vicariously suffering the recurring hurts of a son or daughter through childhood and then into adulthood.

The attitude of many prospective parents is reflected in this full-circle account (a primer for parents?) from the heart of a young wife anticipating foreign service:

> I really feel the basis of a good parent/child relationship is a good husband/wife relationship. I want to be easy for our kids to talk to. I want to be sure they know we truly love them. I hope we trust our kids with their own decisions after a reasonable age. When we feel they're deciding wrongly, I hope we'll pray and not rant and rave. My husband and I are going to trust God to keep us from jealousy when He chooses someone

else to influence the lives of our children. I didn't like family devotions much in our family, so I hope we can make them enjoyable and meaningful.*

Now a weighty question. How many children should a missionary couple plan to have? In interviews with missions personnel, candidates or appointees enjoy every opportunity to think through such principles of family life. The counselors, aware of the all-importance of this particular aspect of overseas testimony, candidly introduce discussion of details from every angle.

Understandably mission societies are loath to set precise limits on a couple's family. When requested, however, the counselors offer sound, realistic suggestions on this sensitive issue. While there's no "right" or "wrong" number of children for a particular couple, the advisors may intimate that increasing the brood beyond two or three gives rise to special problems. Still, when we think our quiver is full, along comes little Jane or Johnnie! (Interestingly enough, the attrition rate of missionaries with two or more children is about half that of those with no children or one child.)

The interviewers may also suggest that the young couple extend their honeymoon for a year or two so that, without the added responsibility and strain of nurturing an infant, they can give themselves to personal and cultural adjustment and language study.

The accessible father. For years we fathers have been getting it from all sides. The main image granted us by the secular media beyond that of a figurehead—a mere fixture around the house creating more disarray than harmony—is a smudged one, restricted to a cautionary, advisory, or punitive role, as well as that of business manager. But contemporary writers are ushering in a new age of Life with Father centered in the concept "Tenderness is strength." As modern society has successfully delivered women from "life-constricting cultural stereotypes," it's now time to salvage men from their mediocrity. This modified role requires Dad to share equally with Mom in the duties of home and hearth. Presumably the grooming of Dad as a fulltime househusband brings a wonderfully new dimension to himself and family life. (A conflicting view claims that men are swinging too far from healthy masculinity and are becoming "wimpy.")

Grains of truth repose in this haystack of secularist ideas. In relation to our present study, it's true that the inaccessible father— the emotionally distant authority figure—isn't an unknown entity among the Lord's servants overseas. While our western culture still places Mom's hand on the cradle, an increasing number of dads, still a mite uncertain of themselves, are enjoying an expanding function in the home, even venturing on occasion into the kitchen. Especially is such role adaptation evident in the case of younger workers, who customarily are more flexible and uninhibited about sharing home responsibilities than we staid oldsters have been. This new interest and accessibility equip them to nurture sons and daughters with easy grace; diaper duty and dialogue are both undertaken with a good degree of casualness. Besides being personally gratified, these dads become an emotional haven for family members, building bridges of understanding. Hence a family without a stranger!

Here are two statements of MKs concerning an issue reiterated in the study: family before ministry. The first testimony comes from one now in pastoral work in the States, the other from a third-grader in Bangkok, written to her correspondence course adviser:

> I find I have a very compassionate attitude toward my children. They *precede* my ministry to anyone else. They will not be sacrificed for any "ministry." I think it's a misguided view for missionaries to yearn for the salvation of nationals and not consider the primary needs of their children.

> My daddy is a doctor. He helps people every day. He also tells them about Jesus. When he is not helping, he does fun things with me. Lots of times we ride bikes to the river. Sometimes I go to the hospital with him. One time I saw an operation! Wouldn't you like to have a daddy like that? Sorry, you can't have him. He's mine!*

Clearly Dad isn't expendable; his is a crucial role. How he handles spiritual instruction and discipline, for example, assumes enormous potential in the development of a child's self-esteem. Mr. Lockerbie expresses the issue this way:

> What it all comes down to is this: A Christian father encourages his child by the example he sets and the standards he upholds, by the faith he represents and the hope he believes, by the love he shows and the joy he shares. That's what it means to be a father.[3]

In this connection we needn't depreciate the posture of veteran missionary fathers toward their offspring. The fact that so many adult MKs are quick to rise up and call their dads blessed reveals that their durable qualities made a significant impact in the home. These fathers might not have verbalized their true feelings, but their priorities and values indicate a deep sense of responsibility in the wholesome ordering of their households. As a boy the noted missionary, J.G. Paton, used to delight to hear his father pray. He was one of 11 children, all of whom became earnest believers. Let's hear, however, from a PK—Tim Stafford of Campus Crusade:

My father's practice of letting us into his world betrays a much deeper attitude that pervaded my upbringing; my parents respected us. We were never their equals in authority, but we were their equals in our humanness. We were not expected to agree with everything they said or thought politically, theologically, or any other way. In fact, I think they would have been disappointed if we had.[4]

Traditionally fathers haven't found it easy to identify feelingly with their growing sons. Daughters have their mothers as a reassuring model and often likewise their fathers. (Puberty may be the most important time for a good father/daughter relationship, even though Dad feels Jane is becoming a young lady.) Whether or not Dad's problem with his son springs mainly from that meddlesome "masculine mystique," whatever that is precisely, he has only a few years for his inspirational influence to bear fruit before the young chap begins to adopt qualities found in others. A good personal relationship with Dad may well eventuate in the son's assuming his essentials of life. Any father would be thrilled to hear or learn of his son's evaluation of him in tones similar to the MK tributes that follow. But first the verdict of an elementary schoolgirl: "My Daddy's a nice and gentle person with feelings like any other person."

I can never remember wanting to be anything else than what my father was. He adorned the doctrine of God (Titus 2:10).*

It became a firm tradition in our home to go on walks with Father after supper. Even when we were off in the jungle, Father would take us on short hikes along the jungle trails and we'd enjoy seeing the moss and ferns and butterflies and things like that. The person who influenced me most in the direction of Christian service was my dad.*

In the midst of any human weakness, I have seen resolve and happiness in whatever my dad is doing. While keeping a firm commitment to God's Word, he has not let his own American cultural background dictate automatic disapproval toward Japanese culture. In him I've seen a man who recognized what his gifts were—and what they were not—and used them accordingly.*

My dad would have to be the one man of God who has most influenced me toward radical commitment and compassionate service. His daily life before me over the past 22 years has exemplified more Christian principles than any class or book short of the Word. I've seen a godly man, totally dedicated to the person of Christ and committed to specific goals. I've seen tremendous flexibility in different situations and people's needs, and a selflessness I'm just beginning to appreciate.*

High-fidelity mother. Scripture employs the strong figure of the human father to typify God as the compassionate guardian of His own dear children. But to portray Himself in His abiding love, tenderness, and patience, the highest and deepest of human roles is used—that of the mother and motherhood with its vast array of worthy emotions. This imagery is present in such passages as Isaiah 49:15 and 66:13. The hymnwriter expresses it thus: "As with a mother's tender hand,/ He leads his own, His chosen band."

Most MKs would confirm this rosy touch in regard to their mothers, even if the latter on occasion resembles a clucking hen shielding its chicks. The "joyful mother of children" (Psalm 113:9) is their first mentor—not merely or always the 3Rs but, as is true in many missionary homes, the basics of character-building. Indeed the pledges in the wedding ceremony—"In joy or in sorrow, in plenty or in want, in sickness or in health"—are fulfilled generally in reference to children as well as husband. Commitment extends to true sacrifice, minus the histrionics—shall we call it secret service? With a hearing heart, Mom's early nurturing and plantings establish to a large degree the emotional climate of the home. A mother herself, this MK cites her own mother's example as bearing fruit in her home:

Like many other MKs I had an *amah* to look after me, but the evenings belonged to Mother and me. We had times of singing, stories and prayer after supper. I attribute my faith to those times when Mother taught me. Now I cannot put my own children to bed without a time of stories, singing and prayer.*

Of course Mom has her exasperating days when she feels she's on a treadmill going nowhere. In a recent article in WBT's *In Other Words* a missionary mother of four youngsters relates how, after a day in which she was given to much complaining, the family had just read the account of the Israelites' grumbling in the wilderness. One little chappie asked, "Mommie, are you an Israelite?" But Dad saved the day: "Mom is the best Israelite God ever had!"

Without focusing on Mom at Dad's expense, we submit that our heavenly Father endows many women, and perhaps most prospective missionary mothers, with innate ability to bear the strain and stress of a life sometimes reminiscent of the godly wife of Proverbs 31. In addition to the multiple housekeeping tasks involved in maintaining a middle-class home in less-advanced countries, the missionary mother in her Mary/ Martha role is usually available, day or night, "being there" when needed.

In this poignant poem, "A Boy's Mother," James Whitcomb Riley reflects on a child's evaluation of his mother. Two stanzas only of the longer ode:

> My mother she's so good to me—
> Ef I was good as I could be,
> I couldn't be as good—no, sir!—
> Can't any boy be good as her.
>
> She loves me when I'm glad or sad;
> She loves me when I'm good or bad;
> An', what's a funniest thing, she says
> She loves me when she punishes.

Though Mom spends most of her time with the children and in the kitchen where she conducts "divine service three times daily," she is free on occasion to express her own gifts in interaction with local people. Along with her husband she was separated in the Lord for service overseas, her adequacy for the work being recognized by her local church and mission society. While conscious of her scriptural place in the House of God, she avails herself of opportunities to serve others within quite a wide latitude.

Nevertheless, balancing priorities isn't always a simple matter. Mom faces the potent decision as to how to relate sensibly to both home and outside demands and still survive with sanity intact. All the while she must guard against spreading herself too thin. In TEAM's *Horizons* for 5-6/71 a mother relates how she resolved this perplexing problem:

> Well, if there's a dilemma, it's that we're both mothers and missionaries. Yet I believe our most important job as mothers is to fulfill the responsibilities of Christian motherhood. At times it's difficult to justify the hours spent in child care and ordinary housework, but the mother who enjoys a missionary career more than her ministry in the home can face real frustration.... Even receiving the quarterly remittance and letters from prayer supporters, "thanking God for the work you're doing," can become a painful experience. She feels guilty for not doing more. Unless such a mother obtains a solution from the Lord, she will often indulge in self-pity and fall into a defeatist attitude.
>
> I've found these three facts helpful in getting directions: First, I know I'm called and sent by God, and I'm where He wants me to be; second, He has given me to my family to meet their needs; third, He has equipped me for just the work He wants me to do.

So we find the missionary mother engaged with her husband in a single purpose to honor Christ in family life and service. Her home, like Lydia's (Acts 16:14,15), is often a center of Christian testimony where young and old drop in unannounced at any time. (Telephones, of course, are still not plentiful in most Third World lands—and, it may be added, not always missed.) While the youngsters with their friends work up simple diversions, Mom listens to the concerns of visiting local women. Then too, with the younger children in tow, she spends many hours in the homes of local friends.

No missionary mother would classify herself as super, though her husband and children may think so. In and through her ministrations, however, she seeks to maintain a fruitful function in the family witness. Having come to terms with herself, any negative musing about being a trapped housewife fades in warm assurance of contributing as positively to the Lord's testimony as if she were constantly out on the front lines of battle.

Prior to introducing the principal personage of our study, let us quote a stanza of a very special mother's favorite hymn (InterVarsity *Hymns II* #131):

> Within Thy grace so tender
> I would abide.
> Thy perfect peace my portion
> Whate'er betide.
> I kneel, dear Lord, before thee,
> Believingly,
> Thy helpless child would trust
> Though it cannot see.

2
EARLY YEARS
Fuel for the Future

". . . joy that a child is born into the world" (John 16:21).

THE BECOMING OF AN MK

Culture & childbirth. A minimum of ado attends the birth of a baby in most underdeveloped countries. While family bonds are usually tightly knit, the perennial baby boom makes childbirth wellnigh casual. A stir arises among relatives and close friends and the priest with his mantras may be summoned, but soon the little one takes its place matter-of-factly in the household.

Cultural superstitions and uncommon national practices abound in relation to the event. Twins are welcomed in certain lands, deplored in others. The dowry system in India means money in the bank for parents when a son is born, a bankroll when twin sons arrive. In other cultures where bartering for brides generates a brisk business, daughters represent tangible assets. In the Arab world a beautiful child is widely thought to attract the eye of demons.

For the most part, however, babies are loved. The grief that accompanies infant deaths, though often expressed in excessive wailing, may be basically genuine. But death is such a prevailing reality in the poorer strata of society that tragedy isn't news. As we would expect, the educated, upper-class parents in every land, with fewer and healthier children, normally bestow loving care on them. And whatever the social status, committed Christian parents typically seek to observe biblical principles in nurturing; they recognize that parenthood is a divinely granted privilege.

Special delivery. Cultural mores of the host country in regard to childbirth don't rub off on missionary parents; their homespun culture is well entrenched. Each child is welcomed with open arms. Still, the first little one could mark "a breakthrough of truly major proportions," to borrow a Xerox slogan for its minicomputer.

At this time parents feel keenly the absence of adult inlaws, half a world away. "How I wish Mom were here!" sighs the expectant mother. Meanwhile in the homeland "Mom" is concerned lest her daughter not know the ropes in caring for herself before, during, and after delivery. Happy and relieved is she when the wire arrives, "Mother and child doing well." Soon photos of the newcomer are excitedly scrutinized.

For those workers in remote places, facilities for natal care remain inadequate. In view of this, some mothers settle in at a mission hospital a week or two before delivery date; often it's a considerable distance from home. In that congenial "launching pad" they're assured of excellent care by devoted nurses and doctors. Others living in or near an urban center avail themselves of the service of an accredited obstetrician. All three of our brood got their first glimpse of the big wide world in an Indian nursing home in Bombay.

The notable day and hour arrive, when the mother's labor pains take over. The soon-to-be father, longing to share the pain, feels wholly irrelevant as sometimes he's shunted off into the waiting room. But times are changing even in Third World countries: the husband becomes a rapt observer of the delivery process, and may in a few cases be quite closely involved in it.

Then comes one of the supreme happenings of family life—the exquisite joy at the first gasping cry and yawn of one's newborn. Squirming in a parent's arms (if in the father's arms, like an unexploded bomb) with no parts missing, Baby becomes the cynosure of all eyes. The hospital staff enter into the spirit of things, possibly agreeing that the little one resembles Daddy in certain ways and Mommie in other ways. As for the parents, however, it's all there and it's all theirs!

To us with love. As the father kneels by the bedside of his beloved, both experience a fresh oneness by reason of their common life already being manifested in this "good and perfect gift" from above. On the threshold of a new stage in their lives, they express thanksgiving to the Giver and renew their dedication to bring up the newcomer "in the training and instruction of the Lord." They're flooded with a sense of wonder at this priceless gift from Him who with infinite ingenuity fashioned, guarded, and nurtured the tiny life in its own secret nook until that moment. One missionary mother, forgivably going beyond the context of Philippians 2:13, was thrilled throughout her pregnancy with the thought, "It is God who works in you." (Haven't we all observed an added comeliness, a queenly touch, in the countenance of a new Christian mother?)

At this juncture it's fitting to empathize with those missionary parents whose child is born with serious physical or mental defects. How patiently these couples minister to their afflicted son or daughter day after day after day! One marvels at how abundantly God meets His people at such a deep level of need. Beset often with the temptation to cry out, "Why, Lord?" they press on in their daily work schedule, awaiting the hour when all will be made plain and they'll communicate fully with their renewed child. An MK friend, father of a cancer-stricken preschooler, writes:

> Few things make us reexamine our own life closer with regard to possible sin than something like this. . . . Nothing has increased our sensitivity to the pain and suffering of others as our little girl's condition. It has been a searing needle thrust deep to activate sensitivity as nothing else has.

Intensive care. Now there are three, but Baby steals the show. For the next months the tiny tyke (already a *pukka* citizen of the country) devotes the hours to sleeping, eating, crying, getting its own way, and having pictures taken for the family album. We're not knowledgeable about such things, but we learn from researchers that from the first week the infant gleans impressions influencing him in later years. (Parental smiles and peekaboos tell a lot to Baby.)

The first month of a child's life is considered the crucial time for it to begin to grasp the sense of responsibility that comes from self-reliance. Most of us have thought we could give ourselves to enjoying the new arrival for six months or so without worrying about impressing on its mind the issues of life. But apparently "as the twig is bent . . . so grows the tree." A real person lurks behind that baby face.

Bringing up Baby overseas requires meticulous precautions. People living in comparatively germ-free areas can't visualize the constant threat of infection posed in many mission lands. The simple matter of thumb-sucking, which most western pediatricians advise parents to ignore, now presents a different picture. Babies born to local women possess an inbred immunity of sorts, though poverty and ignorance along with infection take a heavy toll of lives.

The built-in sturdiness of the normal missionary newborn stands it in good stead in the earliest years. It survives, for instance, the determined activity of cockroaches as they scurry from one dark corner to another. (One missionary maintains that on his field these pests grow large enough to bear a saddle!) Then too the family may share their dwelling with bedbugs, maybe the large, flat-bodied, red type. Picking these off a sleeping, perspiring child becomes a routine task for Mom. A light sleeper with one eye and both ears open, she attempts to quell assaults from all quarters. A mosquito net helps, but some insects such as ants wangle their way past it.

Nevertheless this little one commences its earthly pilgrimage in a fairly comfortable setting. Ordinarily the missionary home is sufficiently stocked with baby things, many from homeside friends indelibly engraved with love.

THE TODDLER & HIS WORLD

Discovering himself. Growing like a weed, the tot takes his first step and soon enters the runabout stage of toddlerhood. Even when he's reined in, this roamer launches out in search of identity with himself and surroundings. The fiesty *buccha* learns new tricks—one, that misbehaving is effective procedure to gain attention. So at intervals he may join the ranks of the Terrible Tempered Twos (TTTs).

The ability to talk, along with a burgeoning sense of wonder and readiness to learn, makes this up-and-comer a source of astonishment to parents. His perpetual curiosity, with a stream of what's and why's, packs his day with activities of absorbing interest. Valiantly he works to articulate his new language. (Our younger daughter struggled long and hard to master "elephant," but until she succeeded we were charmed with "elphilunt.")

From earliest years the growing child is significantly influenced by his environment, but primarily by interaction with his parents. They're his shelter from fears and tears. Whatever happens, whether a stubbed toe or an emotional tumble, he knows where to turn. Later in life he may wonder where *home* really is, but for the present there's no trace of ambivalance on this score. It's where he gets loads of love, a lot of holding and caressing—precisely what he needs most.

Having established himself in his own perception as a separate person, the toddler strives toward independence. Destructiveness at mealtime convinces young parents that this little messaholic didn't spring from an angelic planting. Dr. James Dobson notes, with a deft touch of irony, that "parents who believe all toddlers are infused with goodness and sunshine should get out of the way and let their pleasant natures unfold."

By the way, how do our readers feel about receiving a missionary prayer-letter from a baby or toddler? We mean, of course, one in which the young one is represented as dictating his happy impressions of family life. Another momentous item of news might be that his first tooth has pushed through. No further comment!

Melting hearts. Sharing unconsciously in the parents' desire to identify with the local people, the young child and his winning ways may bear a forceful witness to the love and grace of the Savior. Everyone loves a baby, especially if it can bring forth a beatific smile at the right moment. From the delighted *ayah* (servant girl) to the sternest oldster, this little heart-warmer occupies a unique place in the family circle. A personal family anecdote:

During our first years in Bombay, we had much opportunity to contact Jewish friends. At that time there were over 15,000

Jews in the city, some of whom had fled from the Hitler pogroms. Most of the German Jews remained overwhelmed with grief as a result of having lost loved ones in the Holocaust. Though usually gracious to us when we called at their homes— we also were foreigners—they soon manifested varying degrees of hostility toward Christians and the New Testament; they equated Christians with their German persecutors.

On one occasion, however, a Jewish professor of distinguished bearing visited us in our flat. We had spoken to him about our firstborn child, now slightly over a year old, and this news prompted his visit. As he entered the door and greeted us, our daughter jumped into his arms and kissed him soundly. For the first time we saw the professor's face wreathed in smiles. Following this incident our friendship with him deepened, continuing after he took up residence in Israel.

THE PRESCHOOLER AT PLAY

Street children. Let us look briefly at a less agreeable scene. The delightful prospect portrayed in Zechariah 8:5 ("The city streets will be filled with boys and girls playing there") has yet to be fulfilled, at least in reference to pure enjoyment and peace. Until then multitudes of slum children, even in some major American cities, are left mired in an unmillennial setting. The sad plight of street urchins in Third World cities, especially in Calcutta, is a problem resting at the doorstep of missionary homes—a real-life crisis situation affecting the hearts of MKs as well as their parents. How they would like to put stars in those eyes! Daily they see deprived children, naked or near-naked and reduced to skin and bones, of illusory parentage, grubbing for a livelihood and eking out their waking hours on the pavement.

Oblivious to the noisy, tangled traffic—horse gharries, jampacked buses, bullock carts, rickshaws, cycles, taxis, pedestrians, and perhaps goats and cattle—these youngsters occupy themselves with simple games or with any other activity, good or bad, that turns up. The snake charmer provides an hour of diversion, while the hawkers of doodads and food tidbits attract their attention though rarely their patronage. Theirs is a bleak inheritance indeed; for them childhood ends early. A number of the young boys are already neophytes of the light-fingered gentry.

These children experience little of kindly empathy; they have no formal education or desire for it. But once in a while a heartening scene presents itself: a mother, squatting in a ramshackle hut—a few upright poles holding pieces of scrap tin and set against a filthy cement wall for shelter from sun and rain—fondles her little ones, enjoying their playful antics.

Our focusing on pavement dwellers isn't designed to dramatize the condition, though doing so might be in order. Rather, in keeping with our purpose to relate MKs to their environment, we depict a state of affairs that poses a stinging rebuke to missionaries and their children. Why not bring some of them in for bath and food? Our hearts are open, but taking these needy ones into our arms and homes is something else. Many missionary children, however, would like to do just that.

Explaining to stateside friends why a missionary family doesn't open its home and wallet as well as its heart requires sanctified tact. It appears that reaching out to these denizens of the street would provide golden opportunities for gospel witness. Yet the fences are higher than they look. For one thing, ironically, governments don't view with favor missionary work carried on with such under-privileged children; a few American dollars can mean much to the latter in terms of paving the way for proselytization—so some governments reckon.

Perhaps a freshman missionary friend's experience will in measure attest another major problem in outreach. This dear brother, freighted with low-value coins, began to give a coin to each boy who approached him. Then the inevitable happened. Soon the donor resembled the Pied Piper of Hamelin, minus the pipe but more harried than he, with scores of noisy, pushing youngsters following him wherever he went, shouting, "Baksheesh, Sahib! Baksheesh!" After a few days the brother had to abandon his plan. The incident brings out what would happen in one's home or apartment building should hundreds of street children hear of his liberality and approachability. Certainly some of the Lord's servants and their growing children, not yielding to compassion fatigue, come to grips with Jesus' scary challenge in Matthew 25:34-40 and Luke 14:12-14.

It will be understood by our readers that in emerging nations there's a sizable minority of well-nurtured, happy children who enjoy ample facilities for playtimes. The hundreds of thousands of splendid foreign students enrolled in North American universities represent a microcosm of educated, healthy adults and refined children in their lands.

Busy bodies. Returning to our discussion of the missionary home, we note that, as would be expected, parents provide scope for their youngsters to express their natural disposition for play. They recognize that play is essentially a child's work, so they usually keep enough ideas up their sleeve to fill in slack periods. Fortunately television, the ubiquitous babysitter in the West, isn't yet a viable option in most mission lands; hence "telegarbage" doesn't occupy a place in the child's agenda for diversion. Unless a boy or girl acquires a taste for cartoons and other programs during a family furlough, a non-TV climate is accepted without murmuring. One mother narrates how she keeps her brood interested and happy by means of simple pleasures:

> Surinam is a wonderful place. Our active boy can survive outdoors the year around and ride his bike at any time. There are no places for special excursions such as Disneyland, so other things become special treats. There is hardly anything I do with the children that is not special to them. They are still wide-eyed about life. Even a trip downtown for an ice cream cone is exciting. Our zoo is very tiny, but the promise of a day there with a picnic lunch brings them joy. Give the children a friend to play with and they can spend many happy hours.*

Gospel workers serving in rural or jungle areas normally have a fairly large compound where children can play quite freely— interestingly in Latin America missionary compounds are disappearing in deference to national culture. Where children do have a compound to play in, the tinies have their sandbox, swing, and teeter-totter; the others can build a treehouse for a rendezvous, fly a kite, race with friends, play tag, and perhaps manage a softball or cricket match after a fashion.

Public playgrounds in the cities are generally few, skimpy, and crowded. Only the posh apartment buildings enjoy a backyard or front lawn where youngsters can romp and shout. Nonetheless many of the simpler homes and flats have an open terrace that serves as an ideal playing field in the warm summer evenings. Our building in Bombay had a little extra:

> Between our five-story apartment building and the next there was a cul-de-sac that provided an acceptable playground for our then preschoolers and their local friends. Even the janitor's children, who wouldn't ordinarily be welcomed as playmates because of their low-caste status, were quite well received by the caste children and parents. (While caste has been outlawed by the Indian government, it's another thing to remove it from people's hearts.)

Profiting from play. Christian parents experience difficulty in discerning how much of childhood should be devoted to pure pleasure and how much to practical development, though the two factors can often be blended. Creative play polishes the child's social, emotional, physical, and mental skills. And since the youngster is commonly an inveterate learner in preschool years, parents find that educational play, unhurried and uninhibited, enables them to introduce instruction without curtailing the play feature. This all helps to produce a well-put-together child, developing in him self-control, tolerance, cheerfulness, acceptance of others. Children need to relate to others besides parents.

Throughout the children's early years, the missionary home may at times resemble a beehive. The busy two- and three-year-olds get engrossed in coloring, folding, cutting, pasting. A mother describes the play agenda in their home, permitting youngsters to pull out all emotional stops:

> We involve the children in crafts and games, drama, drawing, puzzles, reading, role-playing, discussions, with ample use of visual material including slides, photos, movies, books, charts and maps.*

But this 10-year-old boy's preferences aren't as primed to sharpen wits as the activities of the younger fry:

> I like swimming and fishing at the Coxipo River in Cuiaba (Brazil). You can do a lot of other things there, like playing soccer on the beach or having a mud battle in the water, or you can even have diving competitions. That's what I like doing best in Cuiaba.*

A facet of play presently at issue among missionaries concerns their older children's exposure to the highly sophisticated electronic gadgetry now popular in the West and already becoming available in some mission lands. A considerable number of parents seem to favor the video devices of the computer age, deeming that their offspring need to be groomed for later involvement in a technological climate. Other parents, reluctant to replace the tools of yesterday with the robots of today, affirm that possession of novel and expensive articles widens the cultural gap between their children and local friends, not many of whom would possess anything but the simplest play material. For obvious reasons, parents are less than thrilled with war toys.

Acting it out. Like boys and girls everywhere, missionary children occupy themselves in role-playing. Pretend play, merging with fantasies ("waking dreams"), isn't only fun; it can develop healthy imagination and creativity. Interestingly, researchers conclude that children who engage in make-believe play become calmer in spirit and less easily frustrated in adolescence than those not animated in this direction.

Should parents be permitted to view the action—a privilege not to be taken for granted—they can learn how observant their child is and how much or how little of their training has taken root. The manner in which a young miss disciplines her doll, for instance, gives Mom and Dad some clues. An episode in one family's calendar, though the participants are somewhat beyond preschool age:

> Several happy hours are spent playing store. A vendor's storefront is erected, with a variety of merchandise gracing the counter, borrowed from the kitchen and elsewhere. Action then begins. A customer picks up an article, minutely examines it, and commences to haggle over the poor quality and the inflated price. In his turn the vendor argues for the unique quality of his product, insisting that the client is getting a superb bargain. More dickering follows. At some point in the process the vendor draws his index finger across his neck, signifying that the customer is cutting his throat. When bargaining is over, though, and the shopkeeper has been beaten down to the minimum price, he'll close the sale and send the customer off with a broad smile of satisfaction, urging him to return. (In real life nobody ever steals a march on these small-shop vendors.)

Pet projects. The missionary child, no less than his western peer, enjoys a wide choice of pets—perhaps a broader selection since his parents aren't generally fidgety about their waxed floors and modish furniture! Some pets serve not only as a friend but as an ally, loyal to its young master even when he's in Mom's bad books.

In many scenes of children playing together in North America, a friendly puppy scampers delightedly as one of the family. But this popular figure is absent in most missionary homes. About the only dogs visible, except in the case of rural missionary families, are the scrawny, fleabitten pye-dogs that make the round of garbage bins.

By fortuity as much as design, the MK acquires novel pets. A young boy may dream of raising a tiger cub, but he may settle for a pet snake. (On one occasion a youngster brought a baby boa-constrictor to boarding school.) A monkey proves a desirable pet so long as the lad serves as its nursemaid—no idle task. Kittens turn out well, though environmental hazards cut down on their longevity. As pets MKs mention goats, chickens, geese, ducks, owls, tropical fish, armadillos, birds (one young girl writes glowingly about her cockatoo), mice (nice mice), and certain insects. We recall two particular episodes in our own family:

> Our daughter procured a harmless lizard for a pet and it was mutual love at first sight. "Lizzie" rested on Anne's shoulder or in her hair during the day and on the window sill at night. It was a trying time when a missionary friend, not realizing the relationship, flipped Lizzie from Anne's shoulder into the bushes.

Then too, at a certain season each year, a female pigeon would build its nest and hatch its eggs on top of our dresser, near an open door and window. The male hovered about just outside. Apparently the couple considered it less dangerous to venture into a situation with humans than to leave the eggs vulnerable to preying hawks. The drama proved exciting for the entire family.

And so to bed. Being normal boys and girls, missionary children hate bedtime. In fact, going to bed may represent Public Enemy No. 1, ahead of being spanked or having to eat green vegetables. Consequently these diplomats par excellence find ways to stave off the critical moment.

Nevertheless Mom normally has what it takes to soothe the child and prepare him for the inevitable. Everything about bedtime, from playtime to snuggle love, is designed to produce a pleasurable environment. The regimen may consist of story-time, singing, and an unhurried period when the youngster relates the trivia of the day. Questions also flow from his lips: "Where did I come from?"; "Where was I before I was born?"; "How can God listen to me when there's so many people in the world and He has so many other things to do?" One two-year-old threw this dandy at Mom: "When we grow up to be mommies and daddies, and you don't have us kids, what will you do?" Then prayer together. Here's a choice morsel from our six-year-old grandson's prayer: "Thank You, Lord, You didn't leave us dangling from Your hand, but You have us squeezed in Your hands."

Finally the nightlite is turned on, or the kerosene lamp turned down, and the bedroom door left slightly ajar to permit reassuring adult voices to be heard in the distance. Reluctantly the little person, perhaps with a favorite toy in his arms, gives up the fight and yields to the sandman's entreaties. The fact that he knows Mommie and Daddy will be there when he awakes helps him to settle emotionally. Then Mom heaves a sigh of relief. Robert Louis Stevenson embodies a child's feelings at bedtime in these familiar lines:

> And does it not seem hard to you
> When all the sky is clear and blue,
> And I should like so much to play,
> To have to go to bed by day?

3
PRESCHOOL DEVELOPMENT
Forging Personality

---

*"I proclaimed a fast, so that we might humble
ourselves before our God and ask him for a safe
journey for us and our children. . . .The hand of our
God was on us"* (Ezra 8:21,31).

FAITH FOR THE FAMILY

A time for strength. Missionary parents, challenged by a deep
sense of responsibility to provide optimal care and teaching for
offspring entrusted to them, recognize that their family testimony is
on the line before an unbelieving but perceptive populace who
justifiably check actions against words. Yet Mom and Dad are also
conscious of having to cope with their humanness. Such was the case
with Ezra and the Israelites committed to his care, described in the
context of the passages noted above. Without visible means of
protection but armed with faith, Ezra brought his charges safely and
triumphantly to Jerusalem.

While acknowledging a proper place for utilizing natural means in
God's service, we needn't water down the blessed principle exhibited
by this sturdy scribe of old. Certainly we desire to trust God on behalf
of our children to the end that, "like a stranger in a foreign country"
(Hebrews 11:9), each will set his or her heart on "the city with
foundations, whose architect and builder is God" (verse 10).

Abundant research has established that the MK's preschool
experiences enormously influence the molding of his adult lifestyle.
Parents can't funnel their maturity into the child's head and heart, yet
it's crucial that as a medium they exemplify those values which please
God, and then that the growing child "consider the outcome of their
way of life and imitate their faith" (Hebrews 13:7). Two adult MKs
share views of their parents' manner of life:

My parents spoke of a Christ who loved, who gave His all for
us. I also saw my parents demonstrate that love. My mother's
way was through nursing, with cases seen once in a lifetime in
U.S.*

I personally am thrilled to have had the opportunity of having frontline parents.*

Nature & nurture. At age four or five the child continues to do everything with gusto. But he's learned that life isn't all peaches and cream. The hurts, disappointments, and insecurities of childhood are very real, not easily handled. At such times the bonds of love between child and parents are more stoutly forged as he receives attention, approval, and affection. (It's been suggested that every child needs at least four hugs a day to survive, twelve to flourish.)

A generation ago psychologists reckoned that nature (heredity) could be five times more important than environment in determining a person's character. In more recent years the estimate has been vastly lowered; nurture is taking on greater significance. While most pre-sixes seem to follow a basic pattern of growth, their reaction to the environment of home and community assumes strongly formative elements. Accordingly the missionary child comes up with certain distinct characteristics. That's not to say that his experience in the training process makes him ipso facto any better than western peers reared in Christian homes. These lines from CAM's *Bulletin* put things in a nutshell:

> Like anyone else, he is capable of laughter and tears. At times he is mischievous, willful, kind, selfish, thoughtful, clever, clumsy, obedient, creative, silly, lovable.

EMOTIONAL DEVELOPMENT

Parent/child & fear. Prudence becomes a key factor for overseas parents at this stage of their child's life. How do we best work toward preparing our youngster for responsible independence and at the same time cultivate in him emotional stability? One of the strongest feelings—the move to protect our child from harm—is heightened by reason of exceptional environmental and cultural conditions. Consequently not a few parents tend to be overprotective to the point of mollycoddling the growing child.

In countries seething with political unrest, missionaries share with embassy staff increasing personal and family hazards. But the Lord's servants move more directly among the local people who on occasion harbor prejudice against gospel ministry, especially that carried on by western workers. So these brothers are sometimes exposed to physical attack. The assurances of host governments with regard to protection of foreigners don't bear the credence they once did. An adolescent MK in Colombia recalls that, when he was four or five years of age, each night he wondered if his dad would arrive home safely.

At such times fear is a stern reality for both child and adult. Like Ezra of old we have confidence in divine protection, yet our frail humanity requires that we maintain a healthy respect for danger and carefully instill the same in our offspring. Providentially the presence of fear registers benefit as well as detriment: it brings to the child an acute awareness of potential danger in his own guarded surroundings.

Then there are the peripheral causes of parental fears to which parents react diversely. A few conjure up a phobia that stations a fearful creature in ambush awaiting their child wherever he goes. Again, one mother becomes panicky when in a neighbor's home her preschooler digs into the rice and curry with both hands, when she knows his usual onceover in the basin hasn't reached the under layer of dirt. (In India everyone eats with the fingers of the right hand, not getting food above the knuckles.) Another mom thinks nothing of a situation like this, convinced that meticulously trying to dodge germs is a losing battle. Perhaps the incidence of infection is about the same in both cases. (Missionary lore has it that when a fly gets into the soup, the first-termer throws out the soup, the second-termer picks out the fly and serves the soup, the third-termer serves the soup as it.)

The vast majority of childhood fears are learned. On that account, since the child is extremely sensitive to parental attitudes, fear can be readily transmitted, possibly generating an innate condition difficult to analyze and for the child to express. Thankfully what has been learned can be unlearned. Still, discerning parents exercise caution in sharing with a younger child their concerns about social and political disturbances in the host country. They also keep a close watch on their servant so that she or he doesn't talk too freely with the child about current happenings. Here's how Eunice dealt with a simpler problem in our family before we'd been introduced to the intricacies of positive thinking:

> Our daughter at two became fearful of moving things like fluttering curtains; even the rustling of leaves disturbed her, and also the rain. Homeside therapy proceeded on this order: As Eunice and Anne walked together from time to time by the sea, they improvised and sang choruses like "Rain, rain, God sends the rain,/ The rain makes the flowers grow." After a few weeks of repeating happy lines of this kind, the fears subsided—so much so that Anne, adult-like, would remind us that God sends the rain to make the breezes that keep us from getting too hot.

Struggling with shyness. At some time or other in life, just about every growing child suffers from a level of shyness. Even one who is attractive and intelligent may be painfully shy, especially in face-to-face encounters with the opposite sex. Yet this personality trait becomes a roadblock to happiness, mostly in the case of boys; a young girl, if shy, is considered cute. In both instances the vexing condition, akin to fear and low self-esteem, needs to be significantly remedied in preschool years. Otherwise the pattern becomes entrenched during school years and the youngster may not naturally grow out of it. He'll avoid taking risks, structuring social contacts around his shyness; and he's a person of few words. His retiring disposition makes it difficult for him to make friends, and social activities are stifled at critical times. Nevertheless some MKs can keep their plight under control, as this seminarian friend does:

> The very Puritan, conservative upbringing of my type of MK was a good but straining precursor to real life. I still am by nature very shy and very conservative, though one may not always notice this. New situations are still hard even yet.

Fortunately missionary children don't live in a fishbowl. The fact that they're sheltered isn't a signal that they're inactive. They get excitingly involved with other MKs and local friends in hobbies and various recreational activities. A shy child, we're told, can gain a measure of aptness in social interaction by playing with a friend younger than himself, all the while working to become an interested, loyal companion. Then progressively he can begin to play with a stable peer group, and still later adjust to more complicated social situations. When his parents set short-term goals requiring a degree of self-determination and then mildly encourage the child's spirit of adventure, shyness should be lessened.

CULTURAL DEVELOPMENT

Identification, childhood style. The MK's early environment determines to a considerable extent how he hits it off later with that alluring world of peers and older people. Many adults familiarize themselves with a new culture as they might learn grammar, in a formal, bookish manner. Ingenuously the preschool MK, with his built-in mimicking faculty and eagerness to communicate, usually identifies with national children as unaffectedly as a child in the West does with his friends.

In hobnobbing with national peers, the missionary child unconsciously applies the pattern of language study followed by adults in overseas language schools. Without worrying about grammar, this linguistic genius grasps the sentence-idea and the intonation of the voice and, lo and behold, in a comparatively short time he's rattling away idiomatically in the tongue of his friends, unaware of his noble accomplishment. He may even pronounce "shibboleth" correctly whereas Dad and Mom meanwhile settle for "sibboleth" (please see Judges 12:6). To be sure, concepts remain elementary, grammar atrocious, and speech content a mere smattering compared with adult capability, but what the youngster lacks in syntax he makes up by meaningful gestures which national children delight in.

As in everything else, however, exceptions occur, particularly if children reach school age before their parents take up foreign service. This informative paragraph by a missionary mom appeared anonymously in a Christian magazine:

> "Children adjust so quickly" I had been assured. "They don't care if other children speak another language. They'll all play together. They'll be speaking the language before you do." My counselors must have had very small children. Our girls, five and seven, have had a rough time. . . . Soon they stuck by themselves. They regressed emotionally. Problems long outgrown now reappeared.*

The missionary child in boarding school, removed from warm daily contact with national friends, loses out appreciably in terms of rapport with them and familiarity with their language and customs. Only special incentive on his part can counteract the trend. The child who takes his schooling at home enjoys closer identification with the wholesome aspects of local culture; moreover he sets the tone for later impressions of different cultures. This CBFMS parent writing in *Impact* suggests ways to encourage a child toward good relationships with neighborhood friends:

> At times we wondered—could we by example, prayer, encouragement and by making opportunities for our children to participate, deepen their love and concern for the nationals all around them? Would they appreciate the Chinese people, language and rich cultural heritage as we did? Or would this be just another experience they would pass through and largely forget, as they found other more interesting pursuits in life?
>
> Prayer, love, the absence of criticism toward nationals' different ways and attitudes, efforts to evangelize and disciple—missionary children have such an ideal first-hand course in practical missions! They should be able to observe daily these sound principles and practices. If parents love their work, the people and the country, it seems natural that this attitude will be transferred to their children for life.

Health & welfare. The World Health Organization (WHO) and other agencies labor consistently with foreign government personnel to eliminate or control epidemics that formerly wreaked such a grievous toll of death. Numerous missionaries of past generations record how one or more of their children were taken. Endemic diseases such as smallpox, malaria, cholera, tetanus, tuberculosis, diphtheria, and polio no longer stalk the masses, though ignorance of basic health measures still prevails among the less-privileged communities.

Protection and the ounce of prevention receive high priority in the missionary home. Parents learn to handle many cases for which folks at home would visit the doctor; some parents might be classed as paramedics. Most households maintain a well-stocked medicine cabinet and Mom or Dad can generally prescribe what the doctor would order. Dental and eye care aren't easy to obtain in rural areas. Children are immunized against the common diseases of the land and learn the elements of good hygiene. Their stomachs, nonetheless, sometimes undergo culture clashes. Perhaps diarrhea, or dysentery, is the greatest threat to children under five, stemming mainly from contaminated food and water. A veteran missionary advises a candidate friend not to neglect bringing three things to the field: his Bible, a toothbrush, and Kaopectate. Then, too, another issue, more annoying than serious, is the hour or so each week that Mom spends keeping the lice at bay in her daughter's hair, wielding a fine-tooth comb.

Missionaries can usually draw on the healthy constitutions they've been blessed with. Probably most of them aren't overmuch concerned about keeping young and trim, but jogging is catching on despite crowded streets and traffic hazards. Some adults find— surprise, glad surprise—that they're free of certain allergies plaguing them from childhood. For this writer the month of August, ushering in the ragweed season in America, passed without a single sneeze in India.

While generalizing on such a sensitive matter is risky, we submit that MKs rate above western averages with regard to mealtime attitudes. Most of them aren't squeamish about food; they don't toy with it, but eat nutritious meals without extended squawking. For one thing, they're not afforded a choice of half a dozen appealingly advertised breakfast foods. Simple menus with low amounts of concentrated sugar and salt, along with whole-grain roughage, might add up to a natural-food enthusiast's dream; so not many parents or offspring suffer from a weight problem. For the record, however, it should be noted that in missionary homes finicky kids aren't rare specimens. And for otherwise normal children, swallowing suspect substances such as cauliflower, spinach, or brussels sprouts is definitely a problem, doubtless inherited from their fathers.

Mission lands often abound in seasonable fruit, and locally grown vegetables are available. (During mango season in India the spirits of the populace rise perceptibly.) Still, both fruit and vegetables may lack the nourishing quality of cultivated counterparts. Imported powdered milk, cheese, dried fruits, and certain kinds of meat can be procured in the larger towns. Ample sunshine for much of the year registers benefit as well as bother in a family's health regimen.

Notwithstanding all these advantages, sickness or accident strikes most missionary children in the course of time. This abridged account describes an ordeal in an Indonesian jungle:

> Each of our five children nearly died, since we lived in an area where proper medical aid was not available. One child suffered from dengue fever, another underwent emergency appendicitis, a third son was bitten by a venomous snake, a fourth became weak as the result of asthmatic attacks in the moldy climate and the fifth fell into a water storage tank.*

Flu, diarrhea, and certain other ailments can often be treated at home, but virulent sicknesses strike children with such suddenness and intensity that qualified medical help is urgently needed. At such times a jungle pilot may be contacted by radio, possibly in an MAF or JAARS plane. Traversing hundreds of miles of treacherous bush, he transports a seriously ill child or adult to the nearest medical center, usually a Christian facility.

The most remembered experience of some missionaries relates to an occasion when, with their child gravely ill and burning with fever, they were far removed from reliable medical help. Waiting before the throne of grace throughout the night, Mom and Dad would commit their little one into the Father's hands, indicating their desire to have His highest purpose fulfilled. A good few of such parents testify to having seen God's healing touch on their child. A WEC father in *Thrust* offers this moving account:

> Barely two months after our arrival in Guinea-Bissau, our only child, Rebekah, caught a devastating sickness that was killing an average of seven children daily and against which the hospital was powerless. For two days our active ten-months-old daughter lay virtually motionless—dehydrating and dying. Then, recognizing the spiritual battle involved, we requested the local national evangelist and our field director to anoint Becky and pray for her according to James 5. They did and the same afternoon she was up, and the next day she was well.

Other parents, still witnessing to God's faithfulness, have laid their child's body in the local church cemetery—a spot and an experience that renew sacred memories long after the workers retire from the field. (Madame Guyon: "I have learned to love the darkness of sorrow; there you see the brightness of His face.")

Undoubtedly at such times the Lord's servants are keenly conscious of the prayer of stateside friends. While frequently uninformed of the specific need, these faithful saints uphold the workers and their families before the Lord. Then too, an experience of severe sickness binds family members more closely together.

PRACTICAL DEVELOPMENT

On-the-job training. Occasionally adult MKs complain that they continue to feel inadequate in the practical business of life. They feel reasonably comfortable in matters of mind and heart, but a shortfall of early training in workaday affairs has left them less capable in domestic and vocational areas. In point of fact, many missionary parents, particularly urbanites, are acutely conscious that their son and daughter need jobs to prove themselves—difficult jobs at times requiring both physical and mental discipline. Children profit much from the "well done" when they earn it. Gordon MacDonald, a New England pastor and writer, explains the procedure followed in his home:

> . . . This is why we constructed a list of jobs which they began to do at the age of four. We wanted them to experience fatigue, inconvenience, frustration, and puzzling problems. Face problems now, or you'll face them later, we said. But in reality we didn't give them a chance; they were going to face them now. This is a form of discipline.[5]

While most missionary parents would desire to implement a similar plan in their homes, it's not a simple thing to find tasks that don't appear trumped up. And of course some boys and girls emulate Tom Sawyer and his methods. It's not unknown for a juvenile to take occupancy of the bathroom in order to savor diplomatic immunity until the danger is o'erpast. The fact that at boarding school domestic duties are cared for mainly by servants compounds the problem.

Nevertheless plenty of youngsters pitch in and pull their weight in the home without a hassle—they've been brought up right. A jungle pilot mentions that at his birth his dad gave him a monkey-wrench instead of a rattle! Rural missionary families with a fairly large compound and a stockpile of jobs command a distinct advantage in terms of exploiting Master Fixit's practical side. The following enumeration of jobs cared for by a jack-of-all-trades and master of some may stand as the ultimate model of MK industriousness:

> I learned invaluable experience in practical areas. I learned to take care of goats, chickens, sheep, dogs, and cats. I milked the goats in order to feed our baby brother, and whatever was left over we mixed with powdered milk. I learned to make bread and fix meals, and of course I learned how to do dishes and clean up the kitchen. I helped as we used dynamite to dig a well and a rain-water tank. I got experience in building when we built our house and chapel. I did all the maintenance of our vehicles and generator. I learned to pull teeth as I watched my father pull all kinds of them; and I learned how to treat wounds and sew up a bad gash in my dad's head. I had a lot of fun learning how to fly the single-engine airplane which was given my dad to use. Along with the rest of the family, I learned to pray, trust and thank God for all our material needs as well as our spiritual and physical needs.

After this broad tallying of skills, any suggestion we might offer with regard to an agenda of home duties would come out on the anemic side. But here's a timely paragraph from CBFMS's *Impact:*

> Some older missionary children work in the villages, hospitals and dispensaries. They also help with typing, cleaning house, working on the car and doing all the odd jobs that help release their parents to do more of their own specific work. We observe that some MKs stay after graduation for six months to a year to help in a fulltime way before entering college in the States.

To reinforce their growing child's practical edge, parents can include him in discussion of finances. Maintaining secrecy about money matters not only deprives the youngster of important training for the future but may give him the impression that God supplies family needs regardless of each member's active involvement in prayer and reliance on Him.

Many parents provide an allowance for each child, divided according to age but unrelated to chores done. By checking his accounts once in a while they train their offspring in the elementary principles of bookkeeping. Knowing how to handle money in terms of spending and giving (or, in the case of a real-life Scrooge, saving in the First International Piggy Bank) proves progressively meaningful to the young person in decision-making.

Servants: status symbol? When communicating with stateside friends, missionaries are inclined to downplay the fact that they employ a servant or two. The homefolks could get the idea that these foreign workers are living in the lap of luxury, like Arabian sheiks. "We ourselves can't afford to hire household help," they reflect, and then, "Perhaps our church is contributing too heavily to their support." They may wonder too why the missionaries' kids can't do the work.

There's a vast difference between the kitchen of a missionary home in underdeveloped countries and that of even the low-income family in the West with its array of time-saving gadgets and utensils. While the missionary household is better equipped than the average national's, coming up with quickie meals still isn't possible or often desirable. (A discerning African observes: "We don't want you to live like us, but we appreciate your living in a style we may attain.")

The culture of many lands is frequently beset by time-consuming practices. Consequently almost all classes of residents in Third World countries, including lower-middle-class families—their average income may be less than $30.00 per month—engage at least part-time domestic help. The wheels of petty commerce grind slowly and queues are a way of life. Understandably a white child standing in line awaiting service could attract unwelcome attention.

Providing the home with staple foods can take several hours of a servant's day. All the while she (or he) puts her knowhow to good use in dealing with crafty vendors, not a few of whom introduce small stone pebbles into rice and wheat to increase the weight. With or without a fridge, much of the family's food supply must be purchased daily. Besides, all dishes and tableware must be sterilized and water and milk boiled. Then, since in a hot, humid climate Westerners ordinarily change their cotton clothes twice a day, there's plenty of washing to be done.

Nonmissionary expatriates usually employ a governess for exclusive child care. The missionary mom, however, wants the joy of caring for each child as much as she can manage to do so. Thus a local girl or boy for general work is enough, though the girl may do some babysitting also—a job she loves. Rural workers often engage a married couple, for whom they provide living accommodation. The single girl or boy is fully content to sleep on a mat on the floor. (Actually, on hot nights, our own three children spent as much time stretched out on the cool tile floor as in their beds.)

True, the presence of a servant brings a negative factor into the parents' training program, diminishing the number of domestic jobs on hand for the children. Worse, the servant girl may dislike to see the fair-skinned child doing menial work so she caters to his whims.

A common, half-humorous observation is heard in missionary circles: "We can't get along with a servant or without one." Through it all, however, the family maintains a kindly attitude toward their helper; she's almost like one of the family. Perhaps at times she's treated too gently by first-term workers, who aren't accustomed to giving orders to another adult.

LITERARY DEVELOPMENT

Readying to read. In their preschool years many missionary children become captivated by books. The important place reading occupies in their parents' lives fosters in them an insatiable appetite for literature geared to their age-group. Certain large-print picture books and storybooks become prized possessions of these pre-sixes and they wheedle Mom and Dad to reread the dog-eared volumes over and over again. Meanwhile the copies double nicely as a security blanket.

This head start markedly influences the child's continuing lifestyle when in the 7-11 age-bracket he begins to read for pleasure. Childhood's God-given gifts of curiosity and enthusiasm prompt parents to provide their eager readers with a good-sized library of priceless volumes.

In previous generations Christian families spent evenings together in reading aloud and discussing the living issues raised. Evidently a fair number of present-day missionary families follow this rewarding plan, going through a variety of entertaining stories and books in the course of a few years. By reading aloud the parent stresses the invaluable nature of the material. This missionary sister in the Lord, an MK, recalls the joy of being read to as a child:

> We grew up with books. The Christmas or birthday presents we would get most excited about were books. Every room in our house was papered with bookshelves. And my Dad read to the older three of us kids almost every evening that he was home. Those reading times are some of my most precious memories—with my older brother putting models together or doing something mechanical with his hands, my sister painting, and me doing embroidery.

Being devoted to reading opens a whole new world to the MK. It's well known that a definite correlation exists between reading and learning; a read-to child not only reads better in school but does better in all his subjects. Besides being entertained and informed, the youngster's understanding of others is expanded. And parents themselves may discover that such times of reading conduce to one of life's sweetest joys.

Fact, fable, fiction. Missionary parents differ with respect to what's better and best in their child's reading material. Aesop's fables, Little Red Riding Hood, Hansel and Gretel, Jack and the Beanstalk, the lovable Peter Rabbit, C.S. Lewis's Narnia Chronicles—do these favorites help or hinder the child's emotional development? One dominant view is that, since evil figures are properly punished and good rewarded, books of this nature provide a wholesome basis for distinguishing right and wrong. Also fairy tales may lend assuring solutions to a child's negative fantasies. Rosalie de Rossett writes of her early reading experiences:

> I grew up with the great secular classics. In fact, I consumed them with relish and intemperance. As a child on the mission field, with no television, no backyard, and an overripe imagination, I plunged into the world of books as soon as my eyes could pick out the story lines.
>
> I wept over David Copperfield's bleak childhood, exulted in the adventures of Robin Hood and his merry men, delighted in the pageantry of King Arthur's court, and was fascinated by the mystery of Hawthorne's house with seven gables. I have never let go of the dream that I, too, will sail lazily down the Mississippi on a raft as Mark Twain's Huck Finn did.
>
> Books were a part of everything. Mother read to us nightly and sometimes after lunch. Dad and Mother brought us books on their trips away. I can still see my brother and me propped against pillows, racing each other through Ivanhoe. . . .[6]

Dr. Frank E. Gaebelein, in his introduction to Gladys Hunt's *Honey for a Child's Heart*, a book that catalogues a host of literary gems for children, accents the joy and value of reading:

> Few things are more important for a child than to discover the joy of reading. Give him a love of reading, and you have given him not only the most satisfying and useful of all recreations but also the key to true learning. The home is still the greatest educational force, and parents who make reading attractive contribute immeasurably to their children's intellectual, emotional, and spiritual development. Forty-one years as a headmaster have convinced me that a genuinely educated person is one who knows how to read and who keeps on reading throughout his life. As Matthew Arnold said, "Culture is reading."[7]

4
UNDER DISCIPLINE
Helping & Harming

"Train a child in the way he should go, and when he is old he will not turn from it" (Proverbs 22:6).

DESIGN OF DISCIPLINE

Biblical "should." The leading word in this text may well be "should." God's people today can be grateful that the New Testament doesn't tabulate a multitude of specific details to direct them in the parenting process. Yet while being released from legalistic minutiae results in gray areas for us, the above admonition is realistic as it stands. We're blessed with a unique foundation for discerning God's guidance in godly disciplining: biblical principles—direct statements and personal examples—that guide, encourage, and warn us (cf. Matthew 7:12). Thus we're provided a strong base on which to build in our child enduring qualities. Perhaps no parent is fully adequate for the task, but with the Helper, the Holy Spirit, dwelling in our mortal bodies, we can bring wholesome influences to bear on our son and daughter to the end that each will be groomed to honor God throughout life.

Moreover the Lord has raised up Christian sociologists and other teachers to counsel us in techniques, though there's considerable disagreement among them on directives. Much of this material, normally designed for western households, is applicable as well to overseas families; "kids are kids" wherever they are. Hence, shunning the frustrations of perfectionism and "the tyranny of the ought," missionary parents can move quite confidently in training their child "in the way he should go." They'll endeavor to encourage qualities such as spiritual commitment, honesty, courtesy, dependability, and self-reliance in daily affairs.

Focus on self-control. A legalistic, monastic flavor attends the term "discipline" when considered merely a euphemism for correction and punishment. To the young boy or girl it has all the earmarks of trouble brewing. Nevertheless the scriptural significance (and commonly the understanding of sociologists today) includes a broad range of estimable features. As a matter of fact, discipline is a special kind of love.

We parents speak of *our* child. Yet actually our son and daughter are a trust from God granted us for a season. However, as we seek to blend firm, dignified instruction with awareness of preparing them for independent thought and action, we soon discover that our sphere of effectiveness, though utterly indispensable, is limited. We can certainly keep our youngsters from growing up like Topsy, but we don't have absolute control of either their character or their destiny. Ultimately the growing son and daughter are personally responsible to collaborate with the various agencies shaping the personality.

Now the basic aims of discipline are fairly clear: to maintain harmony in the home while strengthening bonds of love and confidence between parents and child; to train and mold each boy and girl with a view to forging godly character (cf. 1 Timothy 3:4,5). Veritably our task as parents—striking a good balance between discipline and trust—requires constant grace and wisdom from above. In this undisciplined age it's not easy to keep the child's grubby nature, or our own for that matter, in line. No child ever likes restrictions from the moment of his natal squawk. Consequently, training him can become a destructive war of wills or a most fulfilling experience for both child and parent.

The emphasis in Scripture seems to be placed on the *quality* of the active relationship we preserve with our child. We're admonished, as Ephesians 6:4 implies, not to become impatient or capricious or to be doctrinaire to the point of rigidly applying theories without due regard for practical considerations such as differences in age and personality of our children. Our supreme model for parenting must be our heavenly Father in the disciplining of His own dear children. (Hebrews 12:10: "Our fathers disciplined us for a little while as they thought best; but God disciplines us for our good, that we may share in his holiness." Meditating on the context of this verse may make us parents feel like softies!

MISSIONARY METHODS

Permissive posture. Though poles apart in their extremes, the two main formulas of discipline—permissiveness and authoritarianism—have countless variants, many undoubtedly showing up in missionary households. To carry through with their discipline and gain obedience from their children, younger missionaries, with all the right books, may still seek the advice of older workers. Such open-hearted parents reveal good missionary potential!

The excessively lenient parents request the child to do something, give him the reason for so requesting, and then leave him to juggle the options. ("We have to trust our kids to draw their own conclusions.") The general purpose looks good on the surface and in fact may work out quite nicely when things are going the child's way. Often, too, parents may carry out their plan with honest intent—to evoke self-discipline from the child rather than impose it on him—yet basically we do our child a disservice by placing unfair responsibility on him, maximizing his self-will and minimizing his self-control.

A child exposed to this carrot-on-stick method to gain obedience can easily become the victim of poor habits; for one thing he'll become expert in tuning out Mom and Dad—hearing without heeding. So long as "buddy" parents permit themselves to be maneuvered, the youngster will keep inching, by will and by wile, toward increasing manipulation, until eventually he's being catered to hand and foot, running the house. So the parents end up with a dictator on their hands. Obsessively sweet-talking parents may thus create an atmosphere that breeds malcontents (cf. Proverbs 29;15). As would be expected, spanking is out in this type of discipline; it humiliates the child, destroying initiative.

To be sure, a number of secular surveys claim that in children from two to six the semi-structured permissive approach doesn't produce more spoiled brats than stricter methods. And conceivably some children respond nobly to such overtures and turn out well. (In Third World countries, national children, often raised in permissive homes, appear to be reasonably responsible as teens.) Permissive parents usually employ praise in specific instances meriting it—a prime tool widely recognized as invaluable in encouraging the child toward better behavior.

Ordinarily, however, the baneful effects of this type of parenting don't really show up until mid-adolescence (14-18), perhaps the hardest bracket in regard to parental control compared with the enjoyable six- to nine-year-olds. Besides, the ultra type of tough authoritarianism may be in view in the surveys.

Where then do missionary parents stand in this matter? Our first impulse would be to deny more than token incidence of permissiveness among us, with not the veriest trace of the extreme kind. Nonetheless certain findings point to considerable slippage from the norm. Following is an extract from a report (issued by Harvest Publishers in 1977) of a couple's gleanings during a world tour:

> During our year of traveling around the world, we have lived and fellowshipped with hundreds of missionaries. One observation we made during that time was that some very well-serving missionaries are prone to raise their children in a

permissive home. (There tend to be more melancholics and phlegmatics in the mission field than other temperaments). The feeling seems to exist that their children are giving up so much to live on the mission field that the rebellion and disobedience must be overlooked.

This spirit has been picked up by the children and they begin to feel sorry for themselves and indulge in self-pity. The result will be bitter young people who will always feel that they have been cheated in life.

How much better it would be if parents would dwell on the positive blessings in life and raise their children to respect the rod and its authority.

Are we parents guilty as charged? The number of culpable persons must have been considerable to warrant such a wholesale indictment. In later chapters we'll have opportunity to test this evaluation. Meanwhile, let's look at a sharply divergent view from the pen of Dr. Edward E. Danielson, a clinical psychologist and counselor at Faith Academy (in *Missionary Kid—MK,* 1982):

> What are little MK boys and girls made of? Missionary parents might claim that their children are made of "sugar and spice and everything nice." Teachers and dorm parents working with MKs would probably agree. But a more accurate description might be found in the results of a recent study of MKs in Faith Academy in Manila, Rift Valley Academy in Kenya, and the Alliance Academy in Quito. The MK personality traits may be defined as: emotionally stable, highly intelligent, reserved, conscientious, controlled, conservative, relaxed, somewhat submissive and slightly group dependent.

Authoritarian approach. The extreme form of the other parenting method calls for frequent commands, with each veering from the straight and narrow summarily punished. It's a stern no-ifs-ands-or-buts position that often humiliates the child. A notion lacking certification attributes this program of action to the Pilgrim Fathers; but clearly our forebears weren't insensitive in the nurturing of offspring.

From what we've been able to gather, we conclude that evangelical missionaries generally favor a moderate pattern of authoritarianism—not achieving obedience by autocratic ear-tweaking, finger-snapping, or "glower power," but by dignified disciplining. "My parents were always pretty strict," remembers a British MK. "I was very wilful as a child—didn't know what I wanted. I'm glad now for their disciplining."

While most parents would confess delinquency in certain areas, each child normally receives supervision, guidance, and correction with a firmness and considerateness that foster respect for parents and don't damage his psyche—"shaping the will without breaking the spirit," as Dr. James Dobson phrases it.

When disciplined with loving toughness by concerned parents—those who haven't abdicated their authority—the child becomes conscious of being surrounded by secure love; his dependency is solidly grounded. Dad and Mom have the final say but decisions involving the child are at times arrived at through reciprocal exchanges—talking with, not at, the youngster. Thus confidence in the parents' judgment is enhanced and mutual respect established. Limits tell the child that they're concerned about him. (Two interesting sidelights: Daughters tend to respond more positively than sons to high moral standards—though the latter may at times reach higher ground—and parents are inclined to be overly strict with their first child—they want him or her to be a model for all time.)

Nevertheless good discipline isn't altogether free from casualties; vexing issues still arise. Plenty of MKs defy parental training. We warmly appreciate this missionary father's affecting experience:

> Our relationship with our eldest son had not been bad down through the years. . . . Firm discipline with love had been our modus operandi, and it had seemed to work quite well to that point.
>
> However, his display of smouldering anger had plagued our relationship recently. My heart confessed to an increasing resentment toward Brad. . . . His lifestyle acutely polarized us, and communication was strained.
>
> "God, you have to give me the answer," we demanded. I was hardly prepared for God's answer. He focused His searchlight on my heart attitudes. God said to me, "As long as you choose to reject, resent, and condemn Brad, My hands are tied. . . . You are the real problem. Will you now go to your son and confess your wrong attitudes and resentment, criticisms and rejection? Will you ask his forgiveness for your sin against him?". . .
>
> God wasn't asking me to accept my son's rebellion. He was asking me to love and accept him genuinely and unconditionally as he was, and not as I wanted him to be. . . .
>
> As we found ourselves in each other's arms, tears washing away my built-up resentments, an amazing thing happened. Brad, too, began to weep and with a broken heart acknowledged his rebellion and asked forgiveness . . . and then his mom's forgiveness. . . .
>
> This summer Brad goes to West Africa as a summer missionary. . . . Who can tell what will happen in lives when His powerful redemptive love finds in us a channel?[8]

PROBLEMS & PRECEPTS

Developing self-esteem. The expression "self-love" doesn't sound good to ears attuned to the biblical concept of self-denial (John 12:25); on the contrary, it projects narcissistic overtones (cf. Romans 7:18). But some Christian writers, mainly on the premise of Luke 10:27, affirm that self-love, usually understood as positive regard for one's rights and feelings, is a desirable disposition for God's people to cultivate. Whatever word is used—self-worth, self-respect, self-fulfillment, self-appreciation, self-confidence, self-acceptance, self-esteem—seeking to keep on good terms with oneself is a far cry from arrogant ego-tripping. In fact we daresay that a healthy self-esteem is essential for achieving a fulfilled life.

Two passages assuring us that no basic dichotomy exists between cultivating self-esteem and possessing humility are Isaiah 57:15b and Romans 12:3. Surely there's nothing unseemly in knowing we're accepted, wanted, and loved by the significant people in our lives, so long as we're at rest from inflated self-importance, from doting on ourselves. We live with ourselves and need to be concerned with inward growth, striving to become balanced in attitudes and objectives. The Apostle Paul's experience in this respect is seen in such passages as 1 Corinthians 2:1-4; 2 Corinthians 4:1, 10; 10:1, 2, 10, 11.

MKs don't escape unscathed in this problem of morbid introspection, even if many are only minimally affected. As it is, some homefolks feel that MKs have more than their share of self-esteem! Yet a good percentage of these young people have a smudged conception of themselves, perhaps thinking they're dumb and uninteresting; and they're unduly disturbed by what others think of them. Surprisingly, perfectionist achievers may harbor a harsh self-image, the result of setting unrealistically high standards for themselves.

Sometimes emotionally tongue-tied, these MKs are much taken up with their inadequacies. Even the quiet, well-behaved child may not be happily adjusted to himself and others; and, oddly enough, the overassertive posture of a youngster may be a facade for a sense of inferiority. Yet why is it that adolescent girls who were tomboys in earlier years tend to have less trouble in this area?

In addition to being tainted with insecurity inherent in fallen humanity, MKs are confronted with unique factors arising from contact with cultures, subcultures, and countercultures. Consequently, despite the fact that no one can make a person inferior except by his own consent, the self-identity of many MKs requires shoring up. A missionary mother describes factors relating to their son's image-lag:

I've been on both sides, having been a missionary child in
boarding school and also a missionary parent and dorm auntie.
And I've had our kids go off to boarding school. So I ought to
know a lot more than I do about these things. But it may be of
help to some others to share one of our experiences. I think
some of us parents are so anxious to have our kids know they're
sinners that we don't leave them with a good self-image. As my
husband and I were going over things, we've come to feel we
were faithful in disciplining and loving our kids, but we fell
down in not assuring them of their self-worth.

As an MK myself, I never felt put away and always thought I
could do well if I wanted to. So my parents did a good job on
me. But our own first child, now 11, doesn't feel he can do
anything. It may be his age that makes him feel this way, but
perhaps we were so conscious of the non-Christians checking
up on our kids that we wanted them to shape up perfectly.
Anyway, we've finally caught on to our mistake and try now to
assure our kids of their potential and let them be themselves.
We can't minimize sin, but we should not make verbal attacks
on the individual child.

Disciplining without hurting the child's sense of self-worth,
accordingly, is vital in supportive parenting. Child psychologists
underscore parents' need to respect their child's personal dignity. As
we encourage positive attitudes of our child toward himself and
acceptance of himself regardless of certain weaknesses (he'll have
strengths also), he'll be helped in neutralizing the earliest symptoms
of inferiority—that bugaboo of adolescence that finds behind every
dark cloud a real storm brewing. A tale of two MKs and one PK:

In early years I learned a very dangerous behavior pattern: I
suppressed my own honest reactions and opinions and gave out
that which I knew would please and satisfy people. And
because of this I got to dislike myself, even to hate myself, for
being so mealy-mouthed and spineless and conformist. Then I
would feel enormously guilty at these hateful feelings and try
hard to become "good," to genuinely believe in my heart what I
pretended to believe outwardly. If I were asked for advice by
the parents of the next generation, I might say, Let the child be
himself, be human, and let him feel important for his own sake.
Don't insist that he share your mission. Try to ease up on the sin
and guilt aspect of salvation so that he grows up knowing it is
OK to make mistakes, and that if he does something wrong, it's
not the end of the world.

During the difficult period of settling into life in the U.S., I didn't get much help from Christians. But I think I understand their problem. Some at least wanted to treat me as normal, yet most of the time I wasn't normal myself. So they treated me either as a monstrosity that should have remained in the jungle, or what is worse, a paragon of virtue. Actually I was plagued by guilt feelings because I was so far from perfect. Is it any wonder that MKs find it so hard to be natural?*

I really think that being a pastor's daughter has affected my self-esteem adversely. I feel that no matter what situation you are brought up in, self-esteem can be a problem for anyone. But as a PK, it seems I am always trying to measure up to an unreachable standard—even now despite having recognized the problem. Although never vocally expressed by my parents, I feel I am to be an example of perfect behavior and flawless upbringing. It's my responsibility to reflect my parents' righteous life.

It's evident, then, that buttressing our child's self-confidence, rightfully understood, is an issue of surpassing importance. The youngster thus fitted is healthier, happier, more productive, and more generous and empathetic in friendships than one with a low sense of self-esteem. He won't normally search elsewhere for emotional security in questionable relationships. Fostering congenial friendships by attitudes that go beyond self-interest emboldens the young person to resist unwholesome peer pressure. (Little Jack Horner must have been brought up right. Remember how, having stuck in his thumb and pulled out a plum, he exclaimed, "What a good boy am I!")

The proper kind of parental encouragement and praise (children detect phony sentiment), combined with unstinted expressions of love, won't give the child a swelled head; it lends security. The sharing of appropriate adult thoughts also helps him to bolster self-respect and handle occasional bouts of morbidness. In her crucial teen years a daughter may be profoundly influenced for good by an agreeable bond with Dad. Similarly a teenage son profits greatly from Dad's taking over his discipline in spiritual, academic, and sexual areas.

Assurance of being special and worth much to the Lord can deliver the growing youth from being continually in need of reassurance and approval. ("I look up and feel I'm important.") Looking back also to Calvary and meditating on the Lord Jesus' dying for him should not only enhance his self-concept but encourage the young person to go on to please Him in all things. Despite the multitude of achievers in contemporary society, each MK has been greatly favored in being reared in a home where God's Word is accorded top priority—that Spirit-breathed message that rounds out the basic and ultimate issues of life.

Sibling relationships. The reality of conversion and the effectiveness of parental discipline find practical outgrowth in the cheerful adjustment of brothers and sisters to each other. Yet sibling conflicts arise in missionary homes almost as naturally as day and night. Being thrown together much of the time until or unless some leave for boarding school gives MKs plenty of opportunity to evince Christian grace.

Any survey of missionary families, however, would reveal incidence of spirited squabbles, with pesky brothers and impish sisters sniping at each other or at those of their own sex. From the youngster's point of view siblings provide the safest pecking order—reprisals won't be too serious. And with the green-eyed monster lurking nearby, a child finds another way to capture the attention, if not at this moment the affectionate embraces, of parents. As a rough estimate, we'd say MKs' inter-family quotient might rate 6 or 7 on a scale of 10.

The middle-born of three-stair children can find things rough, unless he or she is motivated to shape up and show the others. Firstborn offspring supposedly are most free from sibling bickering, and daughters foment fewer breaches of the peace than do sons. Here's a case in which the firstborn son, an MK, acts below the norm; seemingly he was weaned on pickles. Also a firstborn daughter's true-to-type reaction:

> Please don't misunderstand me, and don't think my folks are bad in any way. You see, I was the first child and no one told Mom and Dad how to take care of me until it was too late. I was what you might call a trial and error child. Today, you would find that my young brothers are totally different from me. Though they are strong-minded like myself, they are not only *in* the family, they are *of* the family. In any decision that affects their lives, they always get to say their two bits worth and taken into account. Everything my folks didn't do for me, they do for my brothers.

> I never felt particularly antagonistic toward my siblings. Rather, I felt embarrassed that we couldn't be "good" when our parents asked us. I remember feeling so sorry for my mother who had to put up with all the bickering in the home. I think my younger brother and sister had more of a rivalry than I had. He thought I was favored and got more attention from our parents, and my sister thought she didn't have as many talents as I had. Little did she know!

The impact of early sibling relationships, whether positive or negative, often extends into later years. In boarding school a boy who walks friendly-like with his sister is liable to be dubbed Goody-Two-Shoes by peers. And in adult life sibling differences may be accentuated—all going their separate ways without much to do with others—unless a fresh work of grace is accomplished in individual hearts.

Discipline demonstrated. Christian parents intent on carrying out biblical directives usually recognize four basic principles of nurturing. The first is *consummate love.* When we genuinely love our child regardless of anything and everything, we'll discipline him faithfully. Children who know by their parents' words and attitudes that they're loved unconditionally accept discipline with a fair degree of gratefulness; even spanking doesn't blur the picture for long. Putting hedges around the child's activities—freedom within a structure shows up as evidence of Mom and Dad's loving concern. Yet, needless to say, it's not possible or always desirable to insulate our child from all sharp realities that entail periods of unhappiness; shall we call this *good* grief? Life isn't a perpetual party.

Respected writers place *consistency* near the top of any list of priorities for effective parenting. The fact that God Himself is perfectly consistent in all dealings with His people affords us a deep, satisfying sense of stability and safety, and in that climate we can move out to please Him in life and service. A somewhat similar condition obtains when we establish realistic guidelines for our child and faithfully enforce them; his inquisitive, adventurous spirit needn't be thwarted. Even an easygoing temperament can't handle unpredictability.

All the same, day-by-day consistency doesn't come naturally in the missionary home. "Our Day" in parents' lives is frequently marked by change without notice. A mother who maintains a smooth disciplinary pattern for each child over an extended period deserves the "Missionary Mother of the Year Award." Of course there's such a thing as foolish consistency; at times "interruptions are God's appointments." But we can set our sights on the ideal, all the while conscious of the delicate balance between desire and duty. This fine statement by Edith Schaeffer may not be applicable to every missionary family, but it has a message for every parent:

> When asked "What is a family?" and the answer comes, "A door," it seems to me the more accurate definition would be, "A family is a door that has hinges and a lock." The hinges should be well oiled to swing the door open during certain times, but the lock should be firm enough to let people know that the family needs to be alone part of the time, just to *be* a family. If a

family is to be really shared, then there needs to be something to share. Whatever we share needs time for preparation.[9]

Further, creative *communication* is utterly vital within the nuclear family. Good discipline has its source in good relationships, and the latter are built on good communication. Happy indeed are those parents and younger or older offspring who enjoy unhurried exchanges over a broad compass of topics. MKs thus engaged tend to be stable, cheerful, and confident. And parents frequently find that intimate disclosures on their part bring similar disclosures by the child.

In meaningful discussion the son or daughter is given freedom for expression. If it's a particular MK's style, his humorous sidelights will brighten the converse. Still, since parents have a role to play that will sometimes displease the child, they need to maintain a tender but firm authority gap. For instance Dad shouldn't try to enter the teen world as a peer.

Finally there's *correction*. Perhaps we can use a better term than "punishment"; it smacks of hostility. It's clear, too, that corporal chastening isn't to be carried out as a last resort to gain obedience. Yet it's one measure that should normally follow an act of willful misbehavior. Responsible parents will agree that flat-out defiance of their authority demands not merely a slap on the wrist but a trip to the woodshed. Probably children over 10 shouldn't be spanked but disciplined in other ways.

The martyr complex exhibited by some children after an encounter with the rod may be hard for parents to take. Our son of then three years, reacting to a session of this nature, moaned, "You don't love me, Mummie; you might as well throw me out the window." Every child needs to be assured of parental love before and after the event, with the whys and wherefores quietly and briefly explained. (Two related items: Dad shouldn't renege as co-custodian of the rod; and it's the better part of wisdom to keep the strap in a spot not immediately handy so that any touch of parental anger will have time to cool and faulty human judgment can be checked.)

Dividends of discipline. To close on a happier note, let's mention five qualities suggested for parents to instill in their child: a glad heart, a forgiving spirit, an attitude of thankfulness, consideration for others, and a sense of self-worth.

These abiding traits of character mark a well-disciplined child and a wisely regulated home. In a day when the concept of freedom and license, not submission, is filtering down to childhood levels and stimulating outbursts of rebellion even in believers' homes, parents who maintain reasonable, enforceable standards of decorum still help to build a stable base for their offspring's later years.

Summarizing things, we can say that disciplining is something we do *for* our child, not *to* him. And its benefits often extend to the next generation. In the course of time adult sons and daughters, emulating Mom and Dad (plus some fence-mending), will normally strive to keep their own children healthy, pray with and for them, actively listen, remain patient, show respect, inculcate their values. These new parents will also guard against overprotectiveness (that's for sure!). Avoiding criticism and imprudent comparisons, they'll remain sensitive to their child's feelings.

In essence, parents seek to train their sons and daughters "in the way they should go." What a task! Can't we visualize angels who don't have children, or white-robed saints who have had children, entertaining the desire to throw heavenly bouquets, whatever these might be, to faithful parents on this most uncelestial planet?

> Teach me Thy way, O Lord;
> Teach me Thy way!
> Thy guiding grace afford;
> Teach me Thy way!
> Help me to walk aright,
> More by faith less by sight.
> Lead me with heavenly light,
> Teach me Thy way!

> (*InterVarsity Hymns II*, #127)

5
SPIRITUAL INFLUENCES
Crucial Issues

*"Let the little children come to me, and do not
hinder them, for the kingdom of God belongs to
such as these. . . . And he took the children in his
arms, put his hands on them and blessed them"*
(Mark 10:14, 16).

HOME MISSIONS

Sample saints. In his first years the missionary child finds himself
in a setting optimal for spiritual nurture. As previously noted, he
spends an uncommon amount of time with his parents since the wide
variety of outdoor activities available to western children is closed to
him. Even in the youngster's interaction with local friends a parent is
usually stationed nearby. His environment, in fact, resembles that of
the Israelite children of old whose parents fulfilled literally the
injunctions of Deuteronomy 6:7 in respect to teaching the
commandments: "Impress them on your children. Talk about them
when you sit at home and when you walk along the road, when you
lie down and when you get up."

How then do missionary children respond to this favorable
environment? Certainly, as Proverbs 22:15 implies, they're akin to all
other young children in that there's that part of them that can be
readily manipulated for unwholesome ends. The New Testament,
nevertheless, characterizes little ones as sample saints; that is, some
of their qualities must be reproduced in anyone seeking to become a
member of God's eternal family. (G. Campbell Morgan calls Mark
10;14, quoted above, "the Magna Charta of children.") Singularly
unsophisticated, preschooler MKs repose implicit trust in their
parents' instruction, their minds not being cluttered with a multitude
of worldly strivings. And they're sheltered from winds that harden
souls. Eager to learn and remarkably receptive to impressions from
exterior sources, missionary children become a fertile field for the
sowing of gospel seed.

In this formative period the child possesses the faculty of wonder
and the disposition to forget minor emotional hurts. Keenly

conscious of frailty, he's constantly dependent on parental insight and care. Unconcerned with abstractions, the little boy and girl are able to exercise faith in the unseen, often sensing the immanence of God in a manner beyond their years. Of course children vary widely in this respect, not infrequently retaining concepts decidedly off-center. For instance, a preschooler may visualize God as a 10-foot giant whose visage alternates between smiles and frowns according to how he, the child, is acting at the moment.

Safe in the arms of Jesus. An important question: Do our young children belong in God's family regardless of spiritual commitment? And what about children in general? We won't be able to address these enquiries to everybody's satisfaction, but they appear to have a place in a study of this nature.

Many evangelical teachers hold that Jesus' words in Mark 10:13-16 and parallels assure us that all young children are secure in God's grace. Both text and context intimate at least that our Lord had in view a condition beyond that of physical well-being. Perhaps we can assume that the little ones whom Jesus took in His arms were offspring of covenant Jewish parents. We find considerable assurance also from Acts 2:39 and 1 Corinthians 7:14.

At any rate Scripture provides adequate basis for believing that children of Christian parents, until they reach the age of accountability and those who die before that time, are "safe in the arms of Jesus,/safe on his gentle breast." However, no explicit statement in the Word informs us *when* deceased children are born again and thus prepared for heaven. The following passages of Scripture, in addition to those just alluded to, furnish credence to the teaching that little children are secure in God's grace: 2 Samuel 12:23; Matthew 18:1-6, 14; Luke 18:15-17; Romans 5:12-21 (the key passage); 1 Peter 2:2; 2 Peter 3:9. Dr. M.R. De Haan, founder of Radio Bible Class, wrote forcefully on this issue:

> There isn't one verse in the entire Bible to support the idea that God will let any little ones perish. If children die, it's due to Adam's sin, but our Lord's atoning sacrifice took care of that. The only sin which could condemn them is rejecting Christ. Since babies cannot be guilty of this, they go straight to Heaven if they die.[10]

Is there a specific cutoff point at which the child becomes responsible for his own spiritual state? (At the moment we're referring to children of believers.) For at least two reasons the Bible doesn't enlighten us on this point. First, the age of discretion varies greatly in individuals according to the rate of mental development and the nature of their training. Second, should parents know the precise cutoff time, they might become lax in spiritual nurturance until the approach of that period.

Respected Bible teachers diversely suggest that accountability arrives sometime between ages 6 and 20, with perhaps 12 being preferred by most (Galatians 4:1, 2). Nevertheless this question won't engage the anxious attention of missionary parents; they'll move positively in their child's earliest years to lay the groundwork for this personal encounter with the Lord Jesus. We can't begin this assignment too early, but we can begin it too late. (Charles Spurgeon observes that when a child knowingly sins, he can knowingly believe.)

Childhood concern. Almost every missionary child poses this question to his parents: "Do all the babies and little children of the world go to heaven when they die?" Dr. De Haan's statement quoted above seems to assume that they do. (In India it's commonplace to witness a miniature stretcher on which a tiny body is laid, covered with flowers but with the face visible, being borne by two men to the burning ghat.) Not only does the question regarding the destiny of these children disturb the heart of the missionary child; it's a matter of grave concern also to his parents.

The likelihood of our propagating a tolerant view of infanticide, considered almost a virtue in a few cultures under certain circumstances, or of the massive death-rate of small children in emerging countries, may bear on the Bible's silence on the subject, except for those passages previously recorded. The World Health Organization reports that 40 out of 100 children in Third World countries die before the age of five, mainly from polluted water-borne diseases and undernourishment.

We can readily picture our Lord taking in His arms one of the delightful children seen in middle-class societies around the globe. It shouldn't be difficult to visualize His doing similarly with children much less favored. Still, we can't permit our emotions, unfeigned as they may be, to dictate our polity. In lieu of certainty, however, we can rest our hearts on such reassuring words as those in Genesis 18:25: "Will not the Judge of all the earth do right?" These little ones aren't the sport of circumstance.

Are we our neighbor's children's keeper? Phillips Brooks said, "He who helps a child helps humanity with an immediateness which no other help given to human creatures in any other stage of life can possibly give again." One of the signal privileges an overseas family enjoys is warm friendship with national neighbors and offspring. Missionary children act as a magnet to draw neighborhood youngsters to our homes. Our own experience:

During our years in Bombay we had continual contact with children from various racial backgrounds. Eunice conducted kids' classes in our home during the extended season of monsoon rains and at other times in the open corridor between our building and the next. Squatting crosslegged on mats and ready for anything that might occur, this diverse company included toddlers to schoolkids. With enthusiasm they sang gospel choruses to the tones of the tambourine and gestures of the leader. The magic of the flannelgraph attracted not only children but also an adult viewing audience a safe distance removed. From verandas in our own and adjacent buildings, mothers and children watched the goings-on. In relatively few instances did the parents of children attending the classes withdraw them, and then only because their offspring too often hummed Christian choruses at home.

SPIRITUAL GROWTH

The winning of an MK. By the time missionary children reach the middle teens, most have made some measure of commitment to Christ. Between 9 and 12, when children are especially receptive to teaching and concerned about moral and spiritual values, many MKs openly confess their faith. What's more appealing than to hear a sugar-sweet 12-year-old freely expressing her love for the Savior, perhaps in such words as these from the hymn, "In the home and in the throng,/ I would be like Jesus." (Recent research reveals that the great majority of today's missionaries force—not referring only to adult MKs—were converted between the ages of 8 and 12.) But sometimes problems arise as with this girl:

My first real awareness that being an MK is different from being an "ordinary" child came when I was about 10 years old. My older sister and I were sitting under a banyan tree when several church women joined us. I was asked to give my testimony, and I was seized with panic. I knew what a testimony was—I had heard many of them. As for myself, I always assumed I had been saved some years before, though I had no great concern about it. With tears rolling down my cheeks, I got to my feet and fled.

Later my sister said somewhat angrily, "You let the family down! You must never forget you're a missionary daughter!" I had failed as an MK to live up to expectations.

I came to the conclusion that we were special, not for our own sakes but because we were missionaries' children. Other children could make mistakes and be forgiven, but not we. For a finger pointed at us was a finger pointed at our parents and especially our father. But I longed to be seen as just myself, recognized as a person in my own right.

How do early commitments stand up under the force of time and circumstance? Certainly the ultimate proof of a once-for-all experience of salvation must always be perseverance to the end, though no believer gets through life without his share of shaky periods. How imperative, then, that our growing son or daughter's faith be rooted in inward conviction of having been drawn by the Lord to Himself; also that the young person be disposed to please Him in devotion and practical behavior.

It's true that the natural charm of a youngster's personality often resembles the tokens of a regenerate heart. The finely spoken "Yes, sir" and "No, sir" intrigue adult friends. And some of the spiritual feedback we get amuses rather than concerns us. Two such examples in our home:

> Our younger daughter, about eight years at the time, was asked the question in Matthew 9:5, "Which is easier to say . . . ?" Well, Shari began to count the letters in each option to get the answer! Then too, when we used to enquire what she received from particular sermons, she always had a readymade reply, "He told us to be good."

Growing in grace. At times young children react to untoward situations with exceptional displays of faith. Says the Psalmist, "From the lips of children and infants you have ordained praise." A missionary dad serving in Asia relates (in WBT's *In Other Words* for 11/78) how his three-year-old daughter exemplified the simplicity of faith:

> Outside a severe electrical storm jagged streamers across the black sky. Suddenly, without any warning, a sharp bolt of lightning hit nearby, shaking the house and sending me straight out of my chair. Across the hall from me, a Christian Indian girl living with us was tucking our twins into bed and leading them in their evening prayers.
>
> I listened for screams and wails of fright from across the hallway, but only a long silence hung in the room. Moments later I heard Kim's shaky voice timidly, yet somberly, continue in prayer: "And dear Lord, if You're all alone up there tonight and You're afraid too, You just come down here and stay with us."

When nurturing their child in spiritual truth, Christian parents normally major on God's everlasting love, and clearly we should never downplay this blessed feature. Nevertheless every youngster needs prudent grounding in an equally important doctrine—God's holiness. Otherwise he may later join the mass of professing Christians who, consciously or unconsciously, envision God as One whom nobody fears. The hymnwriter knew differently: "O, how I fear Thee, living God,/ With deepest, tend'rest fears." Grasping this aspect of truth will guard the MK from becoming a casual Christian; instead he'll recognize that the gospel is a life-or-death matter. (Childhood storybooks, in which invariably the principal characters live happily ever afterwards, may give young children the impression that Bible incidents end similarly.)

Since the missionary child hasn't experienced a sordid past, as we use the words, his sensibility of sin's implications is cushioned. In Chapter 4, in dealing with self-esteem, we observed how parents require keen discretion in presenting the facts of total depravity and its remedy in Calvary. The first testimony that follows, by a missionary daughter, has grim overtones; the other by a missionary mom ends agreeably:

The most destructive element in my childhood was a sinful consciousness of failure, guilt and worthlessness. With a heightened sense of sin, I believed I deserved to be punished for my hypocrisies. Knowing nothing of human psychology at that time, I didn't know what I was doing to myself, and actually believed I was doing the right thing. My perception of God from my earliest memories was of a terrible and vengeful God. I feared Him. I wanted to be loved, but I felt all the while that I was a hypocrite and that God would spew me from His mouth on the day of judgment. Yet I was more concerned with being accepted in the immediate present.

A vivid moment in our children's experience occurred on Easter Sunday morning after I had read to them about Jesus' death and resurrection. As we talked about how much the Lord loved us to suffer in this way for us, our five-year-old son began to cry. Then he confessed to being a very naughty boy and to have done many things to hurt Jesus. This led to his saying a simple prayer of confession, asking the Lord for forgiveness. Afterwards he felt so full of joy that he wanted to do something for Jesus. He said, "Mummie, I'm going to take a whole bundle of tracts and stand in front of the cinema and hand one to everyone in the line." (We lived just opposite the cinema, and the children had often noticed the people lining up to buy tickets.)

Deeper-life grounding. God doesn't rush the development of His own children; thus a young MK's growth in grace may not often be dramatic. But on reaching the teens, if he has learned to study the Bible independently, he should be able to digest enough truth to assure him of belonging securely in the family of God—of having been drawn tight by cords of love and grace. This should be to him the Biggest Thing in life.

Reassuring indeed would it be if such a young person should have begun to appropriate the preciousness of the believer's standing in Christ, as distinguished from his experiential state that can fluctuate from hour to hour. The former dimension is set forth in Romans 4 and 5, as well as elsewhere in the New Testament. The fact that believers are the best-dressed people is expressed in the first stanza of Zinzendorf's hymn:

> Jesus, Thy blood and righteousness
> My beauty are, my glorious dress;
> Midst flaming worlds, in these arrayed,
> With joy shall I lift up my head.

When an adolescent MK is established in *positional truth* and alerted to the sinister perils of antinomianism—the teaching that, for one thing, magnifies grace to the point of permitting believers much freedom to sin "that grace my increase" (Romans 6:1, 2)—he enjoys a bulwark in stormy seas. Having also laid hold in some measure of the glorious implications of our Lord's resurrection and His present ministry in heaven, he'll normally set himself to "live a life worthy of the Lord and please him in every way, bearing fruit in every good work, growing in the knowledge of God" (Colossians 1:10).

Another imperative of discipleship is *worship*. In a good number of missionary homes undoubtedly the "sacrifice of praise" is muted, although volumes like Tozer's *The Pursuit of God* rest on the family bookshelf. In this C&MA publication worship is cited as "the missing jewel of the evangelical church." Many of us are inclined to define worship much too broadly. A pastor's wife suggests a helpful definition geared to children: "telling God what we like about Him," a thought enlarged upon in such affecting hymns as Sir Robert Grant's "O Worship the King."

When the Holy Spirit has taken considerable ground in an adolescent MK's life and he's learned to devote himself to prayer and praise, he'll realize that something real and different has happened: his faith has become personal rather than borrowed. As a result, he won't later be disposed to relegate his early spiritual experiences to "Sunday school stuff" or "kid stuff." Now with a strong base, he'll cherish the holy privilege of fellowship with his risen Lord. (The hymnwriter asks, "What has stript the seeming beauty from the idols of the earth? . . . What have we to do with idols who have companied with Him?")

An additional aspect of spiritual maturation needs to be touched on—that of *witnessing.* Not a few adult MKs confess to living in mortal fear of person-to-person witnessing; at such times their backbones dissolve. One young missionary intern, now serving the Lord overseas, reflects on her earlier attitude to witnessing: "It violates my academic high horse." Another MK records her former experience: "God pulled the rug from under me. I wanted an easy life. I didn't want to share my faith."

Several adult MKs, however, mention how simple involvement in their parents' ministry served as a precursor to putting their own faith into action as they entered the teens—and to eventually reaching the foreign field. A CBFMS MK recalls an earlier experience:

> My memories of those early years include accompanying my parents to street meetings held every Sunday afternoon in front of the busiest railway station in Japan, Sin-juku. One meeting followed another all afternoon, with hundreds of people crowding around to hear the music and listen to the interpreted message of salvation. I often helped by passing out tracts.

Family council. Since family compactness makes mustering the clan relatively easy at any time, many missionary parents place high priority on arranging special gatherings once or twice a month. One child may report on a particular matter he's interested in; another suggests ways in which the family can share in the physical needs of local children; then someone reads letters from relatives and friends across the seas.

Some families introduce role-playing in such gatherings. For instance, all sit around a table and simulate a situation calling for proper etiquette. Thus the children gain experience and confidence in table manners, conversation, and other social graces. A missionary parent outlines the agenda in their family gatherings:

> Once a month or oftener our family members got together to review matters affecting any or all of us. Each child was encouraged to share his or her feelings and problems, with no restrictions so long as everything was carried out circumspectly. Each speaker was required to stand up and speak clearly in proper English.
>
> The first item on the agenda was always thanksgiving for the Lord's blessing and provision. Then came "objection time," which invariably was greeted with enthusiasm; in fact, this gripe session at times turned out to be the *piece de resistance* of

the meeting, much of it involving sibling problems. But "helpful hints for parents" also emerged for which we were grateful. Following efforts to resolve the main problems, one of the family closed the gathering with prayer.

Family prayers. The adage, "Children should be seen and not heard," has had its day. In missionary homes at least it has been modified. Now even the youngest member may participate in family gatherings if he does so nicely. These are ideal times to have each family member tell what he *likes* about his siblings!

A fair number of adult MKs testify to rewarding childhood experiences in family devotions; others are less than complimentary. Mild grumblings have to do chiefly with long parental prayers; also with the sameness characterizing prayer sessions. Some young people complain that Dad orchestrated everything with a set routine: choosing the hymns, reading Scripture, leading in prayer; and then, at the tag-end when all the young fry were dozy, a homily. Some MKs also demur on grounds that Dad's prayers sounded more like sermons, apparently aimed at straightening out one or another of the children for misconduct.

Other young adults, however, remember family prayers as being varied and meaningful. Wiggling of the preschoolers didn't call forth reprimand. Besides taking a modest part in prayer and Bible study, older youngsters engaged in questioning and dialogue. The passage of Scripture for the next gathering would be indicated and a concordance and other helps provided. Children shared their hurts while parents on occasion voiced their heartaches as well as their victories. "In our rich family life," an MK reflects, "we saw our parents involved in work they dearly loved."

Not infrequently out-of-town friends, national and foreign, would join the circle, adding warmth and freshness. Another MK, whose parents sometimes invited close neighborhood friends to family prayer-times, remarks: "I've seen how they changed when they came to know Christ."

Blessed is that young person who, "brought up in the truths of the faith" (1 Timothy 4:6), remains open to the full thrust of God's gracious workings as he approaches new frontiers of life!

> What shall He not bestow?
> Who freely gave this mighty gift, unbought,
> Unmerited, unheeded, and unsought;
> What will He not bestow?

6
EXPRESSING SEXUALITY
Values & Variants

"I urge you, brothers, in view of God's mercy, to offer your bodies as living sacrifices, holy and pleasing to God—which is your spiritual worship. Do not conform any longer to the pattern of this world, but be transformed by the renewing of your mind" (Romans 12:1, 2).

SEXUAL PATTERNS

Current practices. One can't overstate the gravity of conditions prevailing today in the West with regard to sexual attitudes. Preoccupation with physical sex characterizes multitudes of young people, many of whom, jaded at 15 and soaked in degrading notions of sexuality, have nothing to look forward to in the way of a sane, meaningful adulthood. An epidemic of teenage pregnancies outside of marriage (children bearing children) occurs year by year, at times in the case of young girls who a few years before charmed their parents with role-playing as brides.

Contemporary promiscuity knows no class boundaries; it permeates the moral structure of the masses. Nice, ordinary young men and women, not to mention adults in extramarital affinities, have been caught up in this hedonistic surge—though now they're referred to simply as being "sexually active." Over 100 U.S. magazines deal with sexual filth, some bombarding even primary schoolchildren with coarse sexual images. Apparently these purveyors don't lack resources of women prepared to flaunt their bodies for a price. Then there are the cheap soap operas for children on video tapes ("kidvid").

Loosely defined apart from any suggestion of unconditional commitment to one's partner, love is denigrated to the point of making sexual intimacy acceptable if it's mutually consenting. POSSLQs (persons of the opposite sex sharing living quarters) are steadily on the increase. Chapter 7 of Proverbs has a pertinent message for these days.

Pressing for purity. Denouncing the practice of sexual laxity marks us as antiquated; our vintage is showing. Yet God's people must brand these sexual quicksands as insufferably evil. Apart from being an affront to God and holiness, illicit sex issues in a hardness of life as almost nothing else does. Granted, times are changing, but "the word of the Lord stands forever" (1 Peter 1:25). One reassuring token, however, is that millions of people, not always Christians, view this explicit wantonness with earnest concern. One aroused non-missionary mother verbalizes her sentiments: "We're rearing a society with all the moral scruples of a band of baboons."

SEXUAL EDUCATION

Sex & Sexuality. Respected writers on sexuality deplore the current custom of equating *sex* with sexual intercourse, ignoring other aspects of what it means to be a man or a woman. The physical element is magnified all out of proportion to its legitimate place in marriage and love, which it deepens and enriches.

Sex is properly equated with *sexuality,* representing the total expression of the male and female personalities. Unless this dimension is carried out in a responsible framework, sex education may be little more than a clinical study of human anatomy, reducing men and women to biological and sexual machines. Indeed, the persistence and sweep of this unwarranted contrast, in and outside American public schools, reflects the depth of degeneration marking the sexual revolution of the last two decades.

Costly concealment. While information is understandably sketchy concerning how well missionary parents in the past handled sexual instruction of their children, it seems that present-day parents don't consider these matters the Great Unmentionable. Somewhat reticent and uncomfortable in the process, Mom and Dad are gradually becoming more open in discussing the age-old question of love and sexuality. Actually the growing youngster doesn't mind a bit of embarrassment on the part of Mom and Dad should he observe them struggling with labored candor; on the contrary, he may appreciate their enduring a touch of trauma for his sake.

Missionary parents are being alerted to the necessity of preparing their offspring for confronting an erotically oriented world society. And like certain other postures included in our study, what children don't learn about sexuality can hurt them later. For all that, an adult daughter recalls that as a child on the mission field she had to be extremely careful in broaching any question about sexual things to her mother: "Mom's blood pressure rose dangerously every time."

Sexual education is definitely a family affair, though professionals have taken over from delinquent parents. In boarding school this instruction is cared for largely by surrogate parents, but extended vacation periods at home enable parents to monitor their son or daughter's grasp of sexual matters. The pressing need for frank discussion over a wide spectrum is evident in this missionary daughter's declaration:

> I had not heard of rape. All I knew of sex was that it was something not to be talked about, something to do with adultery and fornication. All I knew was that something of *that* nature had taken place, and I could not bear having loathing poured on me—so I kept silent.
>
> Years later, when I understood, I realized I could have told my parents, but I knew it would break their hearts to realize that in my hour of greatest need and crisis they failed me. I did not see it that way then; I saw it that I had failed them; they were not to blame, for they thought I was too young to be told the facts of life. But they had warned me many times of dangers with strange men, and I could never go out unaccompanied.

Recognizing some of the dangers connected with centuries-old taboos and Victorian prudishness, an increasing number of missionary parents are determined to make themselves accessible and askable with respect to their children's sex-related questions. While no subject is off-limits, they attempt to put things in a wholesome setting. Wise parents won't overemphasize the perils involved in sexual expression lest the child begin to mistrust the beauty and tenderness of sound sexual patterns. Dad and Mom's mutual love, exhibited throughout the day in loving thoughtfulness, may be the best basis on which the child can forge a true conception of sexuality.

Building parental credibility. Preemptive action by parents should begin early, with rudimentary discussion of sexuality undertaken when the child is four or five. Parents will find delicate ways to prompt questions.

No parent expects to generate a lily-pure model of manhood or womanhood. Nevertheless in our child's impressionable years we won't expose him to much in the way of sensuous material. For all that, it's perilous to assume that our growing child is invulnerable to temptation, or that knowledge of the facts concerning physical sexuality will stir up a hornet's nest. Becoming informed won't ordinarily leave him more pervious to experimenting with his body; considerable experimentation takes place anyhow.

The boy in particular may experience his first real trouble when he gets settled into boarding school. Though mainly interacting with other MKs, he'll garner information and misinformation on sexuality, as well as hear scatological morsels bandied about among a sprinkling of students. Interestingly enough, however, several adult MKs recall that during boarding days certain boys held consistently to high moral standards, yet their rugged wholesomeness made an indelible impression on other students.

Obviously, then, the buildup of effective defenses must start from within the individual. When a child at home is groomed in simple but forthright language during preschool and early school-age years, he'll usually deal sensibly with sexual questions as they arise.

Traditionally the teaching of sexuality in the missionary home has been cared for by Mom, but now Dad has broken the ice. He finds no valid reason, psychological or practical, for not sharing in their child's sexual education. Of course the growing daughter will feel more comfortable with Mom in discussing certain sensitive issues. In any event, parents can lay the groundwork whereby the son or daughter's fragile frame, by God's grace, will become "an instrument for noble purposes, made holy, useful to the Master and prepared to do any good work" (2 Timothy 2:21).

TAILORING METHODS TO FITNESS

The preschooler. Family life writers, as they treat the problems, feelings, and reactions of youth, advise that instruction in sexual issues be carried out through dialogue rather than lecture. Youngsters miss a great deal in a lecture; they'll grasp and retain much more when their questions and responses serve as cues to guide Mom and Dad in further discussion. This back-and-forth approach proves especially effective during the pubescent and adolescent stages.

Each of the three principal categories of sexual education introduces parents to varying degrees of difficulty: *when* to teach, *how* to teach, and *what* to teach. We've touched on the first two factors, so now we'll glance at the *what* of sexuality in reference to advancing age-groups.

The time-worn analogy of the birds and the bees has long since gone by the boards, as has the copout that babies are bundles from heaven conveyed by angels. The four-year-old is more interested in how cows, dogs, and cats have babies; he wants explanations particularized. But at that age he's got plenty of more important things on the fire, so he'll file a parent's words in his mind and return in due course with related questions.

The mechanics of sex naturally loom large in a child's mind. In this connection, let us quote by permission from an ad for Health-tex, manufacturers of children's clothing; it summarizes the facts of human birth in language fours and fives can understand:

A baby begins as a small egg in its mother's womb. A womb is a warm, sheltered place inside the mother's body just below her tummy. The little egg starts to grow into a baby when it is fertilized by a tiny seed from the father. The baby grows inside the mother for nine months. It gets its nourishment from its mother through a cord connected to its tummy.

Finally the baby is big enough to be born. Being born means that the baby comes out of the mother's body through a special passageway below the mother's womb. The doctor snips off the cord that connected the baby's body to its mother's. The place where the cord was connected is—your belly button! Some babies are girls and some are boys, but they all are very cuddly and easy to love."[11]

The middle-age child. This stage, from 6 to 10, is sometimes ignored or sketchily dealt with in articles and books on family life; one reason is that it's regarded as quiescent. And indeed, compared with the ups and downs of the preschooler and the turmoil of the teenager, the life of the typical school-age child is marked by calm, steady development emotionally and intellectually. Spiritual growth increases the capacity of the boy or girl to cope with upcoming physical changes.

Since the girl's sexual development is more advanced than that of the same-age boy, she experiences sexual awareness sooner. She may, however, be as embarrassed as the boy in seeking and receiving information; but she'll be grateful and intensely interested in all she gets, such as a book on sexual maturation. The boy also will appreciate material prepared for his particular needs, especially if it contains correct definitions of the "dirty words." He sees some of these inscribed on walls or hears them from older boys but feels too uncomfortable to ask anyone their meaning, even parents.

The preadolescent. Here we glance at some personality traits of the boy or girl between 11 and 13, the period of shifting gears. Just prior to adolescence comes this pubescent stage when the major biological steps toward sexual maturation escalate, with accompanying fluctuation of moods. Both the boy and girl undergo a loosening-up process to prepare them physically for functions ahead; each grows in his or her own way. The girl's body undergoes more complexities than the boy's since she's being prepared for childbearing. Because puberty affects every part of the body, this stage of life has been termed the twilight zone of growing up. Despite a considerable measure of turmoil, the thrill of feeling grownup makes things exciting for many preadolescents.

Perhaps the missionary boy and girl in boarding school enjoy some advantage as they move along the bumpy road to adolescence:

they've got plenty of company day and night in their moments of misery. Doubtless some worry when they observe distinct changes in peers that aren't occurring in themselves. They need to be assured that preadolescents vary much, even over a stretch of a year or two, with respect to processes leading to puberty.

In this stage certain personal and social traits typically appear. The dormparent will be hard put to maintain a modicum of tidiness in the 11-year-old's dorm. In the social sphere friendships come and go with same-sex students. Boys and girls don't get along well together, although teasing one another may indicate initial evidence of interest in the opposite sex. The girl's customary protestations may actually be a cover-up for inward enjoyment even if her reaction extends to hair-pulling. At this juncture boys and girls often have a special one in their dreams. The young man, uneasy with his thoughts, fears that a peer will read his mind.

The adolescent. If parents have early established the child's confidence in their judgment on points of sexual awareness, he'll probably respect their credibility on entering adolescence, when sexually related issues afflict him right and left. In view of this, parents need to keep abreast of things. Today when Christian books, tapes, and magazines are available, Mom and Dad needn't remain ignorant or bewildered in fielding any query posed by son or daughter. They'll frankly discuss formerly hush-hush subjects such as rape and homosexuality. Any consideration of contraceptives obviously brings a double message. Should the teenager throw a real knockout, he'll appreciate being brought into mutual quest for enlightenment.

The adolescent should know that sexual desire isn't in itself sinful; it's God-given and normal from puberty on. The seal of Scripture is upon the sanctity of physical sexuality in the marriage union, not only for procreation but for mutual pleasure and the deepening of the husband-wife relationship. Further, sexual feelings toward those of the opposite sex don't necessarily imply lust.

The teenage MK living and moving in the family homeland would have to cloister himself in a monastery to remain unaffected by the barrage of plastic sexual values abroad today. Much of the paraphernalia of the current erotica is as near as the local drugstore. Consequently the young person must be persuaded in his own inner being that shallow sex erodes every fine instinct for true affection; also that a divided heart in the matter of personal purity has grave implications. He'll like himself much better all around if he can replace his urges with wholesome thinking.

It should be noted, nevertheless, that a single enticement to sexual sin on the part of an adolescent needn't leave his confession of Christ open to question, though his spirit will suffer deeply because of it. He'll now know that indulging in heavy petting, not uncommon with churchgoing youth, makes him susceptible to passing the point of no return. (In this connection, "making it around the bases" in contemporary parlance has nothing to do with baseball.) It's the girl, of course, who usually calls the signals and establishes the ground rules in social relationships, but nowadays a graceless girl may do the propositioning. Christian girls can maintain their virtue only by being settled in their love for and obedience to Christ—and armed with a ready arsenal of unqualified NOs.

The syncopated claptrap of hard rock, the "Pied Piper of Punk" that holds center-stage for multitudes of young people today, isn't for the earnest Christian. Along with other contemporary distortions that arouse abnormal sexual feelings, hard rock music promotes rebellion against all authority, including that of parents and God Himself.

Throughout the ebb and flow of their adolescent's weaknesses and temptations, regardful parents forearm themselves against becoming punitive or accusing—self-defeating actions that bemean the young person in his own eyes and impair later intercommunication. Needless to say, however, Mom and Dad won't become obsequious or intimidated. Working out from the strengths of their son or daughter, they communicate positively in the spirit of responsible love. (By the way, such parents encourage their adolescent daughter to become as attractive as possible, minus an array of cosmetics.)

Intrapersonalizing the sex drive. Previous to puberty and long afterwards, almost every boy and girl is confronted with the problem of masturbation. In the old days the average girl matured at 15 and married at 18; now it's 12 and 20. The boy matures a year or so later. This ten-year span, coming at a time when sensual desires are strong, presents a dilemma for young people. A few MKs have shared with us their inability to control this form of sexuality.

Considerate parents approach the problem with graciousness. Since the Bible doesn't specifically mention the practice (the incident of Onan in Genesis 38:9 isn't relevant here), we're shut up to sane, spiritual apprehension of scriptural principles. The exhortation of the Apostle quoted at the head of this chapter capsulizes New Testament teaching.

A number of evangelical writers believe that masturbation isn't basically a moral issue; otherwise the Bible would have disallowed it. They affirm that, since God has put such a powerful urge within us that often leads to fantasizing, it's virtually impossible for a young person to entirely forego the practice. Thus God doesn't condemn the temperate movement to alleviate the stress.

Most Christian authors, nevertheless, seem to agree that obsessive masturbation stems from a lack of adequate parental affection. The child who savors a giving home environment doesn't ordinarily resort later to extremes of this compensatory pleasure. Accordingly, parents are advised not to react punitively to their young child's habit of probing his body.

A recent book by Dr. John White, an esteemed counselor and Associate Professor of Psychiatry at the University of Manitoba, has proved most helpful to us in analyzing this problem.[12] We're using extended extracts from the volume to fill out the major part of our discussion. Here are some introductory comments:

> People who are anxious and lonely have recourse to it though it affords them scant solace. Children who are under stress at home, adolescents in turmoil, husbands whose wives are pregnant, and men and women away from home all tend to masturbate. . . .
>
> Is masturbation right or wrong? . . . You are not the helpless victim of uncontrollable urges however strongly you may feel to the contrary. You are responsible for your action. . . .
>
> It is an intrapersonal not an interpersonal affair. Its defect lies at this very point: it takes what was meant to be a powerful urge encouraging a close personal relationship but aborts it. That which was meant to be shared is squandered in solitude. . . .
>
> Denied in pubescence and adolescence any reassurance that sexuality was in fact wholesome and that their sexual feelings were evidence that they were becoming men and women, they naturally feel guilty when they masturbate. Disgust and shame are caught as well as taught. . . .

Many young Christians struggling with this habit agonize before the Lord in pursuit of victory. They may experience some relief through physical activities, early morning devotions, and placing pertinent Bible verses on their bedroom wall. Then too, there seems to be correlation between overeating, or bedtime snacking, and masturbation. Dr. White concludes his edifying remarks with additional practical counsel:

> Behaviorists and analysts go a long way toward explaining the grip of habit, but they do not understand that man, made in the image of God, is a responsible being. . . .
>
> Masturbation is not a good thing, but neither is it a heinous sin. . . . *When the interpersonal is lacking, sexual stimulation is promoting the very thing it was designed to overcome.*
>
> The modern urge to reassure ourselves that masturbation is fine in moderation springs from a laudable wish to alleviate the

excessive fear and guilt it causes many people. With this wish I sympathize. But I must not in my efforts to alleviate guilt say that pale shades of gray are white. . . .

The toughest problem is the spiritual one: Why does God fail to answer my prayer for deliverance? . . . To you who are frustrated about masturbation, I would say the following:

(1) God is well able to deliver you. If he isn't doing so at the moment, he may, incredible as it may seem to you, have a prior concern with something else in your life.

(2) Your view of the seriousness of your problem is exaggerated. . . . You hurt no one but yourself by masturbating, but whom have you hurt this week by your sarcasm, your coldness, your forgetfulness, your lack of tact and courtesy? How many minutes have you praised God in the last twenty-four hours?

(3) Thank God for your sexual feelings. Don't hate them. . . . Thank him, too, for the day when you will be master of your sexual drive.

4) Quit hating yourself. Refuse to listen to the endlessly torturous accusations of the accuser of the brethren, who accuses you day and night (Rev. 12:10). If you are cast down, God waits for you with open arms. . . .

(5) Refuse to let masturbation cause you discouragement and self-disgust. . . . Admit no discouragement but ever return quietly to him and wait in his presence.

Leaving a legacy. However difficult it is, our mission as parents is clearcut in terms of instilling in our children a sense of sexual responsibility. We remain the stabilizing force in molding the lifestyle of our son and daughter; they want and need an open, trusting relationship with us.

We parents often meditate on the fact that we're "fearfully and wonderfully made" (Psalm 139:14). We can then persevere in our nurturing to the end that our children, our own flesh and blood whom God has so purposefully formed, will bring honor to Him in their sexual expression. In this poem from *The Keswick Hymn-Book,* Dr. H.C. Moule couches in words the inner longings of one conscious of his frail humanity:

> Come in, Oh come! the door stands open now;
> I know Thy voice; Lord Jesus, it was Thou;
> The sun has set long since; the storms begin;
> 'Tis time for Thee, my Savior, Oh, come in!
>
> Alas, ill-order'd shews the dreary room;
> The household-stuff lies heap'd amidst the gloom,

The table empty stands, the couch undress'd;
Ah, what a welcome for th' Eternal Guest!

Yet welcome, and to-night; this doleful scene
Is e'en itself my cause to hail Thee in;
This dark confusion e'en at once demands
Thine own bright presence, Lord, and ord'ring hands.

I seek no more to alter things, or mend,
Before the coming of so great a Friend;
All were at best unseemly; and 'twere ill
Beyond all else to keep Thee waiting still.

Come, not to find, but make this troubled heart
A dwelling worthy of Thee as Thou art;
To chase the gloom, the terror, and the sin;
Come, all Thyself, yea come, Lord Jesus, in!

7
FURLOUGH IMPRESSIONS
Felicity & Ferment

"Enlarge the place of your tent, stretch your tent curtains wide, do not hold back; lengthen your cords, strengthen your stakes" (Isaiah 54:2).

HOMEWARD BOUND

Potential for enrichment. The context of Isaiah's exhortation relates to both the spiritual and geographical expansion of Israel. In this double dimension it has been fittingly employed in missionary writings to encourage Christians to turn their eyes and hearts, and possibly also their feet, toward the "regions beyond." (We'll recall that William Carey used this portion of Scripture for his memorable missionary sermon in which he gave out the maxim, "Expect great things from God; attempt great things for God.") However, we're restricting the application to the missionary family's potential for personal enrichment and effective ministry during the months of furlough.

Factors pertaining to their children frequently become the major reason for parents' decision to go on leave, at least in terms of its timing and duration. Then for the entire family, the agenda consists of physical recuperation, reunion with relatives and friends, fellowship with local churches involved in their overseas work, and the children's education. All this can add up to spiritual renewal and readjustment of priorities for the way ahead. Some parents engage in continuing education in order to sharpen their adequacy in foreign service; others seek some form of professional accreditation. So not much grass grows under their feet during the months in the homeland.

Nostalgic yesteryears. Before looking at present-day issues connected with furlough, let us review briefly, and to us oldsters wistfully, a scenario of the missionary past. "Memory has its tricks of perspective," but we'll try to keep within the bounds of reality.

The dramatic growth of jet travel has shrunk the globe; foreign workers can now make it home in a day. Forty years or less ago, it often required a month by ocean liner and/or lumbering cargo boat from distant lands.

The hour spent with national and missionary friends on the pier prior to embarking stands out in poignant remembrance. By prayer and song they would commend the travelers to the Lord. If any were given to tears, particularly when the departing ones were retiring from the field, they could shed them without embarrassment. Then the bearhugs of adieu. Long after the streamers stretching from the pier to boat had snapped, those on board would watch fervidly until only the faintest outlines of friends and country were observable.

Thus commenced the homeward trip. On board everything had a novel flavor—the shipboard mystique. The only persons casting a negative vote in this regard were those subject to seasickness, who at times thought they were going to die yet were afraid they wouldn't. Perhaps the voyage would be broken several times by stopovers at major ports, when passengers could disembark for a few hours or days to enjoy exotic scenes.

The last lap of the journey across the Atlantic or Pacific in a luxury superliner like the *Queen Elizabeth, Queen Mary,* or the *United States* brought to us ordinary mortals the impression of sojourning in a floating palace. Even in economy class, somewhere between the barons and the ballast, we were completely satisfied. No tinge of envy struck us with respect to first-class passengers on the upper decks with their gourmet restaurants and ultra-luxurious lounges; instead, we somehow pitied them since many appeared listless and world-weary. The children loved the spacious swimming pool and a host of other amenities such as shuffleboard on deck. The sumptuous meals had no price-tag—it was all in the ticket—though some of us felt guilty about diverging so radically from an oft-expressed desire for "simple living and high thinking."

Each missionary family discovered a fresh consciousness of oneness. If the children had been away at school, the days on board were specially agreeable; they got acquainted with their parents all over again. Then there was the joy of leisurely fellowship with other Christians, including times of prayer and Bible study. Usually a good number gathered for the Lord's table, the breaking of bread, when there was neither high nor low church, Calvinist nor Arminian, but Christ was all in all. Invariably too, fellow passengers comprised nationals from a dozen countries, and meaningful friendships ensued in a most relaxed setting.

Return to native soil. After this spicy tincture of the past, evoking nostalgia that plane travel can't match, we revert for a moment to more recent times. Here are travel accounts of two MKs:

On some furloughs our family travelled east via Europe to visit Dad's family in England. On these trips we visited such places as the Tower of London, St. Paul's Cathedral, Westminster Abbey, and many other great sights of London. Going west we stopped in San Francisco and saw the sights of that great city. Nob Hill and Fisherman's Wharf, the Golden Gate Bridge are still indelibly printed in my memory. Along the way to or from furlough we stopped for a time in Israel to see the holy places; in Egypt where we viewed the Pyramids, Sphinx, and rode on camels; in Switzerland where we spent three days in an Alpine hotel.*

Life as a missionary child has been exciting. How many of you before the age of 14 had crossed the Atlantic four times, or climbed the Eiffel Tower, or gazed at the art works of the Louvre, or walked the halls of Notre Dame Cathedral in Paris? Or which of you has walked right out of the pages of your geography book into the streets of Geneva, Marseilles, New York or Casablanca? I remember the thrill of seeing the Rock of Gibraltar for the first time, framed by a fleet of warships as we entered the Mediterranean.*

The American missionary's sighting of the Statue of Liberty brings a surge of national loyalty. (Currently the lady's iron constitution is undergoing surgery, or rather is being refurbished, after holding high her mighty torch for a century.) Without minimizing his love for the country he has left, this is his native land. An African missionary serving among blacks in England in discipleship training remarked, "I'm going on furlough to Africa." Doubtless the question raised in the protasis of Sir Walter Scott's familiar poem is echoed in the hearts of many returning missionaries, whatever their homeland:

> Breathes there the man, with soul so dead
> Who never to himself hath said,
>   This is my own, my native land!
> Whose heart hath ne'er within him burn'd
> As home his footsteps he hath turn'd
>   From wandering on a foreign strand?

REVERSE CULTURE SHOCK

Unnaturalized citizens. Some of the subleties of acculturation experienced by new workers on entering a foreign environment for settled service are well known; only a few hardy and flexible souls avoid some degree of neuroses in adjusting to a distinctly different culture. Yet from the first the missionary seeks to identify with the people of the land and with as many nonreligious customs as necessity and wisdom dictate. In so doing he's changed both inwardly and outwardly.

But now comes disorientation of a different order. Obviously a missionary's homecoming isn't marked by the trauma experienced by an immigrant. While on the field, through the press and radio, he usually keeps posted on major developments back home, such as the materialistic climate, faster pace of life, cluttered and elaborate homes, and perhaps the new dress styles. (The day of the missionary barrel and the frumpy-looking missionary has almost passed.) Still, he'll sense a measure of conflict as he observes the increased decline in moral and spiritual values. For example, a good reverend intones concerning the "redeeming value" of some X-rated films. In certain ways western society, having rejected the light of the gospel, is worse off than the millions in Third World lands who have never heard the good news (Luke 12:48).

Children's debut. Prior to leaving for the homeland, thoughtful parents don't keep the children breathlessly expectant. They won't build up America as Utopia at the expense of the host country. Good features of each are balanced, with emphasis on factors in which the youngsters have already shown interest. One adult MK comments, "In my experience, children don't want to leave the 'foreign' country for America." Another, now a missionary in Costa Rica, gives an unusual slant on "home":

> My folks never referred to the U.S. as "home" and so we kids never thought of it as that either. That may have been because they too were MKs. For me "home" was where I lived and that was that. That's still true for me.
>
> When someone asks me where I'm from, I never really know what to say! I was born in Korea, but we left there when I was 2, so that's not home. I grew up in Colombia, but we left there when I was 14, so that's not home. My parents live in southern California but, except to the extent they are there, that's not home. My "emotional" home base in the U.S. is Minneapolis, but I haven't lived there for 18 years, so that's not home. . . . You see, "home" must of necessity be where I'm living now. And, fortunately, that's just what it feels like!

The fact that mission societies are advocating shorter terms of service, thus providing more frequent though shorter furloughs, enables most growing children to become reasonably well acclimated to western life. Yet they step into a world of junk food, small talk, and whodunits; of new but patched-up or grease-bespattered jeans, T-shirts with bright sayings, and bumper stickers that broaden their cultural savvy.

The preschooler spends most of his time with at least one parent, so he makes out happily over the stretch. Convenience-oriented kitchens and bathrooms prove a never-ending source of interest to him. An adult MK recollects:

> We nearly drove Mom crazy with our curiosity and fascination. There were faucets and toilets that flushed, and doors with brass knobs in all shapes. It was fun just to open and close them. Some had fancy ways of locking, too. And bright lights everywhere; stores and streets blazed and flashed with them. The cars, big and shiny, went so fast—oh, it was scary.*

The preadolescent, however, encounters problems in meeting new situations. It helps if he's living with a grouping of missionary families at mission headquarters, but still he may not feel altogether at ease. One MK notes that all the kids have to be *so* circumspect in behavior. These testimonies give a perspective of MK sentiments about furlough:

> Many of my clothes came from the missionary barrel and were a little out of style. But some Ladies' Missionary groups made clothes for me which I liked, though they didn't always fit nicely. On the whole, though, people were kind and sympathetic. I'm basically shy and don't find meeting new people and going to strange places easy.

> During furlough I got drawn away from God by the pretty things of the world—the music, styles and friends. I was faced with ridicule in the public school, and sometimes it wasn't easy in the churches. It was altogether different before the nationals. They knew me as I really was.

> In Morocco and Spain I was always the American, while in America I was the one who came from overseas. I grew up unaccustomed to the culture of our own country. The fast pace in America—McDonald's, superhighways, supermarkets, and super-everything—seemed so strange and new in the eyes of this MK. I always felt, though, that when all the frenzied activity of furlough was over, we could go home. Home was Morocco, even though we MKs always talked about life in the States and what we remembered from the previous furlough.*

Back to school. American public school education is presently under strong attack from all quarters for its "rising tide of mediocrity." More than 20 million adults remain functionally illiterate. Teachers, curricula, and educational standards have received a C- or barely passing grade from high-level panels of experts. To mention only one important weakness, the "cafeteria style" curricula in secondary classes, providing an excessive and sometimes purposeless variety of electives, permit students to choose the easiest subjects. A longer school day and school year, as well as more homework, are clearly in the works—more in line with procedures in Britain and other industrialized countries.

The mushrooming of Christian day schools in recent years in America offers missionary children an attractive alternative to public schools. With evangelical headmasters and teachers as well as good discipline, these institutions are finding favor with thousands of Christian families. The charges are moderate, especially when a school is sponsored by a congregation and located on church premises.

It's the pubescent and early adolescent attending public schools who suffer most from cultural factors. They may think other students take them for country bumpkins, just arrived from the boondocks. Additionally, the physical and mental changes occurring at this time of life tend to disturb their emotional equilibrium. But this MK made out fairly well:

> Because of our family standards, we were often classed as "goodie-goodies" (which we weren't). It was hard to keep up those standards against the pressures, but in the end they got used to us and accepted us. The school group was easier to fit into than the church group—I guess because we were in school more.*

FAMILY AGENDA

Recharging batteries. Mission societies advise their furloughites to lay aside time for rest and recreation before becoming involved in deputation. Thus even the emotionally drained worker can get back on his feet. Nowadays the larger missions maintain living quarters for members, with complete housekeeping facilities. Without inconveniencing anyone, a family can then pitch tent and enjoy the spice of homelife. The remark, "We're a family again," or words to that effect, spring from children's lips.

On deputation the homes of local believers are open to the Lord's servant and any family members traveling with him. However, a growing number of missionary-minded churches reserve accommodation for longer use by furloughing workers in whose support they share—an arrangement enabling each family to interact satisfyingly with the church family.

Interestingly, a number of enterprising Christians with practical and administrative gifts have established small communities where furloughing missionaries, besides enjoying household amenities, may take education courses taught by missions specialists. Usually there's supervised recreation for children. Two of these centers operate in New Jersey, one in Ventnor, the other in Laurel Springs.

Reunion days. Visiting kinfolk tops the list of priorities for the first months of furlough. Of course the old haunts change with the years, and there are subtractions as well as additions among loved ones.

Because the missionary family on the field finds it impossible to share the lives of most close relatives, indepth communication with many of these dear ones during furlough is out of the question. Yet Mom and Dad discover afresh that enriching fellowship doesn't wane or grow dull in the case of those standing faithfully with them in prayer for the overseas testimony. An hour together bridges the gap of years.

The youngsters generally need little priming or pumping; as a rule camaraderie with their cousins comes unassumingly. At times, nevertheless, their behavior raises questions and eyebrows. An aunt declared to a missionary mom with reference to a five-year-old son who had started the aunt's car all by himself, "I'd hate to follow that one throughout life!"

Grandparents used to be delightful connecting links with yesterday for their grandchildren, and indeed they're still that for many MKs. But today they're not romanticized as previously; in fact their role is ambiguous. Still, they often continue to remark that grandchildren are the joy of their lives. In some cases there's a Granny Derby afoot—a striving for the most grandchildren!

Despite the satisfaction of reunion with loved ones, time spent with them isn't altogether free of mixed emotions. Some members of the extended family, while appreciating our adventurous spirit in leaving home and adjusting to life abroad, have virtually no interest in the spiritual dimension of our task. As a result, cementing relationships and seeking their well-being in the things of God approach crosscultural communication. Strangely enough, we may feel closer to hundreds of foreign nationals in the family of faith than to some of our kith and kin. While no doubt our own family's witness before relatives isn't always what it should be, we sense the sharp edge of our Lord's statement in Mark 6:4, "Only in his home town, among his relatives and in his own home, is a prophet without honor."

After even amicable periods with relatives, some MKs remain conscious of rootlessness. Three adult girls describe their varying reactions:

> With several other kids in our family, I still often wonder where my roots are. I've seen my cousins, aunts and uncles,

grandparents, and other relatives only a few times on furlough, but this isn't enough to save me from feeling sorry for myself. It's not a big deal, and I'm really not complaining, but it's a factor that has to be handled.

My father is Canadian, my mother American. I was born in India and married an American. But I don't feel like a woman without a country. I have always felt securely "at home" wherever my parents were, and I want our children to feel the same way.

I knew very little about my parents' background, of their childhood or their relatives. So I didn't sense being a part of the larger family circle. It would have given me a sense of worth, security and identity during those earlier years. It would have helped me also to have our own children identify with their grandparents.*

DEPUTATION DIARY

Family on the move. Like many an American family vacation, deputation starts out with rosy expectancy but encounters snags along the way. When the younger brood accompany the parents, all the goings and comings, the startings and stoppings, make it difficult for Mom and Dad to enforce a firm standard of deportment. Unless the children are models of good manners, the hours spent cramped in the back seat (the "grumble seat") of a car can cause multiple decibels of misbehavior; the recurring question is, "Are we almost there?" It helps if one of the youngsters is gifted with infectious humor about the right things.

Yet on lengthy trips with the children along, most parents come through with ways to relieve the tedium. Their repertoire will include a number of games, one of which may be "Places." One family member names a town, state, or country and the next player names one that begins with the last letter of this place; e.g., Boston might be followed by Nevada, and that by Australia. Then too, special duties may be assigned to each child. With a notebook in hand, one youngster jots down a few details about places stopped at or passed through; another notes the people seen and met. Later the children say their pieces with added commentary. Most MKs are amazed to observe *Americans* digging ditches and doing roadwork—jobs for coolies; but the sight signifies how hard work commands respect.

MK on the spot. Getting spruced up to appear before a company of people takes a toll of the younger fry. One preschooler on a visit with grandparents reportedly sounded this note in prayer: "Thank you, Lord, that we could get dirty today." Nevertheless churches appreciate having missionary offspring in their midst; the believers experience heightened interest in the overseas testimony when they gain a view of the whole family.

Some households "adopt" a missionary family of similar age-span. In the *Evangelical Missions Quarterly* for 4/82, a missionary suggests a simple fivefold commitment a church family could make with regard to the new extended family: Pray daily, give weekly, write monthly, send a "care package" quarterly, remember birthdays and anniversaries annually.

More tidying up, of course, is required when the family is invited for a meal in a member's home. The children are duly reminded about table manners: "Whatever is served, eat a little; sit up straight; don't speak too much unless you're spoken to, and then answer distinctly." But things don't always work out perfectly:

On one occasion we ourselves were initially pleased with the deportment of our loquacious son during the dinner hour. He remained reasonably quiet throughout the meal. Later, though, we discovered he had been punching holes in the lovely plastic tablecloth. The hostess gracefully defused the crisis.

An MK mentions a rescue operation carried out by his hostess. Knowing something of child psychology, she had prepared a separate table for her own children and the young guests—screened off from their elders' table and laden with food to fit the fancy of normal youngsters.

Deputational gatherings loom as the nemesis of MKs, most of whom would prefer to get out of the limelight and into the woodwork. They chafe under the image many Christians superimpose on them. Such a young person may be grilled on issues which only his parents could address. Things are somewhat different in churches with a good percentage of young people.

Generally speaking, MKs are relieved when Dad refrains from putting them forward in meetings. Likewise they're pleased if the pastor assures them prior to the service that he'll not call on them unless they request him to do so. Then they're no longer on tenterhooks. Perhaps a teenager may desire to take part in a rapping session with other youths, or explain some of the display scenes.

Run for the money? Deputation has been defined as "the process by which a missionary call comes to fruition." Its purpose is to permit the prospective missionary or furloughite to share his burden for a particular field, thus enabling the Lord's people to maintain prayer interest on his behalf. Rightly or wrongly, however, the issue of finances stands out forcefully in missionaries' minds.

Certainly the typical missionary isn't mercenary. He doesn't relish

the role of fund-raiser, but as Matthew 10:10 indicates, "The worker
is worth his keep." Resources must be secured for passage,
equipment, and support. It's only when the topic of money
dominates one's ministry that legitimate questions arise. On being
asked as a five-year-old regarding the significance of deputation, our
younger daughter explained, "It's when we go round gathering up the
money." We trust she didn't get that from her parents' practices! A
lighthearted volume by Peter J. Brashler relates this story, somewhat
abbreviated here:

> A mother was riding a bus with her little boy. The boy
> swallowed a dime and began to choke. The frantic mother
> called for help. A fellow passenger stepped up, turned the boy
> upside down, shook him vigorously, pummeled his backside,
> until he coughed up the dime. "Oh, Doctor, thank you so much.
> You knew just what to do." "Oh, that's O.K., but I'm not a
> doctor." "Not a doctor! Well, you certainly knew how to get the
> dime out of him." "Oh, I'm a missionary," explained the hero.[13]

The prayer-letters of newly commissioned missionaries reveal
much concerning principles of finance. Enthusiastic in their vision of
foreign service for Christ and determined to follow biblical
conventions, they yet employ distinctly different methods of raising
funds. Some mention outrightly to each congregation the amount
outstanding; others thinly disguise their financial shortages; still
others make no mention and give no hint of needs unless specifically
asked by responsible believers. While we ourselves have practiced it
haltingly, we favor the last method. But whatever the principle
followed, many workers discover that a considerable portion of their
support comes from sources unrelated to deputational meetings.

It's no purpose of ours to assess the different procedures. But we're
concerned that young Christians, MKs included, with a heart for
God's testimony overseas, shouldn't become disillusioned by certain
current practices of an extreme form. We appreciate this statement
by a CBFMS appointee and MK, appearing in *Impact:*

> I don't know how most people feel about going on
> deputation, but I didn't want to go, to speak to people who had
> no reason to listen to me, to be on the road more than not, and
> to raise support for some missionary's kid (me) whose desire
> was to be in Africa.
> I had good reason for not wanting to go on deputation. I
> knew from past experiences that I was a poor public speaker. I
> hated even the thought of it. What could I say to all those
> people that Mom and Dad had not already said?
> And about the finances. I just told the Lord I wasn't going to

tell people about my support needs. In spite of my attitude, God worked wonders for me. He took my inability to speak and turned it into one of the strong points of my ministry.

Sometimes I laughed, sometimes I cried, sometimes I had to tell someone and sometimes I just kept those little treasures between Him and me.

I came away from that dreaded year of deputation enriched and praising God. I loved it, and I hope I learned the things God wanted to teach me.

Unminced words. MKs have much to say about experiences during deputation. From our general reading of missionary literature, we've put together a digest of their impressions, both positive and negative. First the bad news:

> Feeling like part of a traveling circus, with each family member having little acts to perform
>
> Wanting to be treated like the church's young people. "We MKs have many of the same desires and problems—like other girls and boys."
>
> Sensing that church people aren't much interested in them beyond their hearing them quote John 3:16 in the foreign tongue
>
> Groaning when asked by his dad to stand up—being on display
>
> Being asked silly questions, sometimes on adult level
>
> Having to dress up in national costumes and parade around the room
>
> Being expected to remember names of each person who sent them articles of clothing
>
> Craving the companionship of peers and seldom getting it
>
> Finding American kids narrow-minded about those who are a little different from themselves
>
> Being considered something like a freak by peers
>
> Being scared stiff when asked to give a testimony while the church kids talked happily together—and then "not having the foggiest idea of what I was saying."
>
> Being considered model children—ultra polite; then asked by peers if he ever got spanked
>
> Conscious that, since the money came from the churches, he *had* to act correctly
>
> Being asked to describe some experiences—the weirder the better, like finding snakes in his pillow at night
>
> Hearing "natives" instead of "nationals," and noting that many church people tend to downgrade nationals

Being asked why she wasn't black since she was born in Africa

Feeling afraid of pulling a boner and letting his parents down

"People generally come to be entertained with romantic stories of happy mission orphanages, and their imagination is set afire by descriptions of joyful natives singing hymns and rising out of the waters of baptism by the hundreds. Your horror stories of families struggling to survive in one small room and no bathroom except the communal pump in a stinking rat-infested slum turn their rich blood sour against you."

Now the good news:

Witnessing that as a teenager in Africa he was happy with black friends and loved by them; not minding primitive ways since he was born into these

Realizing his lack of experience in communicating with friends in the churches

Appreciating when his parents were taken out for a meal and he and his sister were left with a babysitter

Being allowed to play elsewhere during the meetings

Receiving a few luxury items from folks, different from the usual out-of-style, long-lasting clothes

Gaining open-mindedness and maturity for life by meeting different types of people

Learning that it's not necessary for Christians always to act pleasant even when one doesn't feel that way

Enjoying times of discussion with other young people; being asked about the sports he likes

Receiving short letters from church people, making it easier to communicate with them during furlough

Finding that adapting to different situations, though not easy, is helpful in later years

Looking back and concluding he wouldn't trade his background for anything, in spite of experiences during furlough and deputation

Drawbacks & dividends. Concluding our discussion of furlough, it may be in order to touch on two additional matters. The first relates to the reluctance of some missionaries to level with fellow Christians concerning failures on the field as well as victories. Stable saints value simple honesty on the part of God's servants; they understand that victories are seldom gained without casualties along the way. Parental faithfulness in this area also forestalls the son or daughter's suspicion that Dad is practicing a form of lying. From an earthly viewpoint, of course, silence at this point may be classified as essential diplomacy—so as not to lose a donor's confidence in one's overseas ministry. A pertinent observation by Joseph L. Cannon:

> How come the work is hard going only in the place where I am? . . . Wouldn't it be just a bit comforting to read, "Preacher Returned from Overseas Admits Very Little Accomplished," or "Baptized One Hundred Yesterday; Can't Find Ninety Today."[14]

Another issue pertaining to Things Missionaries Don't Want You to Know can impair parental credibility in MKs' eyes as well as register in all spiritual minds an unhelpful impression of God's work in general. It's the hesitancy with which not a few workers place sufficient emphasis on the increasing number of national missionaries serving in crosscultural ministry. Isn't this the same old story—"It takes more grace than I can tell to play the second fiddle well"? Yet it's gratifying to note that in the last decade or two the literature of many mission societies has been emphasizing the mature lives and service of a host of nationals. While not a few western Christians determinedly retain their stereotypical image of foreign workers, God's people need to know how devoted nationals are filling out the ranks of missionary enterprise in many sections of the world. (We ourselves have observed the anointed ministry of Brother Bakht Singh in India and other countries.)

So furlough brings challenge as well as refreshment to both missionary parents and their children. Many workers would testify that, for themselves, the months in the homeland revealed personal attitudes requiring God's forgiveness and restoration. Along with this, such spiritually revived fathers and mothers undoubtedly perceive an improved family atmosphere.

Thus the Master of the vineyard works to enrich His servants' inner life, preparing them for more fruitful ministry. Meanwhile believers in the churches are similarly encouraged. Previously on hearing of a special need on the field they were disposed to reach for their billfold; now some are stirred to give themselves as Christ's witnesses within or without the borders of their town or country. A stanza from *The Keswick Hymn-Book:*

> How sweet 'twould be at evening,
>   If you and I could say,
> Good Shepherd, we've been seeking
>   The sheep that went astray

8

OPTIONS FOR SCHOOLING
Adjusting to Actualities

*"Do nothing out of selfish ambition or vain conceit.
. . . Your attitude should be the same as that of
Christ Jesus . . ."* (Philippians 2:3,5).

STATUS OR STATURE?

Monitoring attitudes. Of Jesus in His early years it is written, "The
child grew and became strong; he was filled with wisdom, and the
grace of God was upon him" (Luke 2:40). Yet Jesus' parents didn't
promote Him as the Boy Wonder (not so His brothers, John 7:2-5).
On the contrary, neither they nor their Child maneuvered for status.
Though the Bible doesn't specifically mention His attending the local
schul, the few glimpses granted us of His boyhood suggest genuine
involvement in simple, practical activities.

Thus our Lord, God's "visual aid," in His inconceivable stoop
becomes our model of humility—"that sweet root from which all
heavenly virtues shoot." As we consider the MK's education, the
importance of this model can't be overstated.

Few missionaries question the desirability of a good education.
The New Testament commends it as a proper acquisition; even
ambition of the right sort has biblical warrant. But perhaps some of
us parents tend to place educational achievement above spiritual
maturity. Like Mrs. Zebedee in Matthew 20:20, 21, we're more
concerned to have our child conditioned for occupying a notable,
lucrative position in society than to have fostered in him the enduring
priorities of Matthew 6:33.

Reinforcing our child's self-confidence by gentle prompting to
higher achievement has clearly its seemly place; but continuing to do
so all the way up the educational ladder—such as getting a jump on
things by enrolling our son or daughter early in a prestigious college
or university—may leave us with a spiritually sterile scholar. Senator
Mark Hatfield sums up the case in these words: "No matter what our
mission in life, we are called to give our complete allegiance to Him.
He becomes our standard of excellence."

Pondering the imponderables. The young husband and wife embarking for the foreign field with their preschooler face one of the most emotionally laden decisions of life: "How and where should our child be educated?" This is a complex problem. Only the rarest parent anticipates with relish any one of the various options for overseas schooling; there seem to be more questions than answers. In fact, inability to find satisfactory schooling for their children may be a leading cause for workers leaving the field. The supporting constituency back home can hardly perceive the significance of these problems, chiefly that of the child's being separated from parents in the boarding school option.

Nonetheless the committed freshman couple have counted the cost. They couldn't know far in advance all the factors eventually implicated in their final decision—for one thing the mounting tensions worldwide that make our plans subject to change without notice. Yet they're assured that "the Lord knows the way through the wilderness." An OMF mother recounts how she prepared herself for the impact of this searching question:

> We are all afraid of the unknown and untried to some degree.
> I had a baby one year old. I needed an answer. The Lord gave
> the answer. I heard my shepherd say to me in His voice of
> complete authority: "When he puts forth his sheep he goes
> *before* them, and the sheep follow him, for they *know his
> voice.*"

Parents have entire responsibility for determining how and where their child receives his schooling. At the same time missions personnel devote themselves to matters relating to optimum education for their MKs, whether these are overseas, on furlough, or permanently in the family homeland for completing their secondary education. Mission societies supply their members with facts and figures and with whatever further counsel they request. Beyond this, senior missionaries on the field and at home add their mature suggestions; they've been through the mill. A safe principle in discussing a typical MK's instruction is to assume that his needs are virtually the same as any other children.

An OMF booklet notes, "Our leaders have spent perhaps as much time discussing the sticky questions of providing for missionaries' children as for any other subject." In a recent WBT communication these lines appear:

> Wycliffe Bible Translators makes a number of options
> available in the education of the children of its members.
> Because each field is democratic and semi-autonomous, these
> options differ from field to field. But in each case, the Wycliffe

member himself decides what plan to follow. If an individual translator does not feel that any plan suggested by the Wycliffe branch is satisfactory, he may choose another course of action for his children.[15]

Members of most mission societies may also select different solutions for different children in the same family. But most importantly the decision rests with the persons who should make them—the parents themselves. An example of a multi-school family:

> Lisa (12) loves Faith Academy and Richard (9) loves Chefoo. Rachel (10) cannot take being separated from us so is going to a local public school in Singapore. She is doing very well, but we wonder about her secondary education. The Lord hasn't shown us the next steps yet.*

Options outlined. Following are the available options for the MK's schooling, none entirely free of minus factors. Of course not all are available or convenient for every family. Each item listed is enlarged on in succeeding pages, with special attention given to the first two selections:

(1) *Teaching the child at home,* usually with the aid of correspondence courses.

(2) *Boarding school* in the host country or an adjoining country.

(3) *Small-group school.* A number of missionary families living fairly close together, as in a hospital area, may arrange for a private school with teaching shared by missionaries. (A situation of this nature exists when a boarding school, such as Morrison Academy in Taiwan, uses satellite schools so that elementary children needn't board away from home.)

(4) *Parochial Christian school.* In larger cities there's usually a private school sponsored by a denomination or other agency.

(5) *International American school.* In many capital cities of the world the U.S. Government sponsors a school for the benefit of expatriate children. The wives of ambassadors and others may engage in teaching, though often the faculty are professionally trained. These superior schools welcome MKs.

(6) *National urban school* with non-English medium. In areas like Europe, Latin America, and Japan, where the medium of instruction is a major world language, these schools attract a number of MKs.

(7) *Stateside schooling.* This training may consist of a boarding school situation or a day school. In the latter case, the pupil lives with relatives, friends, or in a mission hostel.

HOME SCHOOLING

Promoting a principle. A missionary leader states, "No one will settle forever the debate between resident and correspondence school education for missionaries' children." But the fact that an increasing number of parents are teaching their offspring at home signifies a trend that may not yet have crested.

Convinced that God's order calls for Mom and Dad not to leave their chickens for others to hatch, many parents arrange for school in the family nest. So the moment Johnny jumps out of bed he's in school. They feel that only they can consistently train their child, at least in his primary years, in line with his distinctive personality needs. One mother concisely explains: "Our children are *our* responsibility. We'd be neglecting them if we sent them away to school." Another mishmom: "We have heard stories of bitter MKs who feel they have been shipped off to school so their parents could minister to others." In CAM's *Bulletin* a mother voices the logic of home schooling:

Someone has said, "The home is the unit of society. To this unity God has given responsibility to bring up what it has brought forth. This is God's way—and God's way is the best way." Our main reason for keeping our children at home is that we feel responsible for their training. God gave them to us and we believe we should keep them with us as long as they are children.

How will our children learn secular subjects and spiritual truths? We believe they learn these from the spiritual environment of the home, from direct instruction in the home classes, and from daily associations. The most important lessons our children can learn are learned as they watch us and listen to and take part in the daily conversation of the home.

If teaching their child at home were merely a matter of inconvenience or hardship, nearly all parents would seriously consider the plan. They want to guard his emotional, social, intellectual, and spiritual balance. Very few parents harbor the attitude implied in this MK's caustic comments. (It would be edifying to hear the other side.)

I'm a triangle. Do you know what this is? It's a square with something missing. I have always been that way and always will be. The most anticipated event in my preschool years was when I would get off to school and thus get out of my parents' hair. They then could give their full attention to teaching the natives about the Lord.

Correspondence courses. This central facility in home teaching is a boon beyond price. Accredited correspondence schools, sponsored by colleges and universities as well as independent agencies, maintain close accord with U.S. Government commissions such as the National Commission on Accrediting and the Federal Trade Commission. Thus sound educational and business standards are preserved. (The National Home Study Council, Washington, DC, publishes an annual directory of Accredited Private Home Study Schools.)

Offering instruction in whole or in part by mail, correspondence schools follow a systematic program of teaching and exams, with considerable feedback between instructors and students. They supply written and printed materials, illustrations, diagrams, and perhaps films and recordings as raw material for study; also charts and calendars for the wall. Consequently the parent or other supervisor needn't be an experienced teacher or become engaged in curriculum planning. The normal schoolday is comprised of about four hours of study, plus homework, with breaks for relaxation and recreation.

Each step of study is carefully explained, questions and answers anticipated, and answers skillfully built into the text. As a result, student problems are kept to a minimum, though the need for assistance arises from time to time. Artful reinforcement of instruction through repetition and practice represents a definite plus for student and school. Through personal letters from instructors in the States and by marginal notes on returned papers, the student is challenged to apply himself—a giant step beyond grinding away at bare paper. Commonsense and dedication are the main ingredients for parental involvement.

A special type of home study, known as supervised correspondence study, is presently being used by some families. It differs from traditional forms of home study in that it requires the aid of a teacher or actively involved supervisor who acts as a link between student and agency. The supervisor isn't obliged to be qualified to teach all subjects in the curriculum; he or she receives and distributes materials, collects lessons from the student, supervises exams, answers questions, and keeps the student on schedule.

Another interesting and practical method is being implemented in some countries where missions prefer not to make their presence too well known. Instead of planting a school, mission authorities set apart itinerant teachers to move on circuit, counseling missionary families and encouraging home schoolers in their educational needs.

A currently popular but somewhat controversial course for group study is A.C.E. (Accelerated Christian Education). The international arm of the enterprise, M.A.C.E. (Missionary Accelerated Christian Education) has extended its facilities to over fifty countries. The program provides opportunity for parents to gain expertise in supervising the child as well as in the use of materials. The curriculum is the same as that used in the States. Correlation with Scripture, character objectives, and testing procedures register merit for the course, though not all parents find it meets their needs. A feature of this study course is that instead of 12 grades there are 12 levels of achievement, and students in the same classroom can progress from level to level at their own pace. The address: M.A.C.E., Box 16161, Mobile, Alabama 36616.

Most correspondence programs are designed to prepare students for entrance into high school and/or college in North America. Not only missionaries but also some government personnel and business people utilize instruction of this type for their children.

Ordinarily MKs don't go beyond junior high with correspondence work; they round out high school in boarding school or take up study in the family homeland. The former plan can sometimes enable the young person to finish high school by the time his folks are due for furlough. Three young adults whose education or part of it consisted of home study give a rundown of their schooling and some impressions gained:

My schooling was a combination of correspondence courses (first five years), MK school, then to a Canadian school. I feel strongly that children are parents' first responsibility, even though I know it is difficult for missionary parents to keep in balance their responsibility toward God's heritage and God's work.*

My schooling in Dominico was done by correspondence from Chicago. My mother first taught me, then I was tutored by a missionary teacher from Canada. My sixth grade was spent in the States because we were on furlough. My seventh grade was taught by my mother at home. A teacher was sent down for the MKs that year. My eighth grade was spent with some other MKs much younger than I.*

I took my high school work through correspondence, and previous training was from my parents and older sister. The advantage of this over boarding school might be the development of self-discipline. I was on my own with the high school course—it was up to us to set our own pace. We knew we had five years to complete the course in order to receive a diploma and graduate. Because of developing self-discipline, getting good grades in college was easy. Studying was not always easy, but at least I knew the importance of study and organizing time.*

Advantages & disadvantages. The general competence of home-grown alumni speaks well for this type of teaching and the teacher/parents. The enduring purpose—to achieve a congenial home environment in which education is promoted in its broader and higher aspects—may often cultivate a personality and ability in the son or daughter not acquired in other school settings. Indeed a field director reports, "We are going all the way into home-study courses on our field."

WBT has its eye on computers as a means of teaching children at home. Writers in Wycliffe's *In Other Words* explain:

> One alternative now being field tested involves microcomputers. Students in scattered locations would study with the aid of computers, meeting regularly with itinerant teachers and other students in a central location. This would enable the youngsters to stay with their families, get a quality education and also have valuable peer interaction.
>
> Children sometimes need greater stimulation than is provided by correspondence courses.
>
> Already there are computer programs on the market to drill the student in reading, math and other skills. These well-designed programs with their brightly colored graphics and synthesized speech are attractive to all ages—even preschoolers, who can follow the spoken instructions before they can read. . . . A stimulating, creative curriculum is emerging.

By and large, however, no barometer readings clearly indicate that home-taught students turn out better than those taught by other methods—that is, in terms of emotional poise, Christian character, and fitness for meeting the demands of modern adult life. On the other hand, a significantly higher percentage of homespun alumni later serve in overseas testimony.

Let us then summarize the main advantages of teaching children at home:

(1) *Presence of parents.* These "fulltime" parents, under-cutting the strain of separation, spare the child many hurts that might not be easily erased. Unwholesome peer pressure is minimal in the local situation.

(2) *Modeling by parents.* Many parents consider it a privilege of the highest order to nurture their progeny, maturing them in the important things of life at the most impressionable age. They have opportunity, and usually the aptitude, to exemplify spiritual and practical principles in their own lives, including personal responsibilities in maintaining a home. Submerged at times in interesting discussions, plays, and games, truths may become more living and individualized to the child. The amount of special attention given him normally hastens his all-round progress.

(3) *Witness of family.* A family working as a unit presents a practical testimony to local people, very few of whom would be able or even desire to send their children to a far-off school to be educated. Moreover, the child may well be inclined to embrace in a modest way the vision of Mom and Dad and enjoy sharing in their ministry.

(4) *Identification with national community.* The family circle generally dominates the social fabric of life in Third World countries. So the individual members of a missionary family, through their friendliness, may strike a responsive chord in the hearts of local peers and older people. An adult MK writes: "I learned the ways of the African people and grew to be at home with them. I learned to translate behavior patterns, norms and mores from one culture to another and after a while translation was no longer necessary." Not a few home-study youngsters gain a lifelong attachment to the host country.

(5) *Conservation of finances.* The outlay required to maintain a child in boarding school, also with much traveling entailed, is considerable.

(6) *Availability of teaching helps.* The excellent correspondence courses available from Christian and secular agencies are designed to prepare students for entrance to the better schools of North America. Meanwhile the parents experience growth as they supervise and/or teach.

(7) *Time adjustment.* The same amount of learning can be given in fewer hours. Additionally, the school year can be adjusted to care for vacations and other family outings.

The following extended marshalling of disadvantages of home study isn't as foreboding as it appears at first sight. Perhaps some items listed are fairly positive in nature:

(1) *Shortage of interpersonal relationships.* With Mom and/or Dad exercising discipline in the home and also enforcing corrective measures in study habits, the child may not get enough interaction with peers and others outside the family. If there are several children in the family or nearby, this factor won't loom large. Among national peers too there may be some who will prove stimulating to mind and spirit.

(2) *Problem of non-starters & dropouts.* For one, two, or three children to maintain interest and energy for four or five hours a day, even with several recesses, real self-discipline is demanded. Of course that's what they need for life.

(3) *Absence of competition.* God has wonderfully granted to most children a built-in sharp pinch to achieve. Yet this attribute seems to require wholesome rivalry, especially in subjects the students don't much like.

(4) *Problem of visitors.* National friends may arrive at any time, unannounced and with several children in tow. Even if there's a comparatively quiet spot where the pupil can pursue his study, noises in the distance aren't conducive to concentration. It wouldn't be prudent to hang a sign on the front door, "School in session—please return at 3:00 p.m."

(5) *Capability gap.* Not all missionary parents are good disciplinarians, so home schools can be very good or very bad. Education of our children requires a long-range commitment, with real problems. One mom puts it this way: "How can I teach him to read when I can't even teach him to pick up his dirty socks?" While correspondence lessons usually require only supervision, general principles of teaching need to be recognized and carried out. Parents may in fact over-schedule the child with lessons, not giving him enough free time. And they may not feel well at times, possibly with a contagious disease. The child may enjoy the break but his studies suffer.

(6) *Lack of provision for special subjects.* Music and art, for instance, can't be taught through correspondence.

Certainly it's often possible to get outside instruction in these skills if the parents can't handle them. In science a lab is essential at times; and foreign languages, such as French and Latin, might prove difficult for the parents to coach.

(7) *Shortage of recreational facilities.* Children possess the engaging trait of being able to amuse themselves with the simplest materials. But the growing youngster needs a wider range of recreation for physical and emotional development. The hot climate of many lands accentuates this need. Adequate playing areas aren't commonly found in overseas cities.

(8) *Lure of boarding school.* Some home-study children, listening to the tales of boarding school peers and observing them excitedly preparing to return to school, may cast longing glances at those leaving for that enchanted land.

APPRAISING ALTERNATIVES

Boarding school. The next two chapters deal exclusively with this option, so it will be sufficient at this point to itemize the pros and cons. (The communal nature of boarding life enables us to gain a better perspective of MKs than in any other school situation.) The following listing of *benefits* shouldn't be construed as promoting boarding to the discredit of other plans.

(1) *Superior academics.* Well-accredited teachers provide better training than that offered by public schools in the States and equal to that offered by many private institutions.

(2) *Christian faculty & staff.* Almost all personnel engaged with students are dedicated believers, conscious of having been guided by the Lord into this special branch of service.

(3) *Wholesome competition.* In both study and sports the potential of students is drawn out through emulation and mild competition.

(4) *Cultivation of friendships.* Social relationships begun in school with western and national fellow-students may endure into adulthood (though a number of adult MKs mention they had little close contact with nationals since these were day students and not boarders). Constant association with other boys and girls enables a young person to evaluate peers in the light of future relationships.

It also gives him increased freedom of expression. Further, there is considerable evidence that boarding students make adjustments more readily on their settling down for life in the U.S.

(5) *Agreeable climate.* For the most part, schools are located in regions with invigorating climate—a pleasant change from subtropical summer heat.

(6) *Spacious grounds.* Usually there's plenty of space for almost any activity students want to engage in.

(7) *Constant supervision.* Throughout their waking and sleeping hours, the youngsters are guarded from danger.

(8) *Freedom for parents.* Though rarely a determining factor in the decision to send their child to boarding, parents become freer to press forward in their ministry, even when absence from home is essential. (One mother, questioned as to whether their children were sent away to a boarding school for the sake of the work, reacted typically: "A thousand times NO as far as we're concerned.")

On checking these advantages, the reader may conclude that boarding school is Beulah Land. But there are also *detriments:*

(1) *Experience of loneliness.* Especially in the first months homesickness can become an emotional hurdle. Some children don't overcome it for years, though the great majority begin to feel at home in a surprisingly short time.

(2) *Concern of parents.* Understandably the faraway child is the object of anxious thought on the part of parents, especially Mom. The result can be strain also in marital relationships.

(3) *Meager communication.* Phone service isn't available everywhere in Third World countries, so letters and tapes may be the only means of interchange. A few parents maintain occasional contact with their child by radio.

(4) *Nominal commitment.* Peer pressure and/or compulsory attendance at spiritual meetings can at times cause the student to pay mere lip service to Christian beliefs. At home this attitude would be readily detected.

(5) *Shortfall of love.* No longer is the child a privileged character; he's one of many. Much as school personnel try to make up this lack, there's just not enough love to go

around. Consequently a student's emotional needs may not be fully met.

(6) *Disaffected spirits.* In every assemblage of children and young people, dissension can be touched off by any one of a dozen circumstances, and discord becomes infectious.

(7) *Selection of houseparents.* Mission societies and boarding authorities experience difficulty in securing the type of dormparent they desire. This problem is dealt with in Chapter 10.

(8) *Hothouse environment.* It's been frequently claimed that the boarding school boy or girl, isolated from the real world, may remain less prepared to later resist its harmful influence. Doubtless this is true in measure, yet boarding life liberates the impressionable student from many of the threatening elements of contemporary society and exposes him to positive Christian foundations.

(9) *Expenses involved.* Housing, classrooms, and other facilities must be obtained and maintained. Quite properly, parents of enrolled students are required to share moderately in the expenses incurred. Some missions provide for school costs.

(10) Some schools aren't equipped to deal with unusually bright or learning-disabled youngsters or slow learners.

Small-group school. This option has distinctives that make it adjustable to special needs of children and parents. A situation in which a number of missionary families are stationed in a circumscribed area, such as hospital premises, might call for a school of this type. One or two missionaries would be designated as teachers to complement correspondence study.

Several advantages of this plan are immediately apparent. The family circle is kept intact, students enjoy the companionship of other MKs in study and recreation, and close relationships prevail between teachers, pupils, and parents. A kindergarten class can also be readily cared for. The debilitating climate could be a debit item.

Parochial Christian school. In many urban centers of the world, church organizations sponsor schools with English medium; these may prove acceptable to missionary families residing reasonably nearby. Our own three children attended an Anglican school in Bombay for a few years.

Some of these schools offer instruction from K through 12, with quite a high standard and trained teachers. The curriculum, however, may be slanted to accommodate local pupils without a solid grounding in English. Discipline may be of the spare-the-rod type. Evangelical content of classroom instruction is usually conspicuous by its absence; the teaching of Scripture may be limited to a superficial survey of the Gospels. In this connection we had an amusing experience:

> A teacher enquired of our then seven-year-old daughter, "What is your denomination?" Echoing her parents' words, she replied, "I'm a believer." Later, speaking to Eunice, this teacher said, "Your little girl said she belonged to the beavers; I've never heard of that group."

Nonetheless for some families this option affords a satisfactory alternative to sending their child to boarding school at an early age. Incidentally, the sight of one's daughter walking hand-in-hand with a local girl from school is chockfull of significance.

International American school. The U.S. Government operates a network of 500 or more superior schools in major cities throughout the world, mainly for the benefit of children of embassy personnel and western business people. A number of these schools began as MK schools, but the inflow of non-Christian and nonmissionary elements gradually diluted evangelical standards. To downplay the American presence by a nice piece of diplomacy, this type of school is now referred to as "International School."

Missionary children are well received at these institutions, though the fees are stiff despite the fact that Uncle Sam subsidizes the schools. The exceptionally high standard of education attracts ambitious national students; they covet fluency in English, awareness of western culture, and efficiency in special curricular sections such as science.

The majority of staff and students are non-Christian, yet faculty members are broadly oriented. While the curriculum is almost entirely secularized, the sturdy MK can maintain an effective witness for Christ before his affluent fellow-students. Here's a sketch of one such school:

> The American School in Recife, Brazil, is a comparatively small junior and senior high school designed to prepare students for admission to American colleges. Typically most of the student body come from foreign service families, so interesting friendships emerge between MKs and fellow classmates. For Christian students living at a distance from school, a youth hostel is available, supervised by a missionary couple. The students ordinarily stay there for five days and then

return home each weekend. While not the ideal arrangement, the "weekend parents" are grateful for the distinct advantages such a school presents.

What has become unofficially a Christian adaptation of the International School is SIM's Bingham Academy in Addis Ababa, Ethiopia—for long a missionary school with a largely MK student body. Because of the Marxist revolution in the country, however, much of that has changed. Presently among the 110 students is a preponderance of nationals—children and young people from 26 nations. An article in *SIM Now* gives the rationale for this new facet in the ministry of missionary schools:

> This was a whole new strategy that not only met the need for MKs' schooling in a time of political turbulence, but had diplomatic government people and professionals knocking at the door. They too wanted a place where their children could get a good education—and get it in a highly desirable environment. . . .
>
> The result is that parents from Communist bloc countries, Islamic backgrounds, and today's neopagan western cultures sit elbow to elbow in Bingham's chapel watching their kids take part in special school programs, and hearing the gospel very plainly presented. . . .It's not like the old days, but it sure is a great way to spread the good news.[17]

National urban school. Rather surprisingly, a number of MKs enroll in progressive national schools with non-English medium; and students and parents give them high marks. In industrialized sections of the world—such as Japan (whose public-school graduates are judged as perhaps the most knowledgeable in the world), Europe, Latin America—hundreds of these schools are functioning.

Concerning this unique type of schooling for MKs, a provocative article appeared in the *Evangelical Missions Quarterly.* The writer, Georgina Kladensky, recommends national urban schools as a most agreeable option for missionary children.

Miss Kladensky, a missionary lady, develops her thesis around the number one problem of boarding schools—separation of children from parents and home. Inasmuch as most of the advantages of these schools are stated under other options that permit children to remain with their parents, it will be sufficient to quote items not yet mentioned:

(1) "The child will learn the language without an accent and will be truly bilingual if the parents speak English at home."

(2) "The children accept local culture as their way of living. Sometimes they 'endure hardship' such as cold classrooms and different food. All of this helps the children to understand the way nationals think and react."

(3) "The child who goes to local schools need not experience the shock of reentering the 'world.'"

(4) "Separation [from nationals] tends to stimulate superiority/inferiority ideas. . . . It is also possible that missionary boarding schools contribute to the 'little America' complex which is dangerous where nationalism is rising. . . . 'Just that you chose to go to our national schools shows you want to become part of our culture and not one of the American cliques,' commented a national businessman in Ecuador."[18]

Certainly Miss Klandensky has served the missionary community well in sharing her convictions. (A seminary thesis by another missionary reveals that foreign national schools have a higher percentage of spiritually aware MKs than do other schooling options.) The case for national urban schools is confirmed by these three sets of parents. The focus of the last statement is unusual in that the language medium isn't a world language.

At first our two girls were objects of wonderment to their Japanese classmates, but they soon became part of the group. They learned the language and the appropriate mannerisms. This guaranteed their warm acceptance into scores of homes. In return our children accepted the Japanese and their way of living.*

Our four daughters studied in Argentine public schools from K through 9th. Living in a nation 95 percent literate, we wanted our children to be enriched by Argentina's distinctive culture and literature. . . . In later years they experienced little difficulty moving across boundaries and into other cultures. . . . By keeping up academic skills, our children made a smooth transition to U.S. schools.*

Because our children attended elementary schools in the Philippines, they grew up knowing Tagalog, the national language. This helped them feel included in evangelistic work, and church services did not sound like gibberish.*

Some of the questions parents encounter as they consider enrolling their children in a national school may be suggested:

Will their son and daughter be fully accepted in the school environment, coming as they do from a distinctly different background? National religious tenets and morals, for instance, are commonly taught in such schools. How will they confront the freer attitude in sexual matters? Then too, will not the emphasis on rote-learning hinder their academic and personality development? One missionary mother writes:

It is true that our girl could have had a local education, staying at home with us. But Asian schools naturally and properly have an Asian outlook. Such schooling would have made adjustment to life in America painful and unsettling, possibly resulting in an inferiority complex. Being a fairly intelligent kid, she would realize that she just didn't clue in. To keep her at home would have been selfish on our part.*

And now a final word from a satisfied, liberated MK as he reminisces about life in Japan. It's unclear if he attended a national school, though he's the type that would fit into a situation of that nature like paper on the wall. Curiously too we gain helpful hints on how tables and bathtubs can do double duty:

The Orient was home to me. I remember riding rickshaws to school, playing soccer with Chinese and British friends. I never missed America or thought about hamburgers, baseball, or Fourth of July celebrations. . . . I recall sleeping on the dining-room table or in the bathtub so that weary upcountry missionaries could have a soft bed. My childhood was really happy.*

Schooling in home country. The mere thought of leaving a preadolescent child in the homeland for education arouses tramatic feelings in parental hearts today. Yet many stouthearted parents, Britishers for the most part, did just that in past generations, as did embassy and business people. Factors such as the everpresent danger of crippling diseases in primitive regions and the physical hardships for young in everyday life prompted the decision of missionary parents to bring or send their child home for education. In his biography of a doctor serving in India, Ken Anderson cites a more recent instance of similar decision-making:

It is one of the darkest vales a missionary walks—separation from his children. There was no provision whatever for the Lehmann children to receive their education at Herbertpur, once they became ten years of age, and so they were sent to England. Too often the Lehmanns had seen missionary children growing apart from the faith of their parents, since separation so often fosters spiritual rebellion. It was to be their joy through the years to again and again thank God for children who, through the years of loneliness, kept respect for their parents and found for themselves an enduring faith.[19]

Supersonic jets, shorter terms of service overseas, establishment of boarding schools, superior correspondence courses—such benefits now make it unnecessary for children of school age to be left in the homeland for study except when uniquely personal factors are entailed.

Missions advise that a child younger than 10 shouldn't be left with stateside relatives or friends or in a mission hostel. As for the most desirable or lest objectionable time for the adolescent son or daughter to take up schooling, this adult MK offers some pertinent thoughts:

> Tenth grade, when everyone in the class feels awkward anyway, may be a good time to come home. But if the schooling in the host country is adequate, I would say to wait until university age, though the cultural adjustment may be more difficult then. Much depends on the individual, of course. I personally know of some who have made the transition smoothly at this age. I feel strongly about one thing and it's this: psychologically and spiritually, early teenage isn't the time to be sent away from Mom and Dad.*

So this option seems to be most feasible when the MK reaches mid-adolescence. At least some of the ills will have been remedied. An adult MK recalls his experiences:

> My high school years were spent in a Christian boarding school in the U.S. I experienced real culture shock for the first time. I had never been in an American setting with non-MKs all around me. I didn't fit in, and consequently found myself spending many hours in detention hall on Saturday afternoon as punishment for frequent acts of mischief and sarcastic comments.
>
> "Shape up or ship out!" That was the ultimatum from the headmaster during the summer of my sophomore year. In the tearful session that followed the reading of the letter, my surprised parents helped me to see that my problem was deeper than I had known. I could never expect to change in my own power. I had to commit myself and my problem to God. Mom and Dad told me that if I wished, they would take an extended furlough until I was through high school to be with me.

They were serious about their offer and I was overwhelmed. Expecting a shower of condemnation, I received love and sympathy instead. The following year at school was the best ever as I began to seek God in a personal way.*

Aware of the peculiar needs of adolescents, mission leaders earnestly involve themselves in providing extraspecial arrangements for their MKs' stateside education. Living quarters may consist of a teen hostel near a public or Christian school. Usually a mature, caring Christian couple with a missionary background serve as surrogate parents, making the hostel as homelike as possible. A recent OMF publication explains how mission personnel cooperate with parents in helping youthful MKs retain close family ties:

> As happy and normal as houseparents try to make hostel life for their charges, the separation was too long during such a critical period in the young people's lives. Thus in 1968 the OMF began providing the fares for its hostel kids to visit their parents on the field once during the four-year term, or parents could choose a three-year term instead of four to reduce the period of separation. Beginning in 1974, however, a special Vacation Fares Fund was begun to help parents, especially those with no private funds or special gifts, to fly their children to the field for more frequent vacation visits.

Challenge of change. We're all familiar with Tennyson's observation, "The old order changeth, yielding place to new." Creative review of current procedures in MK schooling is the order of the day; indeed this is serious business. Widespread political turmoil in host countries compounds the problems being faced. Committees comprised of persons from widely based sections of the missionary community—missions personnel, field administrators, parents, and students—meet in order to improve curricula, eliminate defective elements, and forestall potential disruptive influences in the various types of children's schooling.

In early November of 1984, an International Conference on missionary children was convened in Manila, Phillipines. It was emphasized that the political and demographic changes taking place worldwide require considerable alteration in mission strategies. For instance, mission compounds are no longer practical in many parts of the world.

With respect to MK education, the consensus was that, since the missions community is becoming increasingly multinational, assuming that the current pattern of providing a North American education for *all* MKs is unrealistic and insensitive.

The Conference explored proposals as to how missionary families, through alternative educational programs, can remain together on the field.

One favorable outgrowth of change, as we've seen in the case of Bingham Academy, is that schools with larger national enrollment are becoming evangelistic ministries as well as playing support roles for missionary families. Another is that enlightened Christians in the West, recognizing the knotty problems entailed in missionary children's education, are importuned to give the issue a significant place in prayer.

In the course of changing conditions, missionary families follow through with their differing methods of schooling, doubtless at all times witnessing to the reality of God's grace and guidance in such practical considerations.

As we return to the chapter's opening enquiry, "Status or stature?" Ter Steegen poses a correlative question:

> Where is the school for each and all,
> Where men become as children small,
>   And little ones are great?
> Where love is all the task and rule,
> The fee our all, and all at school,
>   Small, poor, of low estate?

9
BOARDING SCHOOL (I)
Rationale & Reaction

---

*"Hannah took the boy with her, young as he was . . .
and brought him to the house of the Lord at Shiloh.
. . . . Then Hannah prayed and said: 'My heart
rejoices in the Lord; in the Lord my horn [strength]
is lifted high' "* (1 Samuel 1:24; 2:1).

WHY BOARDING SCHOOL?

Shared concerns. The issue of establishing overseas schools for
missionaries' children was a priority for prayer and discussion by
mission societies during the previous generation. Personnel in North
America and Britain particularly, convinced of the necessity of on-
the-field training for their children, proceeded to find suitable
locations for schools. This wasn't a simple task in view of the often
difficult and complex problems relating to foreign governments,
climatic conditions, contractors, and other important
considerations. Setting up and operating more than 100 of these
institutions, scattered in nearly 60 countries and educating at any one
time more than 5,000 children, adds up to a massive commitment.

Nowadays parents and offspring are reaping the fruit of leaders'
past and present labors. Still, not a few problems remain. For
instance, in mission lands not served by a boarding school or other
adequate facilities, MKs must travel to an adjoining or remote
country. Some youngsters, to take advantage of their own society's
school, may bypass a nearer school for a more distant one. Then too,
academies vary with respect to Christian orientation, and this factor
bears markedly on parental preferences. Some institutions are
British, and American students leave with a pleasing semi-British
accent and a solid grounding in the classics.

While missionary parents and boarding school personnel realize
that students should be more exposed than currently to the
wholesome features of national culture, thus far only token success
has been achieved. The issues involved are many and sensitive. Some
schools accept a number of local pupils, usually as day students, and
their presence contributes much to the social climate.

Commonly a single sponsoring mission bears major responsibility for staffing its school. Other missions using the facility for their MKs pay somewhat higher fees to compensate for their noninvolvement in the financial structure. Additional schools, however, operate on a cooperative, multimission level—a plan carrying certain definite benefits. Most schools accept offspring of non-Christian foreign business people. Finally, some institutions are independently sponsored, controlled by a board of trustees. Faith Academy in the Philippines, the largest MK school, represents 12 to 15 mission societies, and staff and students belong to over 60 missions and evangelical denominations.

Founding of schools, of course, was merely the first major step in the total commitment. A statement in *The Alliance Witness* (C&MA) clarifies the extent of the task:

We missionaries who are specially trained and involved in MK education have a commitment—to our students, the children of missionaries; to their parents, the missionaries; to the Society and the fields we serve; and to the God-given task of worldwide evangelization. These goals are vitally interrelated.

In establishing MK schools we have the responsibility in the emotional, social, physical, and spiritual realms. In boarding schools we have the unique opportunity to minister to the whole child. We are responsible to provide a place to live which is as like home as possible.[20]

Some schools have two terms each year, others have three. Those located at higher elevations and not readily reached by air, rail, or car usually plan one extended vacation when the weather is fairly comfortable in the plains; this period normally covers Christmas week. At other times the mountain air offers welcome relief from tropical heat. Taking advantage of the refreshing climate, many parents spend their vacation in the hills; then their children normally become day students and live with their folks. The schools located at or near sea-level arrange for three terms, enabling youngsters to get home for an extra vacation. In any event, students spend between eight and nine months of each year in school.

Case for the opposition. Providing acceptable facilities for educating missionary children overseas was carried out in the face of considerable query and outright challenge. Not a few parents and educators, along with knowledgeable believers in the home countries, objected to the program. One stateside mother, more zestfully than others, remonstrated thus with a missionary friend:

Do you mean to say that you intend to bring your young children back to the foreign field—those whom God has given you to train for Him—and then dump them down in some impersonal boarding school half a continent away, where you may not see them for eight months of the year? Don't you love them? Then why do you do it? Your children should be back in the family circle every night.*

This solicitous lady obviously felt that no satisfactory alternative exists to keeping school-age children in the family nest. In voicing her protest, however, she touched on the prime disadvantage of boarding school: separation of children from parents. (Reiteration of this factor in our study will sound like a broken record!) An educator expressed his aversion in strong language: "Separation of missionary children from their parents for schooling has resulted in these children being among the most unbalanced and neurotic of all social groups."

We have at least two statements of MKs attesting the sentiments of the opposition party:

My parents and I have very little in common. I was away at school for about eight months each year, so we never developed an intimate relationship. Now I don't have the loving relationship with my parents that many other MKs have.*

Isolation from everyone in the local culture and being only with other Americans in a foreign country—this I didn't like. This isolation and unreality caused us to live in a dream world of imagination. When we returned to America, it was extremely hard to face reality. We never saw the world at its worst.*

Suffice it to say at this point that a slight majority of missionary parents, having weighed the options before the Lord, send their children to boarding school. Included in this number, however, are some young people who enroll only for the final portion of their secondary education. So, despite certain demerits and perhaps a modest decline as a priority, boarding stands as a viable option for MKs. A bit later these youngsters and young people express their views on boarding school.

PAINFUL PARTING

Heart of the matter. In any culture the breaking up of a tightly knit family structure even for a few weeks results in whacking of the heartstrings. Many missionaries would pay tribute to their own parents who bravely waved goodbye to them as they left for foreign shores.

And now these same workers release their own children time and again for the better part of a year. As a matter of fact, present-day emphasis on family life in the West makes some missionary appointees reevaluate their commitment to overseas service.

Since mothers are typically more emotionally involved than fathers in affairs of home and offspring, it's not strange that many confess that saying goodby to a child is the hardest thing they do on the field. One mom admits, "I get a migraine merely thinking about it!" Another, recalling her first experience of the empty-nest syndrome, concedes that "entering into the empty house was like walking into a tomb."

Those parents who prepare themselves and their children for parting may remain free of trauma, and even experience a measure of enthusiasm, when the hour arrives. The Scripture portion opening the chapter recounts a somewhat similar experience—one frequently mentioned with regard to parents leaving their son or daughter in boarding. But beyond this, many mothers, and fathers too, relate to Hannah in that magnificent hymn of praise. And in line with our present focus, it's encouraging to note that Samuel turned out well physically and spiritually in his "boarding school."

There are those who insist that well-put-together parents needn't flunk composure when seeing their child off to boarding. Well, let it be said that foreign workers don't normally speak of personal sacrifice. Millions of other people worldwide endure much worse physical hardship than missionaries. Yet being parted from one's child in an alien land for extended periods comes close to sacrifice. A mother couches her reaction in the form of a prayer: "Father, I think I have a tiny glimpse of what You felt when You sent Your Son away for our sakes." Another parent, with a twist of irony, declares, "The only good thing about separation is that it takes your mind off other troubles."

Following is a synopsis of parents' feelings at parting time:

Recognizing that parents are the key and tone-setters in the entire process of separation

Not being under pressure to send their child to a distant school; they do so gladly, assured that a good education and friends are worth everything this takes

Finding that tears often came when she wasn't thinking especially of faraway children

Remaining brave through goodbys but shedding a "barrel of tears" during the next week

Sensing a closer family relationship than previously because all family members work harder to keep love warm

Realizing the danger of weeping over the child and dwelling on his woeful lot in having to leave Mommy

Concluding that for the healthy development of their child, it's best to send him to boarding, particularly since he himself wanted to go

Believing that distance doesn't actually separate child and parents when love is understood

Feeling that separation results in *showing* more love

Being sure that their children never doubted the parents' love; they were in on the decision from the very first.

Below is an extract from the diary of Ian Gordon-Smith, a British medical missionary who served in Thailand under OMF. He and his wife Stephanie and both of their children, together with eight other adult missionaries and children, were called by the Lord to Himself in an auto accident in 1978. This account, appearing in a small OMF volume *In His Times,* speaks of the writer's daughter getting off to boarding school for the first time:

I remember as I walked up the road I was holding Rachel's hand. She was very hand-holdy that day—I'm not surprised. On the way up I asked her what she was thinking about, as she was rather quiet, and she said, *"You know,"* and beyond that she wouldn't be drawn—so I didn't probe. . . .

Three minutes to go—Stephanie left, having said good-bye to Rachel—then Rachel, off her bat, came from her place, put her arm round Mark and gave him a kiss—it was very sweet—then walked to me and gave me a big kiss, and we said good-bye. No tears, just very serious about it. . . .

Suddenly, as we know it happens, the train moved off— Stephanie burst into sobs and I endeavored to comfort her briefly. . . . I must confess that I had the greatest difficulty in restraining my emotions, and in the car that evening, there were times when tears seemed so easy to come.[21]

Impact on child. Are MKs themselves conscious of the distress suffered by parents at such times? Many doubtless are. Four young people write about this and their parents' wisdom in preparing them emotionally for the way ahead:

I'm sure my parents felt the twinge of separation more acutely than I did. It wasn't easy for them to let go the molding of an inquisitive kid. But I learned how necessary it is to have a wide range of friendships outside the home; also to acknowledge authority from others besides my parents.*

Maybe we don't know our parents as well as some teenagers, but I think we appreciate them more. We're away from them so much that we don't take them for granted. Often I remember things they said and did, and I'm always thrilled to get home.*

Dad and Mom were both very sensitive to the Lord, and they wanted to bring up each of us in the best way they knew. Because we spent between seven and nine months each year away from them, I'm sure they spent very much time praying for us. Whatever an MK becomes is largely because of the parents, even if they're separated from the kids so much.*

Right from the beginning Mom and Dad made it quite clear that they love me dearly and want me to be with them all the time. But this separation is the best thing for me, and I have come to realize that this is true.*

Should the missionary child be enrolled in boarding school on reaching school age? A weighty question indeed. In spite of intimations to the contrary, controlled studies seem to confirm that, if a child of school age identifies well with the peer group in boarding, his or her self-concept is enhanced and transition is made with admirable ease. Some parents, however, prefer to teach their young child at home for a year or two, perhaps until another nearing school age is able to go along.

However that may be, parting time isn't partying time for the boy or girl getting off to boarding for the first time. Yet many children experience less anxiety than do their folks. One six-year-old, we learn, spoke comfortingly and brightly, "Bye, Mom. Don't worry." The event is often an adventure for that age-group.

It's true that some teenagers in boarding blame all their troubles either on the fact of their being missionaries' children or on the shortcomings of the school. An adult MK recalls her reaction: "When I faced disappointment, discouragement or fear, it was easy to imagine myself as 'the pawn of my parents' devotion.'" Another adult has more positive thoughts:

Separation is more than physical. Many children who have never left home are just as separated, or more so, than many MKs from their parents' love, trust and understanding. It was in preschool years that I absorbed many basic attitudes and principles which have guided my judgments through periods of separation. My parents were the key.*

Headmasters seem to agree that a considerable majority of new pupils overcome homesickness and shyness within a few weeks of arrival. When they become immersed in school activities, negative attitudes tend to dissipate. That's not to say, of course, that dreary days won't turn up occasionally. These statements from a cross-

71986

section of students give us a perspective of their emotional reaction:

The first time I entered boarding school, I missed my folks very, very much. But in a few weeks I got used to it and then began to really enjoy school. I didn't have many to play with at home, so I was glad for all the games we played at school. I even came to like dorm and classroom life.*

My feeling on leaving home for school was one of eager anticipation to see and experience all the wonderful things about Huehue that my older sister related to me, so that my first year away from home was the beginning of a series of never-to-be-forgotten experiences in meeting lifetime friends and learning much besides academic requirements. I have felt that a missionary child loses some of the rich experiences in living and working with other children if he does not go to school with others outside his family. I don't remember ever regretting leaving home to go to school.*

I've never forgotten the feeling I had when my parents left me in boarding school to return home. I have memories of insecurity in the first weeks. I knew I had to cope with things myself. When you feel like crying, you can't just fall into your mother's lap. Like some other kids I was able to deal scholastically with things, but not emotionally. After a year at school, I learned not to divulge myself to others. "Get a fixed approach to life. Speak properly when you're spoken to. Grin and bear it. Make up your mind to cope with it. Come on world! I'm ready to take you on."

I can recall a feeling of excitement mixed with a fear of the unknown that was ahead. And there was loneliness. Separation from home resulted in uncomfortable tugs at the heart, but Mother and Dad must have prepared us, for family bonds did not deteriorate.*

I seemed to get a new sense of responsibility. I knew that Mom and Dad were doing what love required and were trusting us to represent them at school.*

My feeling about leaving home to go to school was that it was the accepted order of things, and therefore very little questioned. My parents had taken us with them to visit the school the year before and I had met many of the kids and the teachers at Missionary Conference. These served to ease the way, and if I was sad about leaving home, I don't remember it.*

Of course everyone in boarding school gets homesick. I cried in secret or talked to the pine trees, or held my teddy bear closer. Sunday nights were probably the happiest and yet with a touch of sadness. Something about church and singing about Jesus—it was like a big hug from my parents. Monday morning was never too bad after Sunday night.*

How do I feel about being an MK? Underprivileged? NO! Neglected by my parents because they sent me away to boarding? Never! Need for pity? Who, me? Rebellious because being an MK made my struggles tougher than yours? Take another look!*

School safari. For youngsters returning to familiar scenes, back-to-school blues are minimal; actually theirs is a bittersweet parting. They're glad when school lets out for vacation but excited when the day arrives to return. Needless to say, anticipation isn't mainly fostered by the prospect of classroom study; it's the thought of being reunited with schoolmates and happy times together.

A parent normally accompanies the young child to school for the initial journey. The mode of travel, obviously differing from country to country, may be partially by air, train, bus, or private car, with indigenous conveyances such as rickshaws for short distances at the end.

Older children sometimes travel by train as a school party. Then there's little evidence of drabness; in fact it all might be termed a happy hubbub or controlled chaos. One boy reports, "On the long train trip to school, we always have a nice noisy time." Additions to the party along the way receive an ardent welcome. Subdued chattering continues long into the night despite the escort's cautionary calls. Here are a few notes about the two schools our own children attended and how the schools are reached:

The first, Woodstock School (the oldest MK school continuing to the present, established in 1854), is an apple-pie American academy nestling in the majestic Himalayas, on a plateau about 7,000 feet above sea-level, near the small town of Landour. When we reach Dehra Dun at its foot, vintage buses take us at a slow but scary pace up the side of the mountain, around a dozen hairpin bends.

The other school, Breeks Memorial, is as British as teatime but with many American and Canadian MKs enrolled. Located in the Nilgiri Mountains of South India, near the town of Ootacamund ("Ooty"), the school is reached from sea-level by a mini-train with toylike engine and bogies open on each side; it zooms along at five miles per hour! (Breeks School is now attended by nationals only, but the MK school is nearby.)

Mention of mountain terrain may conjure in some minds the image of children working their way up precipitous slopes toward class each day. In reality students may continue through an entire day without encountering more than gently sloping terrain. A minimal number of tragedies have indeed occurred when students ventured off-limits, lost their footing, and forfeited their lives; but every effort is made to warn youngsters of hazardous spots. In reality mountain plateaus may be so expansive and free of steep inclines that farmers plant their grainfields, and in some locations tea planters cultivate their immense gardens ("high-grown" on the tea package indicates extraspecial flavor).

Rift Valley Academy, one of the three largest MK schools, was founded in 1905, when President Theodore Roosevelt laid the cornerstone of the main building. This school is located in Kijabe, Kenya, about 35 miles northeast of Nairobi, at an altitude of 7,200 feet above sea level.

On-the-scene report. On reaching the school premises, the girls locate their dorms and the boys theirs. Probably the first staff member they meet is a houseparent, who will have informed herself or himself of each incoming student and some details about him. Then the travelers deposit their luggage in assigned rooms and proceed to remove the grime of the road.

Before long the warm tones of the dinner bell sound. Scurrying in from every direction, spirited young people, some with their parents on this special occasion, converge on the large dining-hall and find seats. Grace is offered, and soon the scraping of chairs takes over. Then all enter with gusto into the matter at hand. The kitchen staff, prepared for the onslaught, outdoes itself to provide savory viands.

The next half-hour is abuzz with happy, uninhibited converse, normal for these lively youth and good for digestion. Bright sayings and witty rejoinders spring forth like water from a fountain. Snatches of personal experiences during vacation, perhaps embellished with touches of fantasy, are lumped together without much coherence. In this gabfest listening is scaled down; the thing is to get a word in edgewise. Occasionally the static crackles fortissimo, whereupon a warning bell may quell the din for a time. (Decorum improves in a few days.)

Parents escorting their young son or daughter to school often depart for home the same evening; others prefer to see their child off to class the next morning. It's thought that a good time for parents to leave is when the child gets settled in class. These adult MKs recall poignant scenes at parting time:

> Dad didn't say much except to remind me once or twice not to lose the key to my boarding trunk which hung so grownup-like

from my neck on a clean piece of string. And for some reason he hugged me a little tighter than usual as we stood, he stooping, outside my classroom door. And then, of all things, he looked in at least a couple of times through the door window after I was at my desk.*

The time for Mom and Dad to leave after depositing us at school came all too soon. When Mom bent down to kiss me goodby, I clung to her and refused to let her go. My body trembled as I tried to hold back the tears. It was of no use; they rushed down my face in torrents. Mom was crying too, and Dad's face was strained and his eyes looked moist. I begged them not to leave as they tore themselves away. I cried all that night and many nights after. . . . I used to hate to open my eyes in the morning, and I would wish it were night so that I could go to sleep again. The staff of the school asked friends in the States to pray for this little redhead, that God would take the empty loneliness out of my heart and replace it with His peace and joy. Somehow, by some miracle I guess, God lifted my burden and left me with a song. It all drew me close to Him who loves me.*

It's been a long, overfull day as the weary travelers resort to their dorms. With heavy eyes, they're ready to call it a day. With "Auntie's" (the houseparent's) goodnight kiss and hug for the little ones, everybody settles in for the night.

In the weeks that follow, houseparents employ discreet methods to relieve some of the children's homesickness, but they know they can't bring full release. And back home a set of parents, with hearts attuned to this bedtime situation, commit their child to the faithful Keeper of children (Psalm 121).

MK mailbox. Projecting ourselves ahead somewhat, we think of methods whereby parents and offspring can keep the homefires burning. In many schools telephones aren't available, though increasingly in advancing countries wires are being extended to once remote places. While some parents at wide intervals contact their child by shortwave radio, letters and tapes do service in bridging the miles between home and school. School authorities tend to discourage frequent parental visits in the course of the school year— the child's emotional tempo can be disrupted when Mom and/or Dad leave. But two or three times between long vacations parents may spend a day or two near their youngsters, possibly when special events are scheduled. Most parents of course would prefer to have it otherwise, and headmasters aren't inflexible in the matter. But one MK at least had his problem with too many parental visits: "I went to a boarding school about 150 miles from home. My parents visited me every five or six weeks. It had its ups and downs—mostly downs."

From the six- or seven-year-old's viewpoint, there's not much to write home about, regardless of the fact that he's immersed in activity from morn till night. However, each student is required to get a letter off at least once a week. Sunday afternoon is often reserved for this assignment, when the houseparent is on hand to help the littler ones pen their epistles. Put to it to express themselves, these children become expert in making large xoxoxoxoxo's.

If they're reasonably short and very sweet, letters from home are welcomed and shared. Parents understand that it's better not to try to direct their child in school details; he's now under another authority in that domain. Of course moral principles in moderation and warm encouragement are in order. An adult MK remembers: "When my parents went into the jungle for some weeks and couldn't send me a letter, they prepared five or six letters with instructions that I should get one each week."

A parcel from home containing toothsome morsels never lacks interest for the child and his dormmates; and he'll discover a number of other fair-weather friends. Two parents suggest items deemed likely to catch a youngster's fancy:

> We wrote our children in school once a week or oftener, and sent them some goodies or fruit once in a while. Even older children love that. Letters should contain news about their pets, animals, national boys and girls they know; also brief information about what God is doing through their parents, national pastors, and other Christians. Ask them to pray about these matters as well as for their parents.*

> In our letters we try to help our children become as self-sufficient as possible. We encourage them to seek the help of houseparents and obey them, and to try to express their problems on paper.

Let's note too the reaction of three students to letters and parcels from home:

> Soon after my parents left me in boarding school, I experienced inner hurts. But everything faded into the background when a letter came from home. For those few minutes, through words written on paper, the family was together again, though physically half a world away.*

> After school we run to our dormparent to see if there's a letter from home. My family has been just great about writing. Mom's the best, but Daddy writes often enough to let me feel I'm his and he loves me. One thing I much appreciate is their

listening when I write and their asking me intelligent questions about things at school and how I feel about life there. They don't just tell me how things are going for them.*

A box from home! Everyone in my side of the dorm was waiting excitedly until I opened it. Yum!—tamarind balls, guava cheese, and mango chutney. Everyone chorused, "Are you going to eat that stuff?" I quietly chuckled inwardly with greed because now I would not have to share it with anyone else.*

Inasmuch as we've already devoted several chapters to the MK's home life, perhaps we can dispense with an account of vacation periods spent as a family again. But excitement reigns throughout the school as vacation time approaches. Anticipating the spice of homelife, Mom's cooking, and gentler discipline, boys and girls savor the pause in classroom proprieties—the teachers also share the exhilaration of these days. And few students are tardy as the bus driver toots his horn; even he becomes impatient to get off to the railway station. Elsewhere in the study the train trip to school is described. By adding a few decibels of excitement to that journey, we can summon up a picture of this present safari. A student recounts the feelings of herself and siblings as they were nearing home for their winter vacation:

For an hour we watched all the landmarks that brought us closer to our train station. We went crazy when we saw our parents waiting for us. Vacations meant swimming almost every day in the ocean and seeing our good friends again.

Life in God's house. According to New Testament analogy with a little stretching and sublimation, the boarding community qualifies as the House of God (Ephesians 2:19; 1 Timothy 3:15; Hebrews 3:6; 10:21; 1 Peter 2:5). The confines of the school, obviously, are to be understood in a less literal sense than the child Samuel's brick-and-mortar domicile. It's been suggested that boarding school is a state of mind!

Yet if in Exodus 3:5 God cites the portion of foreign Gentile wilderness as "holy ground" on which He met and instructed His servant Moses, the alien environs of missionary schools may be considered territory marked by His special presence and watchcare. May we not say, then, that an area where offspring of God's servants study, eat, play, pray, and sleep, and where others of His servants minister to their physical and spiritual needs, is holy ground?

OMF's Sheila Miller in a study traces the 100-year history of Chefoo School from its founding in China in 1881 to its present site in

Malaysia. The latter school's Centennial Hymn acknowledges God's faithfulness in the lives of students and staff:

> Thankful friends from far and near,
> Celebrate this joyful year;
> Chefoo born on China's shore,
> Grown through days of peace and war;
> Lessons learned in class, at play,
> All have led us in His way.
> > Hearts and voices let us raise,
> > Our Jehovah-Jireh praise!
>
> Now in highlands valley cool,
> Worldwide prayers surround our school,
> Fears and laughter, tears and joy,
> Love for every girl and boy.
> Crafts and skills and half-term fun,
> Inward battles fought and won,
> > Guide and guard through all our days,
> > Our Jehovah-Jireh praise![22]

10
BOARDING SCHOOL (II)
Life in an MK World

> *"By wisdom a house is built, and through understanding it is established; through knowledge its rooms are filled with rare and beautiful treasures"* (Proverbs 24:3,4).

FACILITIES & AMENITIES

Postcard view. Wherever located, at or near sea-level or atop an air-conditioned mountain, the typical boarding school complex presents an attractive picture. One writer describes a particular school's cluster of buildings as "gleaming white edifices circled about and under by lush-green semi-tropical trees and flowers. Crowning deep-blue roofs and fresh-washed sky make it a scene of artistic splendor." [23]

Not far from schools at a higher elevation there's usually a town with dozens of pokey little shops. These serve the kitchen staff as a partial source of supply for staple commodities like rice and wheat, and candyholic students for sweet tidbits. Schools located at mean level generally have access to larger centers with superior conveniences.

School equipment. Solidly constructed academic buildings enclose classrooms, library, teachers' lounge, administrative offices. Then there are the dormitories, faculty quarters, dining room, additional lounges, chapel, gymnasium, music rooms, and probably a student store.

Classroom equipment, while kept in good condition, doesn't equal that of homeside schools with their creature comforts and superbly printed textbooks, few of which are appreciated by pupils. Audiovisual and other learning aids are now standard equipment, with films from embassies at times supplementing textbook material. As we would expect, computers are showing up in some schools.

The number and scope of library offerings in most schools leave something to be desired, chiefly in the sphere of contemporary literature and current events. There may also be a lack of student exposure to the history, geography, and culture of the host country. In addition, many schools don't reach accreditation standards in lab science equipment and courses, vocational studies, computational skills, and industrial arts. One parent, however, shares a grand thought:

> We found it isn't necessary to have a million-dollar building and all the latest equipment to have a school. When we have teachers who love to teach and students who desire to study, we're fully content. . . . The staff of our boarding school have enriched the quality of our parenting.*

ACADEMIC AIMS

Educational standards. A good education is comprised of a variety of learning experiences, both organized and informal. While conscious of the need for a more broadly based curriculum, administrators consider one element indispensable: the rounding out of students in Christian principles by teachers, houseparents, and other staff members. In our judgment, most schools pass muster in this category.

Several other distinctives mark overseas schools: a low pupil/teacher ratio (averaging about 8/1), arrangement for students to room and study with those from different racial (western) backgrounds, and the absence of distracting influences such as television in the dorms. The larger schools are moving toward meeting the express needs of both handicapped and gifted children.

Constructive criticism of academic standards, however, isn't wanting. In an incisive evaluation of 15 overseas schools visited in 1974, Mr. D. Bruce Lockerbie of Stony Brook School remarks:

> Although we can testify that each school has its brilliant students, we find the general range of accomplishment to be less than might be expected and considerably below the laudatory self-assessment of some administrators and faculty.[24]

Only five or six of the 100 American schools, including about 30 secondary schools, are accredited by any one of the three main U.S. regional accrediting agencies, each of which certifies schools in a particular area of the world. A good number of the non-accredited schools remain small. Students of well-rated institutions can readily transfer credits to U.S. schools and colleges. Almost all secondary teachers are regionally state-accredited before they commence their work abroad.

Most schools would welcome certification and some are proceeding toward that goal. The main hindrance is shortage of qualified administrators, counselors, librarians, and nurses, in addition to insufficient equipment and courses as previously noted. Some administrators and boards may have financial or theological reasons for not seeking accreditation.

It's worthy of mention, nevertheless, that traditional educational methods aren't necessarily shackles of the past. Currently the battlecry in America is Back To Basics, echoing the "no frills" curriculum of missionary boarding schools from the beginning. Most graduates read and write well, a respectable percentage exceptionally well. With reference to scholastic standards, many alumni consider their schools worthy of high marks. This MK specifies her school as a barometer for other schools:

> The high academic standards in MK schools produce high achievers. For example, out of a senior class of 26 in our school, 14 are honor roll! Seniors had an average of over 1,000 on their SAT scores, which is significantly higher than the U.S. average.*

Diplomatic headmaster. Since operating an overseas school continues with the sufferance of the host government, the headmaster and his administrative associates are responsible for a number of uniquely important functions. Besides essentially school-related responsibilities, they must be skilled in the art of public relations in order to maintain goodwill with various national functionaries—government and embassy officials and perhaps others. Relations with national officials are easily strained, particularly in the aftermath of political unrest.

From personal conversations with adult MKs and testimonies received from others, we view the typical headmaster as approachable and sympathetic as respects individual students and their problems. Students may not always love him, but they like him! Being ushered into his august presence doesn't result in trauma. This versatile headmaster attempts to keep parents informed of what's going on at school and how they can encourage their child toward better adjustment to school life. In the matter of learning problems or physical disability, he works to bring affected pupils into the mainstream of school activity.

Testing teachers. In many schools the teacher exercises a multi-role, at times outside his area of certification. He may serve as athletic coach, music instructor, counselor, supervisor of study hall and mealtime, or even as houseparent. Thus he relates to students over a broad plane. Parents feel free to discuss with him the strengths and weaknesses of their children.

Despite not being subjected to indiscipline in class and tense relations with parents—the main causes of burnout among western teachers—the attrition rate of expatriate teachers is high. As a rule they're not career people dedicated to prolonged service overseas. In some cases, eagerness to travel abroad prompts a young teacher to assay a stint of this nature. Or a short-term worker may be constrained to answer the call for a fill-in. Occasionally a field missionary with teaching aptitude is reassigned to the classroom. Whatever the reason, the high turnover rate proves a grave impediment to the smooth functioning of many schools. Faculty members with a long-range commitment are sorely needed; such teachers, by attending seminars during furlough, can keep up with current educational advances.

A teacher in ELWA Academy in Liberia, where children of ELWA radio staff are enrolled, comments: "Teaching isn't an easy job, but it is a way to consistently witness for Christ. The children see your life each day. They test you and try you to see if you really mean what you teach." In a more general reference to staff requirements, a writer personalizing Rethy Academy in Zaire states:

> I need dorm parents and teachers, secretaries, elementary and junior high teachers, French teachers, and remedial specialists, art teachers and music teachers. . . . I want people who come because they have a heart for people, for nationals, for missionaries, but especially for children. I need people who are flexible, who can adjust to doing without, who are willing to learn the local language and love the nationals. I need those who will not consider their job second-class because they are support missionaries in that they minister to missionaries rather than to nationals. Those are touchy qualifications, aren't they?

Teachers leave their impress on students; most MKs retain warm remembrances of some of them. These alumni discover too that teachers look better with the passage of time. Our own children concur that with rare exceptions the teachers were "tops." When students on furlough write to friends at school, they'll often close with "Give my love to the teachers," specifying two or three.

HARDY HOUSEPARENTS

Shock absorbers. Supervising a dormitory ranks as one of the crucial roles in missionary service and certainly one of the most taxing. These surrogate parents are engrossed with their charges for the better part of each 24-hour day. Thus a boarder's cheerful adjustment to school life frequently depends on the helping hands and hearts of "Auntie" and "Uncle."

Many schools entrust this role to single ladies as well as to married couples. Others, like Faith Academy in Manila, normally select couples in order to strengthen the idea of family life. This particular academy actively recruits houseparents in the U.S. and Canada, thoroughly screening each applicant. No more than 20 students are assigned to a couple, and houseparents aren't permitted to engage in regular teaching or serve in other posts.

Still, administrators find difficulty in enlisting the right type of persons for this vital ministry. As with teachers, the rate of turnover is high. Adult stateside Christians anticipating foreign service tend to shrink from seriously considering what seems essentially a menial, behind-the-scenes task. On occasion missionary mothers with children in schools serve (as Eunice did) for a year or two. And strikingly enough, some alumni offer themselves as houseparents. Two of these appointees describe their motivation:

> "If only I hadn't been separated from my parents. If only I had had a normal life instead of a life in a boarding school!" These "ifs" and many more have been the theme of my life and the source of much bitterness. . . . Praise God He is allowing me to see the "whys." He was preparing me for my life work—the special appointment as housemother to a school of missionary children. . . . Through these seemingly negative experiences the Lord has been preparing me to understand and love the MKs He is going to entrust into my care.*

> When asked to consider serving as houseparent, my first reaction was negative. The Lord was calling me to *missionary* service! That evening my Bible reading was 1 Corinithians 12. Suddenly I realized that I wanted to be a hand or a tongue when the Lord wanted me to be a toe—a toe covered by a shoe and unseen, but necessary to the balance of the body.*

Servant of all. The following rundown of a houseparent's day by a CAM veteran, designed to inform parents about dorm life, won't be construed as a glamorous ad for recruiting personnel for the job:

> Let me answer your questions, allay normal doubts and fears about your children as you consider the field and sending them away to school. The Lord is served in caring for your child and giving the proper attention to every situation—broken bones or glasses, bump or bee-sting, tummy or toothache, under the weather for any reason; all get treatment. Someone is always responsible every minute of 24 hours to see that the children eat and sleep well, play, study, practice the piano, take their medicine, are taken to clinic for checkup, are pulled out of

swimming hole a bit sooner if they begin to shiver, brush teeth, have nails trimmed, are covered up, tucked in at night.

Someone always sees that they are bathed, ears scrubbed inside and out, clothes changed or put away, hair combed out, bangs trimmed or curls in place, sash tied, shirt tucked in, have offering for Sunday school, Bible verses learned, shoes polished, tied.

There never fails someone to spot a feverish brow, shoe with hole, missing strap or lace, broken toy, that button off; to make birthday cake, supply jar for tadpoles, string for kites, shelf for pine cones, stuffing for dolls; to address the letter home, check sweeping job done, read bedtime story, that call in the night.

We could elaborate on hikes and holidays, chapels, plays, singing programs, and devotions by the fireplace. . . .[25]

For all that, no dormparent can be all a child needs or wants; to be this would require a person's becoming a perfect blending of babysitter, housemaid, nursemaid, loving and tender (and tolerant) disciplinarian. One 10-year-old offers his suggestion of what would constitute a good supervisor: "If I were a houseparent, I would want cats, dogs, rabbits and other animals. I would allow days off from school on every birthday." Veritably, these servants of the Lord, committed to round-the-clock ministry, can be forgiven if their patience wears thin once in a long while; their hearts are in the right place. A housemother recalls an experience in comforting a little one with the "lonelies":

One night while tucking in one of the smaller ones, a little girl whispered for me to pray with her. With my hand in hers, we talked to the Lord together. It brought to my mind a poem I had long before pasted in the front of my Bible: "Lord, give me a little hand to lead."*

Restrictions don't always set well with their charges, so it's not surprising that dormparents come in for considerable carping. In fact, probably a majority of past and present students feel somewhat equivocal about their dormparents. One adult MK describes an uncommon experience:

During my fifth-grade year I got along well with the houseparents—they were my mom and dad. But getting along with my peers got harder. Before it had been "us against the houseparents," but now I was outside the circle. I had suddenly in their eyes become the informer.*

Typical of kudos received from adult MKs, however, is this comment:

Fortunately I had very good houseparents, understanding but quite strict. Their strictness actually gave me a sense of security and also respect for them. At least I knew where I stood. In general I have no complaints about boarding school. My dormparents were of the best possible caliber.*

SCHOOL ETCETERAS

Balanced discipline. Regulations have to do with activities such as the use of the swimming pool and other recreational facilities, attendance at meals (no skipping unless by permission), visiting local shops, church attendance. Some rules are firmly but fairly enforced, while others are in the nature of guidelines. Here's an atypical statement by a recent graduate but with a promising conclusion:

It was a terrible struggle for me to learn to accept authority. I saw many kids who lived by the rules, never questioning anything for fear of being labeled rebellious. Their individuality and critical thinking were stifled in their struggle to stay on the good side of the staff. I've known kids who were completely bewildered when it came time for them to leave school and begin to make their own decisions and set up guidelines.They realized they didn't know how.

I went to the other extreme of rebelling against everything. I couldn't see one good thing about the school. Finally, however, I realized I had to accept the staff and their God-given authority. Once I learned that and started offering creative alternatives rather than complaints, I became content.

In my four years of boarding school, I've grown to love the school and its people. Through my conflicts with the rules and authority, I've learned to accept and even respect them.*

The "unsparing rod," prudently handled, has its honored place in MK schools. British academies, with their spartan discipline, practice caning oftener than American schools do, though it should be added that the British operation is carried out with a dash of empathy—the functionary places a book under his arm to soften the strokes.

Peer pleasing. Is it possible for baneful group pressure to exist in a boarding school? Indeed it is, though not often entrenched. Not a few MKs have that within which disposes them to become compliant allies of a peer group bent on breaking rules and railing at school personnel.

On first entering school a child isn't troubled by what others think of him; he has a loving authority figure in his parents and he sees himself as they see him. But since acceptance by others in his age-bracket stands out as the overriding desire of most growing children, a youngster lacking gumption and self-esteem tends to weaken when slick-talking peers bear down on him to conform. Especially vulnerable is the early high schooler. If he has to risk displeasure, he may feel it's easier and safer to displease his parents than being rejected by his peer group. He wants to be considered a regular guy. At such times a girl is ordinarily more intent than a boy in standing with parents.

A number of adult MKs mention that they observed little evidence of this type of behavior in their schools. Several others indicate that a nucleus of schoolmates was able to quietly cut down to size any offender who initiated softening-up techniques. Our hat is off to the members of such a voluntary "anti-mischief group"!

Teasing and friendly banter, of course, are inevitable in any company of youths. But a timid child continually badgered by a peer group about a conspicuous habit or condition can suffer lasting emotional hurt. Sticks and stones can cause less injury than name-calling.

If a student remains a low achiever in classwork, he's generally free from taunts, but if he plays up to the teacher he's a prime candidate for the full treatment. Three MKs give their impression of peer influence in their schools (we wonder if they have ever seriously checked their own attitude):

> Boarding school is in many ways an extreme example of "Small Town, USA." Everybody knows it if a teacher yells at a boy or girl in class, or if a girl and her boyfriend break up. People build fantastic defense mechanisms and masks to hide their true feelings about life. Some kids have left our school not even knowing themselves because of the roles they have played for so long.

> There was a lot of peer pressure in our school. When a new kid came, we worked on him to make him conform to our way of things. One special kid we wouldn't tolerate—one who liked to eat and play with his sister. He was really weird, and so was she. But both finally came around.*

> In boarding school we had to fend for ourselves. We didn't have our parents to check us, and our dormparents couldn't be everywhere at the same time. So we learned to give and take and to get along with others.*

Spiritual life. After the above discussion we'll want to enquire about the spiritual climate at boarding school. Prefatorily let it be said that if faculty and staff had the practical wisdom of Solomon and the spiritual discernment of the Apostle Paul, the school community would still suffer from some degree of spiritual malaise. Nurtured by believing parents and thus above average in terms of deportment, missionary children don't often arrive at a settled faith by the time they enter school. Scriptural truths may ricochet off their heads and harmful notions take root in their hearts; and then there are always the few who purposefully don a cloak of spirituality. Doubtless some students experience springtime in the heart throughout much of their school life, but perhaps the majority fluctuate between ho-hum and hallelujah.

Communal living at its best tries the fiber of the staunchest believer as much as it satisfies his social instinct. Boarding life is no exception, either for students or staff. Along with the delights of fellowship come interpersonal problems. It's all too true that, as British friends in India used to quote:

> To live above, with saints we love,
> Won't that indeed be glory!
> To live below, with saints we know—
> Well, that's a different story.

Boarding school, sometimes termed the halfway house between the home and the world, is neither a Bible institute nor a public school, though it partakes of the nature of both. Ostensibly study material is biblically oriented, but this premise may not be immediately apparent in some schools. Yet we surmise that most staff members take pains to erase the unnatural dichotomy between spiritual and secular instruction, since all genuine education is God-centered.

Elementary students devote a portion of each day to classroom prayer and Bible reading. Secondary classes vary in this respect from school to school. In addition to daily chapel (weekly or semiweekly in some cases), pupils may gather for family prayer in their dorms each evening. The older boys and girls, with or without a staff member in attendance, may on Sunday evening join one of a number of groups such as Pioneer Girls, Christian Service Brigade, Awana Club, Young Life, Campus Crusade.

In British schools particularly the students wear uniforms throughout the week. A good fashion equalizer, this practice helps to solve dress problems for both students and parents. If a vote were taken of student preference for or against uniforms, the ayes would probably win out, though most young people like a change into street clothes once in a while to know what they feel like.

On the Lord's day each boarder dons his or her best bib-and-tucker for Sunday school and morning service. It's a pleasing sight to watch a company of children and young people in their spiffy go-to-meetin' uniforms marching in loose file to church.

Meetings may be held in the school chapel, or perhaps the students as a group attend an English-speaking gathering fairly close to school grounds, usually following western modes of expression. Generally speaking, however, they don't join assemblies of predominantly national Christians, even if the messages are translated into English. To many of us, doing so would represent a friendly gesture on the part of students and school, but as one missionary explains, "An influx of scores of blond-haired American teenagers is too much of a distraction to a local congregation."

A good number of young people mention receiving blessing during Spiritual Emphasis Week, when an outside speaker ministers on evangelistic and discipleship themes. At another time a well-known conference speaker from Britain or North America leads in a week of deeper-life ministry. The latter meetings attract vacationers, including missionary parents with children in boarding.

The condensed statements that follow, originally appearing in mission literature, give a varied view of spiritual life as it's manifested in some schools:

Being taught the most important thing in life—knowing Christ personally

Attempting to make his testimony be what people like to hear, just to get them off his back—thus learning the language of hypocrisy

Rebelling at Bible classes and chapel, Sunday school, devotions—"Religion is being stuffed down my throat"—but later seeing everything differently

Concluding, after much spiritual struggle, that boarding school is what the individual makes of it

In absence of parents, having to rely more personally on the Lord

Beginning of desire to be controlled by the Spirit

Expressing gratitude for many hours spent with a group of girls—at Bible clubs, in the dorms, in walks to the hills— "challenging, praying, singing, sharing, and loving each other."

Being delivered from spiritual defection through assurance that his parents' faith was sound and solid and worth following

Enjoying happy years at school after, at seven years, being raised "to walk in newness of life" during Easter services

Arriving at school in a period when spiritual things were spoken of in whispers, but blessed through revival when many boys and girls began to bear witness to their faith. "Spiritually I was born here and, like a babe, hungered for the Word and grew."

Being extremely unhappy at having to be separated from family, but during a time of severe sickness seeing her parents and their love in a new light

Feeling a burden for the lost, especially her close friends

The sound of music. Scripture accents making music as one of the believer's highest privileges and befitting pursuits—first as a sacrifice to God, then as a means of personal enrichment for His people and of communicating the Good News to prepared hearts. This "universal language of mankind" occupies an honorable place in Christian testimony; the voice of praise is virtually never silent in hundreds of languages.

A young but growing university course, ethnomusicology, may be loosely defined as the study of music in its social and cultural context, with a view to communicating with other cultures. And, of all things, recently a Wheaton MK on short-term service in Ecuador wrote music in the Quichua genre; then she put lyrics to it promoting hygiene and health care for radio broadcasting!

As we would expect, many missionary children early acquire a consuming fondness for good music—not often the toe-tapping species. From the initial establishment of overseas schools, therefore, administrators have sought to exploit this trait for the Lord, igniting latent talent. So most schools utilize music in the various phases of daily study. An alumnus has this fine word to say about his school:

> The music program and presentations in our school gave plenty of opportunity for finding one's talent. Almost any kind of instrumental music could be learned. Our bands and choirs were first-rate. I think music is more original when done by MKs—it has a flair all its own. They enjoy music and art, with little thought of competition and reward, so everything is creative and not mechanical.

Truly a musical education is a distinct privilege in these days. The diversity of contemporary styles in vocal and instrumental music prompts school authorities to introduce students to tasteful expressions of each type. Through training in notation, rhythms, and harmony they're afforded a basis for appraising current trends. A missionary mother writes concerning a special problem at school:

> I really thank the Lord for our kids' dormparents. They're just right for these big kids. They're sharp and into things and yet they're firm too. They've had to have a big comedown on rock music this term. You wouldn't believe some of the music that comes with the kids from missionary home! Several are having a rough time taking it since rock is their hobby. One 9th grade kid brought 100 tapes of the stuff.

It's widely understood that music appreciation and acquaintance with the world of estimable music favorably affects the student's general learning and speaking ability. And of course melody helps to heal the drooping spirits of performer and hearer. A missionary expands on this thought:

> Music tears down barriers for communicating Christ, and makes inroads into people's hearts both at the intellectual and emotional levels. I believe music can be crucial in opening hearts to the Lord as well as convincing them of their need of Him.

At another point in D. Bruce Lockerbie's study previously mentioned, this educator gives his impression of music programs in the MK schools he visited:

> Most impressive to us are the programs in music—classroom, performing ensembles, and private study. Some schools have as many as 60 percent of their students receiving piano lessons, for instance. Several schools are equipped with music teaching and rehearsal facilities to rival colleges ten times their size. The quality of choral and instrumental performance confirms the value of this investment. In some cases a school's music program offers the European community its best opportunities for enjoying Western music. In at least one instance, the school choir appears annually in concert before the head of state.[24]

EXTRACURRICULAR ACTIVITIES

School athletics. Authorities generally find that strengthening athletic programs results in fringe benefits for the school, notably better morale. The normally docile student may take on new enthusiasm on reaching the playing field. And perhaps an obnoxious youngster will undergo a distinct change of attitude, as happened to this young chap:

> I looked forward to having playmates at school, but I didn't have them. I hated school until the 6th grade, when soccer came into the picture and changed things. I believe to this day that, because of this, being sent away to boarding school was the best thing for me.

The moment classes are over and students finish off their tea and cookies, streams of avid enthusiasts, minus flashy playgear, head for the sports field. These boys and girls generate excitement; they make it happen. Soon an intramural game is in progress with lesser gymnastics on the sidelines.

Obviously the type of games depends on the school and the season. A listing of them might include versions of baseball and softball, basketball (on the field or in the gym), football, field hockey, soccer, cricket, tennis, badminton, volleyball, rugby. Some students engage in track, wrestling, mountaineering, hiking—not to mention walking on stilts. Then each school has it swimming pool or an agreeable alternative such as an ocean beach.

Supervisors and / or coaches stand guard against injuries, chiefly to the young children. Youngsters who experience difficulty in handling defeat are counseled, though the formula, "Cheers today, jeers tomorrow," pertains only mildly to the present scene. Heroes aren't demoted to goats overnight and nice guys don't always finish last. One team doesn't report having "scalped" opponents when they hand them a drubbing.

Coaches strive for excellence among their charges but encourage fair attitudes; they stress that competition and cooperation go together, even when a team ends the year with an occasional winning streak of one or two. Thus team members normally find that all this is good training in coping with the lumps of life. "Athletic experiences with the kids," muses one alumnus, a coach, "were better than I could ever hope to find elsewhere." (Boarding school students and alumni will probably consider this account entirely too idealistic, that there are plenty of temper flareups from time to time. Surely this can't happen in a company of *missionary children!* We have at least three students and a graduate with non-fictional statements.)

> There's no need for dull moments. Every Friday or on alternate Fridays we have clubs or hobbies. Each one can choose what club he'd like to join, whether camping, cooking, woodworking or leather-craft. The clubs then run for a semester when kids switch to another club. On Saturday night there may be junior high games, when the entire junior high classes are divided into teams and play against each other.*

For our Saturday night activities we have parties and coffee houses and films. Each day we climb trees, build tree houses, ride go-carts, play volleyball and soccer, and all kinds of fun things like that. Midterm weekends are usually the most fun of all because the parents come and visit and we have picnics, musicales and Field Day.*

We have hikes in the woods and picnics, and once or twice a semester Pioneer Girls camp out for two or three days and nights. Then there's the Yearbook and the newspaper to work on, choirs, sing-a-longs, folk groups, social events. MKs are puzzle fans, so there are plenty of these going on throughout the week.*

Marbles were the big event of recess, and you had to be able to shoot overhand, not underhand like beginners. Alleys were hot trading items, with beautiful marbles of all sizes and colors available. We also played "gilly dandu," when you sharpen a small stick at both ends, then flip it up and hit it with another stick. Throwing a ball against the wall and doing something before it came back must have taken an average of an hour a day—plainsies, clapsies, round-the-world, to-backsies. We run into variations of this game in America.

Finding friends. In a world where so many social relationships are superficial and transient, blowing hot and cold, boarding school offers young people a unique opportunity to cultivate secure friendships. The fact that the makeup of many schools resembles a mini-United Nations conference, with students from perhaps a dozen countries, makes friendships unusually stimulating. Of course some MKs are more gregarious than others and acquire friends more readily. Is this because they work at it? Certainly those who don't take friendships for granted but contribute generously to the relationship find enrichment in both personal and school life. An RBMU missionary daughter evaluates her experience:

Has boarding school life mattered much to me? Has it made me feel unwanted or unloved? Yes, it's mattered a great deal to me—so much, in fact, that I wouldn't have it any other way. Where else could I get such personal, loving attention from teachers and counselors? And where else could I have so many friends around me so much of the time? It is through these teachers and friends that I learn how to get along with others— in all sorts of circumstances and how to share with others— not only of my belongings but also of myself.

No one questions the significance of same-age friendships, but casual older friends often have much to bring to a relationship—values such as humor, good sense, spiritual freshness. As for social times with national fellow-students, most MKs seem to lack incentive in availing themselves of golden opportunities. An adult recollects:

> The school I went to was fortunate in that there were many national students in the classes (about 50%), but unfortunately none, or very few, were in boarding. Looking back on my class pictures, I don't recall the names of any national classmates. I cannot remember any particular discrimination on the part of the teachers; it's just that the boarding world and the world of day-to-day life hardly overlapped. I would have liked, in retrospect, for the teachers to encourage more interaction with local kids.

Dating daze. When in the course of human events the boys in boarding shift gears and retreat from their strong aversion to the opposite sex, social relationships take on a new dimension. Though still somewhat uneasy in their company and unable to initiate sparkling dialogue, the young gentlemen want to be well thought of by the ladies. And they may wonder what the girls are doing to make themselves look so much nicer than a year or two before. As for the young ladies, the subject or object of their conversations increasingly resorts to boys.

School authorities accept and frequently encourage boy/girl friendships. The confining nature of the community, however, makes it imperative that relationships be monitored. A chill or impropriety in a particular friendship could bring wide repercussions. So official permission for dating is required in some schools. Two other important factors hinder the expression of romantic sentiments: Days and evenings are usually filled with curricular and extracurricular bustle, and the lounges provide about as much privacy as the school picnic.

Still, a boy and girl may talk together after supper until the study bell rings. And there are normally a few semiprivate spots on campus where a twosome can enjoy a few fleeting minutes of freedom from prying eyes and plying tongues. The school grapevine is highly developed and never overloaded, and dating news spreads like a prairie fire. Two young people explain how these momentous matters were handled in their schools:

> Previously we could date about once a month, and any socializing between dates had to be done in groups. A "date" meant sitting on a bench and talking alone—and holding hands

if you so desired. Dating was an institution reserved for those who were going together, and down-to-earth talking between boys and girls was unheard of. . . . Now things are different. Dating regulations are more relaxed. Double dating is allowed. For instance, we can go downtown to eat and bowl. Boys and girls are learning to talk to each other about things that really matter, not just the daily gossip.*

It wasn't so much the rules against dating as much as having very little opportunity for it. We were marched back to the separate girls' dorm immediately after school was over. But there were frequent visits from boys, usually under cover of darkness. I remember being in the senior dorm and seeing the girls open and close the back door as a signal to boys who had come from the boys' dorm. Guy Fawkes night was the social event of the year. Again, under cover of darkness, boyfriend and girlfriend could meet. Other than that, very little social life was allowed or encouraged.*

Pleasantries & pranks. What would a school of active youngsters be without fun? Clearly wit and humor, including the sharing of outlandish minutiae stored away in the mind, aren't wanting among boarders. To be able to see the humorous side of life's foibles and to laugh at one's own represent a step forward in maturation. Presumably instances of off-color jesting appear among a few students, yet lightheartedness and innocuous banter distinguish the social life of the student body. (Worth mentioning is the fact that no graffiti adorns the walls.)

A once-in-a-lifetime event of common interest in school can set excitement astir. Here's one that could prove unique in boarding annals:

At Chefoo School in Malaysia about six years ago, Penelope, the ever-popular she-goat, was due for delivery. Grades 4 and 6 were summoned for the occasion. By the time these students arrived however, the newly born kid was struggling to stand, and Penelope was licking it. But, just imagine, again Penelope lay back panting, and before the eyes of all gave birth to another kid! Cheers arose from the entire group. Penelope became quite a heroine.

Now a brief word about pranks; many of these could be tallied. There are the covert operations, coups and countercoups. In addition to the time-honored practice of short-sheeting the houseparent's bed, fertile minds concoct novel schemes. The houseparents of a missionary school in Brazil report a nefarious happening: A student painted lizard eggs to resemble candy and passed them to friends! Over and above student artifices, Auntie and Uncle may on rare occasions move in conspiracy with their charges. A reliable witness records this episode:

> One Friday night our housemother took us girls after lights-out to scratch on the boys' dorm window to scare them. When we were outside, the housefather and boys locked all the doors of our dorm so we couldn't get back in. We had to climb through the clothes chute. The next Friday we locked the boys out.*

Grand finale: Graduation: This major milestone in the MK's life, termed Speech Day in some schools, signals a full round of activities—generally stirring but at times a little wearing. Every senior's parents and special friends who can possibly make it are on hand for the gala occasion. Those afflicted with "cameraitis" click away to freeze the event for posterity.

The graduating MK knows only too well that this day marks his bowing-out of face-to-face companionship with most of his classmates. A good few of the youngsters who tearfully left home and family ten years before now become misty-eyed at the thought of school friends being scattered far and wide for further education and lifework.

The guest speaker at the graduation service gives his observations and advice. More often than not the speech deals with some variation of the concept "The world needs you!" and may be long on bliss but short on specifics. Students are reminded that, though they yearn to get out of what sometimes seems an unreal world and into a world where the action is, there's a fairly small "Welcome" sign out there; but each graduate is needed. He'll find that life isn't a bowl of cherries; still, God's man in God's place won't lack God's blessing, so he can make a difference.

To add a further word: As the believing MK leaves school and enters college, meanwhile taking additional steps toward full independence and career involvement, he'll want to align himself heartily with the highest goals. The more estimable the enterprise, the more satisfied he'll be. And what is more worthy than being numbered among God's faithful "fellow workers" (1 Corinthians 3:9), whether he's engaged in industry or vocational Christian service.

The believer is inextricably associated with eternity's greatest Worker in a success-laden purpose: One day the whole creation will join in the Hallelujah Chorus, "It is finished. . . . The kingdom of the world has become the kingdom of our Lord and of his Christ" (John 19:30; Revelation 11:15).

Missionary parents and offspring alike become freshly conscious that a new juncture in family relationship is imminent. In view of the perils besetting young people today—even those carefully reared in truths of God's Word—parental concern and confidence are echoed in these petitions of Amy Carmichael on behalf of early adolescents of Dohnavur Fellowship in South India as they step out on their own:

> Father, hear us, we are praying,
> Hear the words our hearts are saying;
> We are praying for our children.
>
> Keep them from the powers of evil,
> From the secret, hidden peril,
> From the whirlpool that would suck them,
> From the treacherous quicksand, pluck them.
>
> From the worldling's hollow gladness,
> From the sting of faithless sadness.
> Holy Father, save our children.
>
> Through life's troubled waters steer them,
> Through life's bitter battle, cheer them,
> Father, Father, be Thou near them.
> Read the language of our longing.
> Read the wordless pleadings thronging,
> Holy Father, for our children.
>
> And wherever they may bide,
> Lead them home at eventide.

11
TEEN TIMES
Struggling to Mature

---

*"Don't let anyone look down on you because you
are young, but set an example for the believers in
speech, in life, in love, in faith and in purity"*
(1 Timothy 4:12).

PREPARING FOR PLUNGE

Teens on tenterhooks. The normal life-span has been likened to a
passing breath—a birth, a breath, and then the bier. To the teenager,
however, the stretch between what has become drab childhood and
crossing the threshold into that enchanted land of adulthood seems
interminable, a lifetime in itself. Sometimes called the tadpole stage
or the "ouch" generation, this interval is often fraught with
uncertainties. In the process of learning to deal with fluctuating
feelings, the young person doesn't know whether he's a boy or a man,
a girl or a woman. Worried about what others think of him, the youth
feels like a stranger to himself.

Adolescents act the way they do because they're troubled.
Nevertheless, while these are tough times for teens, we can
overemphasize the element of teenage turbulence, painting things
with too broad a brush. Hosts of youths move into adulthood
without constant tumult. The majority may be reasonably happy
most of the time; they're learning to unravel their hangups. Phasing
out a good degree of parental authority and yet unencumbered with
major adult responsibilities, these "keenagers" scent adventure in the
air. As Agnes Machad poetically renders it, "The untrod ways of life
are touched by fancy's glow."

The mid-adolescent MK often experiences trouble, particularly if
his earlier years were spent in rural or primitive areas abroad.
Removed from his parents and adjusting to a whole new run of
things, identifying with today's peers in high school or college may
not be easy—even when these are Christian institutions. In an article,
"Who's the Strange Kid?" in *The Alliance Witness* for 12/18/74, a
high schooler sizes up a new student, an MK; also a few perceptive
words from an MK in Senegal:

There's this new guy in my geometry class, you know. His hair is shorter than most kids. The first day his boots were polished real nice and his jeans were new! Every day he comes to class with his homework done. And when it comes to jokes he isn't with it. Somebody said our teacher is a real "Archie Bunker type" and this guy just looked blank.*

A lot of people have told me that MKs often have the attitude that the world owes them everything. If we MKs could be courteous and show gratitude, it would help our image with people here, and perhaps the response of church people would be better.*

All in all, this is a time when emotions run high and strong—a period when there's as much dejection as pleasure. The young person doesn't like what he sees in the mirror. Shooting up in height, gawky-looking, and walking with a gangly gait, he's uncomfortable with his inner feelings and their outward display. In speech he's pestered by "foot-in-mouthitis." Not the least problem is the struggle with erotica. And through it all he may not recognize that this is normal for the course.

Sociologists usually consider adolescence to extend from the early teens through the early twenties. Nonetheless, since in western society no solo birthday marks entrance to adulthood, for our particular purpose we're thinking in terms of the years 17 and 18 or 19 as the median period of adolescence. During these years the MK realistically commences the quest for independence from parents and identity with his new cultural environment.

Early teen years. Yet what about the years 13 and 14? For a variety of reasons we shouldn't neglect this stage, which some esteemed writers place alongside preschool years as chiefly determining future stability of character. On the brink of adolescence, the early teen's difficulty in dealing with deep physical and chemical changes may be reflected in unpredictable behavior. If the MK spends these crucial years in boarding school, in company with scores of others similarly affected, the reaction will be less pronounced.

This digest of testimonies gives an overview of how MKs react to high school life in America:

Appreciating his parents' judgment, and not developing bitter feel-
ings, when they returned to needed ministry on field
Facing the turbulence of teenage America an entirely new experi-
ence—not dressing, talking, or thinking like his former peers
Having opportunities to share travel experiences and parents' work
Finding that classmates eventually realize that he's an ordinary

person, not living in an exalted sphere—all this happening when he
himself began to open up

Being shy but intent on showing friendliness, thus being well accepted

Feeling that a teeming African jungle was less threatening than
American high schoolers

Observing lack of student interest when shallow curiosity is allayed

Being told nicely that she did things quite a bit differently than other
students

Gaining help from the Lord to see her part in parents' work—by
studying contentedly in the U.S.

Learning that an MK doesn't always attract attention because of the
American student's exposure to different racial groups with their
different lifestyles

Weathering cliquishness, materialism, and other characteristics of
high school life—then sensing maturity for life ahead

Displaced persons. Following this glimpse of early teens, we turn
to observe the 17- and 18-year-olds now interacting with Mom and
Dad in the movement toward full independence. (Incidentally, as we
learn from several sources, there are approximately 10,000 MKs
today under 20.) How does the environment of the missionary home
influence the young person's ability to establish a becoming lifestyle
in a world estranged from the living God?

One adult suggests that "a handbook for 'scared MKs' arriving in
the U.S. would help." Of unique significance is the probability that
such young people are coming of age at the most complex period in
human history. "The world is ever near," the hymn says; it's much
nearer today than when these words were penned. An adult MK
writes about MKs' reentry problems:

> You wonder why the MK is homesick, very homesick. He
> wants to return to his family, his big mission family. That was
> the only place he's ever really belonged. He was part of them
> and they understood him. The funny little sayings and
> mannerisms that slip out now and then meant something to
> that family, something important. . . . His new friends try to
> picture what he shares, but all they have are stereotyped ideas.
> What the MK needs more than anything else is a friend that can
> help him fill the empty void of fellowship that he is missing
> from home. Someone willing to listen and not be bored.
> Someone who tries to understand and who is willing to admit it
> when he doesn't. Someone who cares.

Normally the adolescent MK is engaged either in completing high
school or about to enter college. He'll be examining himself in the
light of new demands being thrust upon him, with the need to settle

on at least some priorities for the upcoming stage of life.

The committed Christian won't go alone into uncharted seas. Without doubt he's meditated on the Apostle Paul's two letters to Timothy. (While Timothy was no longer an adolescent, he's not urged to "run the show" in his fellowship with God's people but to witness by a godly life.) Then there's John Bunyan's allegory *The Pilgrim's Progress,* which virtually every MK has read. Far from being outdated after 300 years, the volume can prove a boon companion for the present generation of youth. In his perilous journey along the King's Highway toward the Celestial City, "Christian" confronts the same general types of temptation young people face in these final decades of the 20th century.

Let's check the downbeat feelings of a mid-adolescent girl on being left by herself in the U.S.:

> How did I react when my parents left me at home and re-turned to the field? I was indifferent and almost rejecting in my attitude toward them; but it was only a cover-up for the deep hurt. It's still very hard to think about it. I knew in my head and assented to the inevitable—it was right for me to continue studies at home and Mom and Dad were needed back on the field. We went through all the supportive Scriptures we could find, and I felt it was part of my share in the missionary work. But I never got over the deepdown sense of abandonment. The houseparent at our mission home tried to fill the gap, and the Lord has given me other mothers and fathers in my parents' place, but it was never the same.*

Another missionary daughter depicts some of the sweeping changes she observes in western social values as opposed to those practiced in her childhood home:

> My parents opened our home and hearts to everyone who came to us, regardless of the time of day or night. But most people aren't like that in the West anymore. People don't care. They lock their doors and their pantries and their hearts. . . . And don't bare the agony of your heart; these people haven't seen or heard the things that hurt you, and they may think you are a little insane. Don't touch too much on the poverty and sickness and anguish of the country you were raised in, for it touches the conscience of the woman with a houseful of luxuries and a garbage can full of thrown-away leftovers and she doesn't want her tender conscience disturbed.

Countdown to independence. The cutting of the umbilical cord commences the parental process of letting go, usually completed when the son or daughter marries. When parents unnecessarily prolong childhood, however, seeking to keep the young person perched on the edge of the domestic nest, detriment follows for all concerned. Childish things must be put away in their proper time. For one thing, Mom and Dad should respect their early teen's privacy, forgoing snooping. We surmise that awakened missionary parents and offspring move on about the same wavelength along Freedom Trail. Yet the parents of MKs like these would wince to hear their murmurings:

There are still some subjects I find difficult to discuss with my parents. They weren't there when the subjects were of vital importance to me. The important things of my life happened at boarding school, not at home on vacation. I was saved at school, my friends were at school—all this happened while I was away from my parents.*

I never felt free to confide in my parents because I always got a sermon. When I told either Dad or Mom my problems, they didn't seem to be listening—they were planning their sermon. If I had a boyfriend problem, I wanted some practical advice and understanding, not a sermon. I want to teach my own kids how to "win friends and influence people," as a Christian ought to do.*

My parents never understood that I was different from other missionary kids. I was small, weak and not as smart as others. But I was expected to adjust like all the rest did. I didn't and was miserable.*

Still, only the rarest son or daughter limits communication with parents to grunts, or belligerently pulls up stakes and strikes out on his own before gaining a clearcut plan of action. Practically speaking, the loosening of family ties should embrace *interdependence* of the part of the MK. The discerning youth will consider his interaction with parents and older friends an opportunity to gain breadth and balance in the affairs of life. An adult daughter articulates her sentiments:

In my experience as a teen I found it a real problem to hear the unrealistic expectations people had of me. . . . We MKs have fears about the future, about coping with life today. We are sensitive about all those eyes on us and worry that we will let someone down. . . . But through the advice and prayers of loving parents and others who understand us—and don't expect perfection—we can take our place as responsible, productive citizens.*

A significant number of missionary parents, putting to good advantage the arrangements set up by their mission societies, take leave of overseas posts in order to see their son or daughter through high school or the first year of college—that is, should the young person sense the need of this. Mission boards generally provide public ministry for parents while on extended leave of this nature.

Blessed are those parents who refrain from bailing out their offspring as soon as a difficulty arises but instead encourage them toward personal decision-making and responsible action. If a son or daughter at a distance shares a special problem, Mom or Dad won't catch the next plane to be Johnny-on-the-spot.

Blessed also is that MK who, having stepped out into full independence, continues to extend to his parents the respect, patience, and understanding he would give to his best friend (not a reference to the family dog). He'll discern that they themselves are undergoing a peculiar type of adjustment pains.

Far from being detached spectators, parents have their valid place at this time—one mainly hidden from eyes and ears. (Matthew 18:19, 20 proves a bulwark to many parents.) A missionary mother, having relinquished her earlier role, affirms, "I will support, love, advise, pray, hope and believe, but I won't control."

Should the young person of 18 or 19 appear to lack an adequate sense of responsibility but insists on moving out into complete independence, it's befitting in most cases for parents to send him off with their blessing. We can't protect our offspring from all error and evil, nor can we continue to live in and through them as if to provide chart and compass. Wrong decisions may be made by our son or daughter with respect to friendships and futures, and perhaps there will be years filled with more defeat than victory—all deeply felt by the MK—yet these experiences are frequently, though sometimes needlessly, part and parcel of life.

We parents have had opportunity to state and restate biblical values to our child, but we can't maintain that the adolescent will pursue them. Regardless of how solidly the Christian base has been laid, our son or daughter will be trapped to some extent in value conflicts. Only the young person with a true heart for God, who doesn't fear being a minority of one at times, possesses the sure safeguard for purity. "The grace that sought and found me/Alone can keep me clean." Not marching to the world's drumbeat, he continues his quest for independence within the context of commitment to Jesus Christ as Lord.

THE SECULAR SCENE

Youth of the 80s. For the past century or longer, youth has had its place in the sun. The hope of society focused on the role of its youth; they would bring in the social millennium. Exposed to all the advantages and skills that any other society might covet, in a country unexampled in privilege and opportunity, American youth would far surpass their forebears in pursuits that matter.

It might be urged that every generation has a similar dream. Yet one is alarmed at the disparity between yesterday's dream and today's reality. A *Newsweek* editorialist describes the current crop of American youth as "silent, selfish and tractable." They're silent in being averse to searching out enduring values; selfish, in insisting on immediate gratification of sensual desires; tractable, in being susceptible to prevalent fancies such as situation ethics ("If it feels good, do it"). And the harvest? One tragic outcome is that suicide now ranks second to traffic-accident deaths in the U.S. among 15-to-19-year-olds—5,000 each year.

We can't overlook the millions of sturdy young people, often tucked away in comparative anonymity, who stand tall in terms of character and responsible life-goals. A recent broad survey by a secular group reveals that American young people today are relating better to their parents then those in past decades. But there's the other picture, concerning which yesterday's parents bear a major share of blame. Trading idealism for materialism, they've sown the wind in loveless parenting and are reaping the whirlwind in capricious offspring. Adolescents frequently see themselves as their own authority; they think this attitude is just fine. Absolutes are obsolete, traditional values distrusted; everything is relative. (We have no desire to pontificate on societal corruption, but the reader will remember that we're viewing the Life and *Times* of an MK.)

A sweeping evil of the day is youth's experimentation with illicit drugs—marijuana, cocaine, LSD, PCP (angel dust, superpot), heroin. Such drugs are used by one third of all American youth, often on a daily basis. Clearly missionary parents, well before their offspring move out on their own, need to arm themselves with proper information on outlawed narcotics, helping their son and daughter realize the ruinous nature, emotionally and physically, of these drugs. Parents can write for full information on drugs to National Federation of Parents, 1820 Franwall Avenue, Silver Spring, MD 20902, or American Council of Marijuana, 6193 Executive Blvd., Rockville, MD 20852.

Another mind-altering drug, representing the third largest health problem in America, is *alcohol*. The lives of one out of every four or five people, younger and older, are being directly damaged by this scourge. Frightening also is the fact that there are 10 million alcoholics, many of whom at one time were positive of never experiencing a drinking problem. Not a few of these are quasi Christians who may have felt that, since early Christians used fermented beverages, they should be free to do likewise.

Multitudes of teens, touched off by the idea that drinking is cool and adult, are heading toward alcohol addiction. In this connection MKs can be grateful for their having been sheltered from the drug scene; also that their parents are non-drinkers. Being aware of alcohol-related problems, probably almost all MKs shun even social drinking.

As the poet phrases it, masses of people are feeding on "earth's dark poison tree—wild gourds, and deadly roots, and bitter herbs." Of course there's never a famine in that type of food. "Name the perversion, the amusement, the foolishness," posits a *Newsweek* columnist, "and sooner or later someone will bottle it and sell it at a profit." It's no longer necessary for the lustful—and those just flirting with porn—to frequent the sleazy sections of a city; the merchants of pornography are reaching into the home by means of raunchy video cassettes. One of the latest perversions is "kiddie porn," exploiting children through providing them with pornographic tapes and literature specially designed for them. Indeed the soul merchants of Sodom couldn't have devised more warped practices to attract the ignorant and loose-moraled to their wares.

Notwithstanding this evil maelstrom, God continues to draw out a people for His Name. The Holy Spirit touched the life of John Newton, a wicked slave-dealer, and transformed him into a vibrant preacher and hymnwriter (he wrote "Amazing Grace"). Somewhat similarly the Spirit is awakening hosts of young people to their spiritual need—so remarkably that not infrequently newly converted Christians under 35 comprise half the membership of evangelical churches.

Quest for identity. Into the depraved climate of our day the MK enters to hammer out his educational, social, and vocational objectives. He won't find much with which he can wholeheartedly identify. The world displays its best image for a time, but fairly soon the spiritually minded young person perceives he must fight to be clean in a society where often it's cool to be dirty. (J.C. Ryle: "The World's frowns have slain its thousands; its smiles have slain its ten thousands.") The media long ago discovered that vice is more in demand than virtue.

"Our parents left the world deliberately, knowing what it was they left," explains one adolescent, "but we missionary kids don't really know that world we are told not to love." And a young non-MK voices her impression: "Of all the kids I know here at school MKs are some of the easiest to be swayed to do something wrong. They've never thought things out." In the light of these statements, the numerous postulates in the following paragraph, reminding us of our Lord's words in Luke 6:27-31, may stand as an incisive true-or-false quiz for MKs, or indeed for us all:

An MK is more sensitive and receptive to all human qualities. Sometimes too much so, and people take advantage. But I believe the quality of sensibility and tenderness and compassion is too rare in this rushing, selfish world. Better a few situations of being taken advantage of than to reject one of the finest and noblest human qualities—the awareness of another human being's needs. An MK is more tolerant and forgiving, too. There is almost a lack of prejudice, especially racial prejudice, and a concurrent interest in the ways and customs of other cultures. But that very quality of being different the MK finds so painful.

In earlier years parents observed with keen delight how their children related so artlessly to national friends—though of course a teenage girl wouldn't insist on having her nose pierced in order to wear a large ring like many of the village women did. But now as adolescents in the U.S., some of these same offspring become susceptible to seductive influences—for instance, moving on the "cocktail route" in making and keeping friends. Other MKs make the grade moderately well, while others come through with flying colors or, to change the metaphor, with a second pair of eyes to distinguish between the wheat and the chaff. Having a good believing friend at this time would introduce the young person to a circle of other friends.

MK boys adjust to western life somewhat more readily than do girls; more options, such as various sports, engage their interest. Yet they may not stand against worldly practices so effectively .Still, a good number of boys and girls attest that their background (and assuredly their backbone) enabled them to stand their ground against the "bandwagon syndrome"—secular peer pressure. As voices in the wilderness they witnessed by their walk and talk to an altogether different way of life. These lines from our vintage scrapbook by an unidentified poet may reflect the reaction of acquaintances:

Who are these that come among us,
    Strangers to our speech and ways;
    Passing by our joys and sorrows,
    Singing in the darkest days?
Are they pilgrims hurrying on
    To a land we have not known?

THE EVANGELICAL SCENE

Quest for fellowship. When we censure the secularist for his ways, he may turn the tables on us by enquiring, "And what does one find in your more favored garden?" We may respond in positive terms—and through God's sovereign grace there's plenty to report—but inwardly we feel like hanging our heads in shame. Not the least dubious spectacle, and one that has become fair game for satire in the secular media, is the feuding flock. When we remind ourselves of the divisiveness existing even among conservative evangelicals, we won't be disposed to draw our righteous robes about us and refuse to admit our weaknesses. We speak and sing and feel good about our faith— our particular branch of the evangelical tree—but still quibble over minor distinctions in doctrine and practice among us.

If the adolescent MK has grasped something of the preciousness of that beautiful word *koinonia,* "fellowship" (cf. Psalm 133), he'll relate as fully as possible to any of God's people seeking to walk faithfully and fruitfully in the light of Scripture. On marginal issues dividing believers he himself may be suspect should he ignore a few sacred fences (cf. Luke 9:49,50); but the "more excellent way" (1 Corinthians 12:31) is still wide open—illustrated in part by Edwin Markham:

> He drew a circle to shut me out—
> Rebel, heretic, a thing to flout.
> But love and I had the wit to win;
> We drew a circle that took him in.

For local fellowship the resolute MK—we say "resolute" since surveys reveal that an inordinate percentage of missionary children neglect this vital pattern during their first years in the West—will seek out a company of Christians, preferably a missions-hearted assembly. This congregation won't be perfect, so he should feel at home, except that he may have to muffle his Amens and Hallelujahs if animated doxology of this type is part of his spiritual diction. Nevertheless, under no circumstances should the MK isolate himself from local church fellowship—"No good if detached."

When removed from his local church for periods in college, the young person profits greatly from his fellow believers' prayer support. But wherever he resides, being actively linked with "God's workshop" affords him facility to discern and hone his spiritual gifts. While maturing in the things of God, he'll seek to implement the Apostle Paul's exhortation at the head of the chapter. Continuing along the rocky road to adulthood, then, the MK will savor some of the unique privileges of the "good life" viewed from Heaven's perspective.

Settling on a lifestyle. Undesirable overtones tend to cluster about the expression "Christian lifestyle"; it smacks of a stereotypical framework lacking freedom and creativity, not to mention spirituality. Yet if we understand the designation as a blending of Christian graces in the process of growth, it becomes proper and meaningful. The practical unfolding of Paul's lifestyle is evident in Philippians 3:13: "I press on toward the goal to win the prize for which God has called me heavenward in Christ Jesus." (As we write this, the Olympic games in Los Angeles are concluding in which the buzzwords were "Going for the Gold [medals]." Each winner, through all his long, rigid practice had a *mindset* to excel.)

In conjunction with church fellowship as a priority in the MK's way of life, the matter of his *acceptance of authority* arises. Obviously in business life this is utterly essential. But since authority has to be learned, slow learners predominate in our society; consequently a widespread crisis of authority exists in both secular and spiritual areas. If the young person has learned to accept and appreciate human authority, his capacity to obey God is remarkably increased. As for missionary parents, some of those who have wisely nurtured a family may feel like novices in coping with their teens' distaste for discipline. While the latter need models more than criticism, the parents need daily the wisdom and grace of the Lord in carrying out their limited but vital role.

In line with this principle of authority (cf. Judges 17:6-13), the stable MK will be unmistakably clear concerning the ultimate authority of his life as he leaves the family circle. Diverse viewpoints will compete for his approval, not merely in peripheral areas such as preppy clothes and macho hairstyles, but in issues affecting his loyalty to the Master.

The young person can't hope to ride out the storms of western hedonism unless his cardinal standard is allegiance to Christ and the Scriptures. "Aim at heaven," writes C.S. Lewis, "and you get earth thrown in. Aim at earth and you get neither." (A recent Gallup poll shows that 65 percent of teens in evangelical churches never read their Bibles independently.)

So a genuine Christian lifestyle embraces a wide variety of satisfying pursuits, all pleasing to the Lord: choice of friends, life partner, vocational objectives, and other short-range and long-range issues. Thomas H. Gill clothes in words the inner stirrings of a young Christian's heart as he commits himself to a Christ-honoring lifestyle:

> Lord, in the fulness of my might,
> I would for Thee be strong;
> While runneth o'er each dear delight,
> To Thee should soar my song.

. . . .

O not for Thee my weak desires,
  My poorer baser part!
O not for Thee my fading fires,
  The ashes of my heart.

O choose me in my golden time,
  In my dear joys have part!
For Thee the glory of my prime,
  The fulness of my heart.[26]

12
IN COLLEGE
Fiber Testing

---

*"This is my prayer: that your love may abound
more and more in knowledge and depth of insight,
so that you may be able to discern what is best . . ."*
(Philippians 1:9, 10).

IN PURSUIT OF KNOWLEDGE

Love & knowledge. The Apostle's prayer for the Philippian
Christians heaps one superlative upon another to underscore the
importance of increasing love; yet it then urges that the resulting
attitude be continued within a framework of "knowledge and depth
of insight." And the expected fruit of this type of perception?—"so
that you may be able to discern what is best." What a fitting
presentation of goals also for the college-bound MK!

"A little learning is a dangerous thing." The truth of this familiar
maxim is all too evident in these days of specialization; it's not merely
a scary concept for the student cramming for finals. But conversely,
despite the need for MKs to be well posted in our increasingly
informed society, can't we absorb too much knowledge? In this
regard a revision of the above adage reads, "A *lot* of learning is a
dangerous thing." Now if such a dictum pertains to the generality of
people, does it likewise apply to a missionary daughter? Let's give
heed to one girl's side of the story:

> Intelligence is rated low in the qualities suitable to a girl MK.
> I was often told, "Be good, sweet maid, and let who will be
> clever." And it was made clear to me that intelligence could be a
> dangerous thing to have. Yet it was one of my few talents, and I
> knew it. I decided I would be one who willed to be clever, and I
> didn't especially want to be a sweet maid. I knew intelligence
> was dangerous. For one thing, there was curiosity, the hunger
> to know how and why and when and who and all the rest of the
> answers. . . . Curiosity could get you into a whole bunch of
> trouble.

Where then is the balance between a dunce and a pedant? We
presume to state that anyone, including an MK of the feminine

gender, may be considered learned in the best sense of the term who blends spiritual vitality with academic excellence. Thus knowledge is meshed with humility, forbearance, and love. It then becomes serviceable for God's purposes (a writer speaks of the "utility of humility"). In 1 Corinthinas 8:1 Paul declares that "knowledge puffs up, but love builds up." The context reveals that the reference is to pseudo knowledge, which as Way's translation phrases it, "blows up the windbag of empty self-sufficiency." In the Bible verses that follow, Paul warns against this type of knowledge while James asserts that true knowledge consists of more than mere rhetoric:

"See to it that no one takes you captive through hollow and deceptive philosophy, which depends on human tradition and the basic principles of this world rather than on Christ" (Colossians 2:8).

"Who is wise and understanding among you? Let him show it by his good life, by deeds done in the humility that comes from wisdom" (James 3:13).

Risky scholarship. Not every MK has the capacity to forge ahead to acquire a Ph.D. or Th.D. all to the glory of God. Scholarship needn't affect one's spiritual disposition but in many instances it does arrest our productivity as Christians. Having as many degrees as a thermometer can't be equated with lifelong learning at the feet of the Lord Jesus Christ. The business world requires intellectual manpower, yet knowledge in and of itself won't bring abundant living and may not noticeably change behavior. Perhaps it's prudent to keep the heart a little softer than the head.

Myriads of unregenerate scholars snobbishly employ their native intellect to promote moral confusion, calling evil good and good evil; and gullible students hang on their words. Moreover, alas, some Christian pundits tend to befuddle us by multiplying (cf. Proverbs 8) salvos of five-dollar words in dealing with relatively simple truths. (Time out for confession and explanation. A young missionary, on reading our manuscript to this point, blurted, "Teacher, teach yourself!" We insisted we're "middle-brow" in the use of language, like most of our readers.)

HIGHER EDUCATION

A MUST for the MK? The typical missionary family answers this query almost automatically in the affirmative. For the most part college graduates themselves, parents desire to have their son or daughter enjoy the benefits of higher, tertiary education. This privilege is afforded comparatively few in less-developed countries; in the U.S. too only 50 percent of young people enroll in a four-year program and many of these don't complete the full schedule. Quite remarkably, about 90 percent of MKs proceed to some form of higher studies, a good number to schools their parents attended.

Nevertheless some MKs entering college in lockstep at 17 or 18 haven't been really aroused to learn. College just seems to be the natural turn to take. As early as the ninth or tenth grades, these young people should have asked themselves such questions as these: "Do I possess all-round fitness for taking this decisive step? What should college do for me? To what extent will the college of my choice meet my realistic goals in life?" Or to put things succinctly, "What do I go for and what do I go with?" Parents also need to keep posted on pertinent material in order to stay ahead of their teenager. Catalogs are readily available from colleges and universities.

Missionary parents don't ordinarily seek to enhance their egos through getting their son or daughter enrolled in a prestigious university. But some other-minded parents still covet a competitive edge for their offspring in today's achievement-oriented society, so they press their teenager to choose job-relevant courses of study. The specter of a son pounding the pavement looking for work causes the job market and salable skills to loom large in their thinking. An educator indicates that "the most popular course on the American college campus is not literature or history but accounting."

Choosing the right career may start with choosing the right college and the right major. The resourceful MK, then, will take note of the skills he possesses and enjoys using, lining them up with career prospects. He might well select a "comprehensive" college or university—one having a good liberal arts program as well as job-related courses. In this connection, Dr. Ward Kriegbaum writes:

> The colleges doing the best job of educating students are those which have a "general education" banner, says a new report from the Carnegie Foundation for the Advancement of Teaching. The payoff for students, says the report's authors, is schooling that enables graduates "to understand themselves, their society and the world in which they live."
>
> It is my desire that we will educate students—not just train them. We must focus on the value-added dimension of a college education—improvement in self-image, social maturity, interests and competency. The goal of Christian higher education is that those who are taught shall live in such a way as to carry out other responsibilities to God and find joy and delight in so doing![27]

Institutes of higher learning, Christian or secular, should be considered precisely that—places where learning occupies paramount status and the student is called to the joy and rewards of contemplative study. Administrators and professors don't assume the role of surrogate parents. Each school has its counselors who, while they are warmly accessible, avoid mothering practices. Dilettante students aren't welcome; learning is hard work and there's no way to make it easy.

The MK's previous academic profile, of course, generally discloses his aptitude for productive study, as well as his strength of character and endurance potential. Still, a prospective student needn't score in the 95th percentile of the College Board's Standard Aptitude Test (SAT) to fit him for the classroom. For a moderately bright student with, say, a SAT score of 1,000 (the U.S. average was 893 in 1982-83), there's a likelihood of his gaining admission to a good college; moreover, he may get more out of his years on campus than some others with sharper minds.

A viable option—stopping-out. Boarding school MKs frequently complete their secondary work by age 17. It would be unrealistic to assume that every graduate is equipped psychologically to enter the college community at that age. Most young people would be able to care for classroom requirements, but many of these might encounter serious personal problems in their exposure to today's avant garde youth, even in Christian institutions. An MK writes in *Good News Broadcaster* for 3/82:

> Coming from a rich crosscultural background with a prescribed set of standards and with limited job opportunities and financial knowhow, the MK is full of world-changing potential—yet begins college vulnerable and fragile. As one veteran of this reentry crisis put it, "It's a time when you have to grow up fast and trust God—or go off the deep end."

Not a few high school grads avail themselves of a plan whereby they gain admission to a particular school but delay their entrance through the ivy-mantled portals. The prospective student may engage in foreign travel—a pastime that won't appeal to every MK at this particular juncture—or take a paying job. The arrangement of deferring college has been given the name of "stopping-out," to distinguish it from such negative concepts as "copping out" or "dropping out." Many educators acknowledge the value of stopping-out in certain circumstances; it's no longer a novel procedure. The majority of large colleges and universities incorporate this plan of action in their literature.

Advantages of stopping-out are peculiarly applicable to MKs. Even young people with a robust makeup may feel good about adopting the plan. Deferring entrance for a year or two allows time for the boy or girl to adjust gradually to dress and behavior before facing the subculture of campus life. Within the warmth of the family circle—provided the parents are then on furlough or special leave— the MK can move about largely on his own. Ordinarily he'll enjoy a breathing period after ten or twelve years of continuous schooling. While he may have his heart set on the heady experience of freshman life, eventually he'll recall the stopping-out interval with few regrets.

A plaintive note frequently sounded by MKs relates to their having been deprived of practical training in childhood. This time of stopping-out offers opportunity to make up this deficiency in part. For instance, the youth might find a job in a supermarket where he's involved with the ebb and flow of community life—and getting his first paycheck. Then too he'll be able to care for a dozen matters he's had long in mind: learning to drive, corresponding with school friends and others, acquainting himself with the local culture, leisurely enjoying friendships and dates, reading those books he's never been able to get around to, brushing up on math. He may also want to nose about several college campuses to get oriented for further decision-making.

As with most commendable plans, stopping-out has a few minus factors: the arrangement may not fit in with the parents' furlough; the student's frame of mind for study could suffer and some essential groundwork lost; or he could get involved in lesser interests and imperil his initial vision. In view of these possibilities, it may be wise in specific cases to postpone the stopping-out period until halfway through undergraduate study. Nevertheless, after unbroken precollege instruction, the young person should appreciate a slower tempo so as to gain a broader view of his new homeland.

Christian or secular campus? There are no easy answers to this question. Each type of institution has its pros and cons with respect to what it can give a particular student. Accordingly it may be helpful to look briefly at three main types of colleges: the Bible college, the Christian liberal arts (or comprehensive) college which has been touched on a few pages back, and the secular campus. A fourth alternative, the postsecondary two-year vocational school—the least expensive way to go to school—is discussed in Chapter 14, "Vocational Interests."

For the present, let us check two clear statements shedding light on the diversity of opinion existing on the subject of Christian versus secular schools. The first, by Karen D'Arezzo:

> The Christian college is alternately condemned as an intellectual hothouse that breeds only plants too fragile to survive in the real world or defended as a haven of safety in a

godless world—the only responsible choice for a discerning evangelical. Conversely, the secular university is depicted both as the haunt of irresistible temptations for the 18-year-old innocent and as the only soil in which to grow sturdy, reproducing Christians capable of meeting effectively the exigencies of life in the twentieth century.

Is a freshman teenager better able to construct a scripturally informed world and life view in the midst of constant challenge at a state university or under the encouragement of professors committed to Christian faith?[28]

Then a paragraph by lecturer/author Rosalind Rinker:

"Well," someone says, "he might lose his faith and become an atheist." Strange, but it doesn't seem to work that way. As a counselor for Christian students in secular universities, I have watched two kinds of "Christian" students come on campus. Those who "lose" their faith in college are mostly those who had no personal convictions when they arrived. They were Christians by "persuasion" or by "association." They really had little to lose. Arriving on campus they immediately sought friends and campus activities which did not bring them in touch with other believers. Those who came with real faith, convinced Christians, soon found other students who were believers and together they found the answers to questions that bothered them. The very contrast seemed to develop maturity and spiritual backbone. I have seen hundreds of Christian students on secular campuses mature into strong Christians.[29]

THE BIBLE COLLEGE

Prior to liberal arts? For 17- or 18-year-old MKs planning to enter a four-year college, a worthy alternative to stopping-out or in addition to it is a year or two in Bible college. In order to strengthen their grasp of biblical Christianity, many young Christians opt for the one-year general curriculum offered by most Bible colleges.

This procedure shouldn't be understood as pampering the MK. On the contrary, it's most realistic in view of the multiple crosscurrents of thought sweeping through academia today. With the Word of God firmly rooted in his mind and heart, the young person will be better qualified to resolve to his own satisfaction the conflicting assumptions currently propagated.

Four years in a Christian liberal arts school gives the student perhaps six or eight hours of Bible survey, though some schools offer three or four additional hours of religion courses. In either case, that isn't sufficient to ground the young person in the Word. Of course he can study on his own and with others, but he'll miss the thrust of daily exegetical study of Scripture and its correlation with lecture material of a semi-secular nature. Consequently a year in Bible school could make a real difference in his post-secondary studies and indeed in his entire Christian life.

Along with this advantage, the MK will find that the social climate of a Bible college represents the closest approach to what he experienced in boarding school overseas. The schools radiate an atmosphere of friendliness, since students are generally less sophisticated and more open and communicative than those on liberal arts campuses. With so many MKs enrolled in some schools, the situation resembles Old Home Week. One can visualize a group of MKs getting together for an evening of fellowship and wide-ranging reminiscences. It's also a prime place for meeting one's match!

Complete Bible college education? From its inception a hundred years ago, the Bible school movement has fulfilled a distinctive role in strengthening young Christians for the challenges of life. The 300 or more schools in North America (about 85 of which are accredited) have produced 75 percent of all evangelical missionaries on the field at present—though after Bible school some of these will have proceeded to seminary. Somewhat more than 50 percent of graduates are in fulltime Christian service. Not surprisingly, Bible colleges aren't seriously affected by dwindling enrollments common today in the case of certain other educational institutions.

Three distinctive purposes from which few schools have swerved reveal the practical carrying out of the original vision. First, students are prepared for vocational Christian ministry as pastors, missionaries, teachers in Christian schools, and local church musicians. Second, a program of biblical and practical education, coupling classroom study with Christian service, presents a sound biblical philosophy of life. Third, authorities strive to maintain a strong and deep spiritual posture in all classroom and campus activities. So students enjoy a wholesome sense of community.

Bible college gives the MK perhaps his first exposure to systematic inductive study of Scripture based on "Thus saith the Lord." The academic qualifications of the faculty of accredited schools and the number of library holdings have increased so markedly in the last two decades that often graduates can advance directly to seminary or other postgraduate study. It's only in areas related to science, art, and math that Bible college students lack training. (A difference usually exists between a Bible college and an institute. The former may offer two years of liberal arts, double what the institute provides.)

Despite this reassuring scene, the subjective reaction for some students to sustained Bible teaching and strict discipline issues in a few problems. Here are four testimonies:

Right after my first year in Bible college in Canada I backslid for a while. That was the first time I was really on my own. But my MK friends and I had been warned about all the problems of changing to a western culture and we decided we'd adjust positively.*

My Bible college days brought some turmoil, mostly because I wasn't prepared to let the Lord Jesus have His way in my life. But later I dedicated my life to serve Him wherever He wanted me. He in turn gave me a wonderful husband who feels called also to Brazil.*

After graduation from high school I entered Bible school, where many of my preconceived ideas of what a Bible school would be were dissolved. I expected everyone to be truly seeking after God, but as I looked for that heavenly atmosphere and aura of spirituality I was disappointed. I found others just like myself, some closer to and some farther from God. . . . I learned much and got to know myself for the first time at Bible school. Frustration set in as I began to see many of the problems which continued to hang on in my life. I saw the devastating inferiority complex which pervaded my thoughts, resulting in a negative outlook on life in general. The frustration led to bitterness, because I believed the rough experiences of my life had made me what I was. The whole boarding school experience—being teased by the other kids, a strict high school education in a boarding school in America— these were the factors responsible for my problem. I had no interest in missionary work. . . . But in spite of my wrong attitudes, God was at work in my life and allowed me to grow and mature. . . . I realized that the things I had been bitter about which I blamed on my past environment, were just the sinfulness inside me coming out when faced with tough circumstances.*

Never had there been any doubt in my mind but that the Lord wanted me to go to Bible school. These past three years were a time of growth and challenge. What a privilege it has been to have teachers who teach the Bible and also live it before us! One lesson the Lord is still teaching me is the importance of using the Word in times of temptation.*

THE CHRISTIAN LIBERAL ARTS COLLEGE

Integrating faith & learning. Private Christian colleges in the States, especially church-related institutions, have been encountering severe reverses of late. Within the last ten years or so approximately fifty of these schools have closed their doors. Yet the cream of the crop are still in business, pledged to give young people an integrated world view, biblically based, relative to the great issues of life. Commitment to Jesus Christ is stressed and the dignity and worth of man respected.

Tragically, however, broad and deep differences exist between some church-related schools and the soundly evangelical type. Moral permissiveness and erosion of Christian values—for example, ambivalence in acknowledging the inerrancy of Scripture—represent two leavening factors in the former institutions. Their academic brochures don't always reveal the extent of departure, the nuances of language concealing inroads of secularization.

The faculties of evangelical colleges seek to preserve a curriculum in which biblical values are brought to bear on each area of study, preparing the student for life and ministry. A writer in *The Christian Reader* calls it "education with a purpose." Science, presently the favored child of U.S. education, occupies a more prominent place in the curriculum. Finding room for technological subjects, of course, requires cutting back somewhat on liberal arts courses, but the additions often meet the special needs and desires of students. Computer, health, science, and business management courses strive to meet popular demand.

A growing number of Christian colleges are no longer inferior academically to secular universities, at least in the available courses. Faculty members are normally well accredited in their fields and stay abreast of new techniques. Dedicated to their mission, they're genuinely concerned for each student's total development.

So the MK is well-advised to consider the Christian liberal arts college. Instead of being caught up in the "clammy grip of the future" by fastening his eyes on the job market, he can be launched as a liberally educated person equipped for meaningful service in his vocation. A liberal arts background develops the individual's aptitude in carrying through with interpersonal business relationships. In short, the general quality of his life is enhanced. The typical student or businessman tends to deliberate better if he's familiar with the arts, music, and literature.

Spiritual & social life. The MK who anticipates being carried along sweetly in the flow of spiritual vigor at a conservative Christian college will almost certainly be disillusioned. Intellectual stimulation may remain at peak level, but dry periods occur in every student's spiritual experience. Whatever the cause, group exercises such as chapel begin to lack challenge and meaning.

Frequently, too, an MK's lack of a warm social life lowers his spiritual temperature, particularly if his self-image already is suffering. But if he reaches out understandingly to make friends, sharing their joys and sorrows, the result can be a freshening of his entire personality.

The freshman year, taken up mainly with classroom work and new scenes, apparently passes quite happily for most MKs. But the "sophomore slump" is something else. The initial incentive wears off to some extent and graduation is far off. Consequently a sense of alienation may set in, disrupting the student's emotional equilibrium. School breaks may prove difficult as one MK confesses, "I feel like an orphan with my parents far away." Another MK describes how arid places in her life were watered:

> Four years at a Christian university tremendously altered my life. Through a speech class assignment during my freshman year, I realized my need of complete surrender to my *Lord*. He used Psalm 51 to break my heart concerning my hypocritical spiritual veneer. I began to realize that God desired "truth in the innermost being" and a "broken and contrite heart." The Lord was teaching me the importance of a genuinely spiritual life— one in which my inner relationship with Him was so meaningful that it was outwardly evident by the way I lived and acted. By God's grace, this precious lesson, as well as many others, I continue to learn, believing that He will continue to perfect the work He began.*

THE SECULAR UNIVERSITY

Sheepskin shock. While the secular school can be dismissed as a pillar of integrity insofar as Christian values are concerned, it may well have estimable distinctives. Not a few faculty members, counselors, and deans are people of idealism and good will.

Probably the thing that strikes the entering MK the hardest isn't the expansive grounds or the masses of students, though these scenes tend to flounder him also; it's the bewildering smorgasbord of courses, programs, activities, and societies. A good number of courses are now available which most of us never heard of. Majors are multiplied in order to provide a broad education in the sciences, humanities, and arts as a basis for professional skills. Additionally the "Waspy" (see Index) young person will be amazed at the cosmopolitan nature of the student body; in certain larger schools foreign nationals represent a hundred different countries.

A respected Christian writer maintains that a secular university can be "the safest place on earth" for the sturdy Christian. And indeed an MK may discover it's much less fear-producing than he imagined. Ability to adjust is largely determined by whether or not his backbone contained the "antidotes for freshmanitis": a happy childhood with plenty of affection received and reciprocated; a favorable classroom and behavior record in high school or in correspondence work; a healthy physique and a good mental attitude toward life in general; aptness in adjusting to new situations. With a good rating in these areas and a solid Christian base, the MK should be a fit candidate for the secular campus.

Still, every Christian student needs to be alerted to destructive influences, often subtly staged. These will include the following: a depersonalized atmosphere, the result of a mass-producing process; the "illusion of the classroom," the idea that scholarly profs must know what they're talking about, even when they promote alien, humanistic reasoning—each prof is virtually a law unto himself; the penchant of some teachers to satirize Christian things, taking potshots at the Bible, especially in relation to creationism as opposed to evolution.

No apology, except for the ellipses, need be offered for quoting extended extracts from the winning essay in a recent youth-writing contest conducted by WBT's *In Other Words*. Submitted by Karen Loving, the title is "Girl Without a Country," relating to her entrance to a secular university:

> Numbly I stood watching the car drive off into the distance. All that was familiar was fast disappearing over the horizon. . . . I wanted to run after the car and cry, "Take me home. . . . I don't belong here!" but I couldn't move. . . .
>
> Home was Ukarumpa, our mission center in Papua New Guinea, an island that most of those students around me had never heard of. I'd been born in PNG and lived there until just a few weeks before, when I'd graduated from our Wycliffe high school. Mom, Dad, and my younger sister had come back with me and planned to be in the U.S. during my first year of college. . . .
>
> During the next few weeks I had so many new experiences that I often felt confused and out-of-place. The five girls I lived with were not Christians. One of my roommates was involved with a married man, one girl spent five or six nights a week at her boyfriend's, and one of the girls eloped. Another became pregnant, and a fifth girl was fast becoming an alcoholic. . . . But the thing I dreaded most was the age-old question, "Where are you from?" I didn't really know. . . . I felt like a person

without a country. I made a lot of friends, and outwardly I seemed happy and well-adjusted. But inside, constant turmoil made me confused, lonely, fearful, and homesick. . . .

I learned quickly that my life depended on the early morning "meetings," when I'd find a quiet place and spend time with God. I dreaded each new day, but as I took it to the Lord, He gave me the strength to meet the tasks before me. . . .

For the first time in my life I began to understand a little of what Christ's coming to earth really meant. I could identify with His feelings of loneliness. Christ had gone through so much; He understood and I knew He could help me. I gave Him my confusion, loneliness, fear, homesickness, and culture shock. In their place He began to fill me with love and peace. Things didn't change overnight, but He was always there guiding me over the rough spots, comforting me in my times of homesickness, and being a friend in times of loneliness.[30]

Undoubtedly a good number of other MKs in secular schools, like Karen, feel like nonconformist Daniel in the lions' den. Yet they have Daniel's (and Karen's) God to guard them. What a peaceful night Daniel must have spent with Leo's tummy as a comfy pillow!

Building relationships. Rarely recognizing a familiar face on campus, the freshman MK may remain socially marginal with respect to the mainstream of school life. Gradually, however, he'll begin to meet some whom he'll greet with more than a "Hi." College years are times for extending social rapport—in class, lab, dorm, and on the grounds. The number of Christians the MK can warmly relate to will increase, including a few profs who gather with Christian students for informal fellowship and counsel. And of course he might seek out a few fellow MKs.

Assuredly this young person will interact well with outlanders on campus; he himself feels outlandish at times, and he's color blind in regard to ethnic groups. Presently there are more than 200,000 foreign students enrolled at U.S. colleges and universities, so MKs have plenty of opportunity to bring their entire social background into play.

God has raised up a number of vibrant testimonies that prove most supportive of freshman Christians—Campus Crusade for Christ, Young Life, Navigators, Inter-Varsity, and others. Concerning the witness of these companies to the rank and file of students, however, one member says, "It's like being a Christian missionary in a Muslim country."

PRACTICAL MATTERS

Countercurrents in admissions. Of late a widespread movement has been underway in America toward "minimum competency testing" for high school seniors. All this comes in the wake of slumping reading skills and accompanying low-achievement scores, especially in minority communities. (On SAT's verbal section, scores average about 425 out of a possible 800; math scores average about 470.) Dwindling enrollments in many colleges is one cause for flexibility in admission standards. It's a "buyer's market" in the case of most colleges.

Welcomed by some parents and prospective students, this watering down of academic standards is strongly opposed by those who insist that current and proposed modifications send a negative message to high school committees and students. Almost certainly admission standards, instead of being softened, will be tightened. High school diplomas should mean something.

Meanwhile colleges are waging a recruiting battle for students, mainly those of the top-notch variety. While academic performance in secondary and SAT scores is still the overriding factor for acceptance (though SAT layouts are also under fire), braun as well as brain is bid for, and in some cases paid for in the way of scholarships; athletics feature college life. A senior with both advantages will find college doors opening automatically for him. High school grads with a SAT score of close to 650 on each of the two sections shouldn't experience much difficulty, even in one of the Ivy League "think-tanks," though these schools don't lack enrollment.

One distinct edge enjoyed by most MKs is a good grounding in English, reading, writing, and related subjects—the verbal section of SAT. Incidentally, writing isn't a forte of the typical American senior. As one droll educator remarks, "He don't rite so good." A few U.S. secondary schools are restoring to the classroom the good old McGuffey's Readers, long considered quaint.

Faith & finance. One of the toughest issues of the college-bound MK is the question of finances. Costs continue to escalate year by year for tuition, fees, boarding, and books—and financial aid is down somewhat. At present, costs at Christian colleges come to between $6,000 and $8,000; at secular universities these run well above $10,000. State universities, with expenses partially underwritten by government except for boarding, charge about $1,500 for residents of the state.

Missionary families don't generally squirrel away a nest-egg for college expenses. Then what happens when more than one in the family are ready to enroll at approximately the same time? Some missionary parents are averse to going in debt to care for school bills; others feel free to do so within reasonable limits. Both sets of parents would doubtless testify to God's faithfulness and the reality of the supernatural checkbook. Understandably mission societies can't pick up the tab for their MKs' undergraduate expenses, but they keep up-to-date information at their fingertips concerning scholarships, low-interest government loans, and other financial issues. "The aid is there," says one writer, "for those willing to seek it out." Specific criteria are currently being revised on government loans, and the future is somewhat clouded.

Despite financial stringency, the MK should avoid endangering his health and academic progress by taking on too heavy a load of outside employment. Of course he'll avail himself of any part-time job open on or near campus. The employment office at college maintains a listing of job opportunities. Obviously city colleges have more job prospects than those in rural areas. The MK might deem it wise to take an extra year in college and thus be able to carry more hours of employment. At any time, however, he'll love to see Dad's handwriting, especially on a check inscribed "For personal use."

Then too, "The Army Wants You!" Likewise the Air Force, the Navy, and the National Guard Reserves. Upon the student's qualifying, Uncle Sam will finance a good part of his college education in return for some of his or her time before and/or during school years in the R.O.T.C. (Reserve Officers' Training Corps). After graduation the young recruit must undertake a stint in the service.

Speaking of mandatory service, our Lord calls each of us to yield our entire being to Him for His sovereign purposes. Dr. Handley Moule's hymn expresses the heart prayer of many MKs. One stanza only:

> Yes, ear and hand, and thought and will,
> Use all in Thy dear slavery still!
> Self's weary liberties I cast
> Beneath Thy feet; there keep them fast.

13
IN A FAR COUNTRY
Cause & Effect

"On hearing it, many of his disciples said, 'This is a hard saying. Who can accept it?'. . . From this time many of his disciples turned back and no longer followed him" (John 6:60, 66).

DOUBT: *Help or harbinger?*

Missionary forum. When a group of older missionary friends gathers for an evening of social fellowship, the broad common ground of interest provides much fuel for discussion. One subject, however, inevitably arises—family joys and sorrows. Most of those present share news of their offspring, now on their own as adults. There's a lot of good news concerning the activities of sons and daughters in missionary service and of others settled into meaningful secular work that affords scope for spiritual witness.

Up to this point the impression might be generated, were a nonmissionary friend within hearing distance, that whatever missionary parents are doing in the way of child-training, it can't all be wrong; evidently they're giving their young people what they need to cut the mustard in adulthood.

But not all the parents have good news to report. One or two couples remain conspicuously quiet as discussion of family members proceeds. The reason for this attitude holds no secret for the others; putting it mildly, some of their offspring aren't in good shape spiritually. Before the company breaks up, petition is blended with praise in a season of waiting on the Lord.

Shadow of doubt. Most missionary children, it appears, make a commitment of their lives to Christ before reaching the teens. Whether this profession of faith results in new life is of course sometimes unclear. The natural charm of childhood when operating at full thrust resembles the expression of a regenerate heart. The child's confidence may be based more on a parent's words than personally directed to the Savior. But we needn't belabor the point; the child responds as a child. The commitment usually satisfies the youngster until the early teens; for the present he's taken up with more exciting things. Mom and Dad, nevertheless, are often thrilled with their child's sayings and actions springing from spiritual impulses.

As noted earlier, the seemingly quiescent preteen years are immensely important in setting the stage for the youth's personalization of everyday affairs in and outside the home. Concepts issuing from observation and experience bear heavily on his ability to handle doubts when later they begin to crop up. Five adult MKs recall their reaction to incidents in early teen years, the last quote the heart-cry of an adolescent:

> Digging back into my memories, there are many images rising to the surface of the inconsistencies of adult Christians. Where was the truth we were supposed to always speak? When some old lady complained of illness while devouring large amounts of food at our table, I did not see the necessity to ask politely after her health. When some young brother delivered a sermon got almost word for word from C.S. Lewis or some other book, I did not see the truth in calling it "from the Lord." It would have been more honest to read it directly from the book itself. Once an old brother fell asleep during a very long and boring sermon and I commented afterwards that at least he had the sense to do openly what everyone else was doing inside their heads. I was rebuked, and told that the old brother was maybe not asleep but listening with his eyes closed. Ah!

> When I was a kid in boarding school, I used to daydream about doing something blatantly bad, just because everyone expected me to be so goody-goody. I used to visualize myself jumping up and down in church. . . . How many times I wanted to give a true testimony! I did go through a period of rebellion, which turned out to be a crisis for my parents. I rejected everything I had been taught. But the result was that Christianity became something I personally believe, rather than a way of life I took for granted.

> Beginning in junior high, Christianity didn't make sense to me. I had questions but the answers I got didn't satisfy me. So then I just quit asking. I didn't say anything because I knew immediately there would have been prayer circles praying for me. I didn't want that. I wasn't happy during that time. I remember times at college just sitting on my bed and crying from built-up misery. (*Writer's P.S.* Through the understanding of several teachers in college, this girl came to see Jesus Christ as the solution of her problems. She later served on the foreign mission field.)

I have no idea when I first came to know the Lord and to be born again. As far back as I can remember, I knew about Jesus and loved Him, and knew He was my Savior. But when we moved to the States when I was 14, I began to hear all sorts of conflicting things from people I knew to be Christians, and that really threw me for a while. The one that concerned me the most was when I would hear people say that if you couldn't pinpoint the moment of your salvation, you weren't saved. That had me in turmoil for years. Until finally, with the help of Scriptures such as John 5:24, I began to see that I was manufacturing difficulties where they didn't exist. . . . How compassionate a Savior He is, and how patient with each one of our idiosyncracies!*

Hello,
I have heard very much about you.
Some people say you made us to have somebody to love
And to love you.
Because I admire the world they say you made—
The people with hearts that cry for you,
The furious wind,
The people with eyes that laugh with you,
The sky,
The weak people who pretend they're made of steel,
The strong people,
The tired, happy, self-controlled, beautiful, dark world—
I don't want you just to do things for me,
Because I figure you're doing what you want with me already.
But I think I could love you.
I would like to meet you some day.

The following abridgment of questions that MKs ask has been gleaned from many sources, including items brought up by our own children:

How can I, a junior in high school, be as sure as I was earlier in life, when I get mixed up by the things my teachers say?
Am I a Christian only because I was born into a missionary home and was taught nothing but the Bible?
How can I hold that Scripture is inspired by God when there are so many ambiguities, paradoxes, and difficult portions that I can't understand?
Why are so many questions arising in my mind not answered in the Bible, such as where God's work for me ends and my own responsibility starts?

Christians seem so narrow-minded and defensive when I speak of problems in the Bible.

So many intelligent teachers and writers, like Freud, deny the authority of Scripture, calling it manmade.

Is there *anything* that all true Christians agree on?

Why do my parents refuse to discuss the place of evolutionary teaching?

So many fatal accidents happen to Christians as well as to non-Christians.

I have so much trouble meeting temptation under social pressures, though I'm told that the Holy Spirit dwells in the Christian.

If God is love, why so much cruelty, injustice, and conflict in the world?

Missionary parents will be able to answer such reasonable questions, although not always to the satisfaction of a son or daughter. Later Os Guinness sets forth some helpful principles. At this point, however, two simple suggestions may be in order. First, the person with doubts may clarify vague issues by jotting down his problem and perhaps a possible solution. Further, it's good to know that our Lord Jesus didn't condemn sincere questioners (cf. Matthew 11:3-5, 11; Luke 24:13-27; John 6:53, 66-69). In the course of time, through fellowship with Jesus, these disciples had most of their problems cleared up.

The preteen youngster normally follows the doctrinal persuasion of parents. Except for a few disturbing moments, he feels comfortable with their body of teaching. Any problem is resolved through mutual confidence and discussion.

Not surprisingly, however, some missionary parents view with alarm the first intrusion of doubt in their growing child's mind; they perceive this as a telltale symptom, the tip of the iceberg. For his part the youngster may be reluctant to share his problem outrightly; doing so might hurt Mom and Dad or bring reprisals upon himself. So he learns to answer parental questionings evasively.

On taking up residence in the West, many adolescent MKs don't enjoy settled assurance of belonging to the Lord. Their background of teaching isn't unimportant to them, but it lacks positive, personal dimensions in heart and experience. Furthermore, while they remain relatively tractable and continue to grapple toward making faith their own, the distinctive features of adolescence—physical awkwardness, emotional distress, social uncertainties—can cause spiritual interest to flag.

Several other significant factors enter. First, MKs are coming of age at a time when the attractions and pressures of the world are uniquely strong and insidious. Again, the submissive temperament characterizing not a small percentage of these young people leaves them vulnerable to the voice of the crowd. Then too, differing interpretations of Scripture by evangelicals certainly don't help to confirm the MK in his struggle for assurance.

The down-drag of the flesh may similarly cause the young person to question the validity of an earlier commitment to Christ. He begins to feel that God isn't really much interested in him. Viewing the multitudes of outwardly motivated, uninhibited people all around him who make no profession of faith, he wonders if there's much difference between himself and them with respect to the basic issues of life. Feeling sorry for himself, he loses the inclination for prayer and the Word. Bible verses memorized and hymns sung cease to stir him. So he lapses into indifference.

Value of doubt. Two things a young person with doubts may not fully realize. First, that every Christian in the course of life encounters periods of doubt and drought that seriously affect his spiritual bearing. We're all still under Spirit construction and consequently have our valleys as well as our peaks. Ter Steegen confesses, "I aim at God, yet from Thee stray." And the hymn affirms, "They who fain would serve Thee best/Are conscious most of wrong within."

Besides, doubt is often a prerequisite for achieving steadfast faith, the initial step toward validating a previous avowal. The early teenager may say, "Dad, how do you know the Bible is true?" The wise father won't reply, "But we've been reading the Bible together since you were three and we've talked about its being God's own Word." Instead Dad will draw out his son or daughter with the strength of quiet reason.

The time has come for the young person to gain personal assurance. Biblical truth isn't so fragile as to discourage the most determined probing by an honest enquirer, younger or older. What other fortress but Scripture has withstood the battering rams of unbelief and denunciation for millennia? After years of questioning, C.S. Lewis asserted: "I believe in Christianity as I believe the sun has risen, not only because I see it, but because by it I see everything else."

In his excellent book, *In Two Minds,* Os Guinness discusses the value of doubt. Here are a few paragraphs from the volume (pp. 47-49):

> The value of doubt is that it can be used to detect error. . . . The Devil's stock in trade is the world of half-truths and half-lies where the half-lie masquerades as the whole truth.
>
> To the mind that is morally and intellectually healthy this positive value of doubt can work to its advantage. If there were

no disease in the world, inoculation would be unnecessary. If there were no lies and half-truths in the world, doubt would be superfluous for everything could be believed. But just as a tiny dose of poison is sometimes the best antidote to complete poisoning (though too much kills), so a modest dose of doubt—limited, temporary and constructively used—can be an excellent preventative of unbelief (though excessive doubt is fatal here too). . . .

Doubt, then, is a problem for both faith and knowledge. As long as the presence of doubt is detected anywhere, neither faith nor knowledge can ever be complacent. But though doubt may be normal, it should only be temporary and it should always be resolved. Wisely understood, resolutely faced, it need hold no fear for the Christian. To a healthy faith doubt is a healthy challenge.[31]

Tim Stafford in *Moody Monthly* also concludes that doubt can be serviceable in the life of growing and questioning youth:

For a parent, a teenager's doubts should be seen as a birth process; he is bringing into the world a new faith. And you can't have someone's baby for her; your teenager has to ask his own questions and find his own answers. (They may be the same answers you found, but they will be *his*.) Having babies is dangerous, yet this danger doesn't keep people from having kids.[32]

Darkening of doubt. Presumably many MKs move through the various sub-stages of childhood and adolescence with quiet confidence and little serious doubting. In this connection, an adult MK recalls: "I have nothing but pleasant memories about childhood. Maybe I've just blocked out the bad ones. I'm sure there were some." Others suffer agonizing seasons of quandary. For a few others, displaying doubts becomes a heady experience bringing a sense of maturity and independence; they may even take delight in shocking their parents verbally.

In principle, the deeper the earlier commitment—of one who has known the beams of the Father's love and wanted to do everything right—the more acute the anguish. The later in life doubts arise, the more protracted they become. Assailed by serious doubts, the adolescent may be reticent in seeking the fellowship and counsel of mature Christians; he feels he must deal with things himself.

'Twould be gratifying to dispense entirely with a discussion of this nature as being unrealistic. Yet a disquieting number of MKs, though probably not large percentage-wise—no accurate appraisal is possible—have reneged on a prior confession of faith and dropped out of the Father's fellowship. The vital question as to whether a particular defecting MK was saved earlier in life or has never experienced new life in Christ must be left to Him who judges the thoughts and attitudes of the heart. But, we repeat, one can't move far from the principle set forth in Hebrews 3:14 to the effect that ultimate proof of salvation is perseverance to the end. A missionary friend of long standing relates circumstances attending the spiritual breakdown of his son:

> Our eldest boy gave no problems at all. Until recently he was a delight spiritually, academically and socially. He was always so spiritually minded that we had to sort of put the brakes on regarding baptism, going to Bible school, etc. He was baptized at 15. After finishing high school in this country as an A student, he went to Bible school for the one-year course it offers. Then he expressed the desire to go into the Lord's work, possibly as a full-time teacher in some foreign country. After Bible school he very successfully completed his training as a teacher.
>
> During his last year at university, he married a girl in the church whom he had known for five years. She seemed a real dedicated Christian, but has shown hardly any interest in spiritual things since the marriage, and really doesn't want to have much to do with our side of the family. She comes from what you might call a partially Christian background, also a divided home. Though the parents are not separated, they go two different ways in all things.
>
> In the course of our son's first year of marriage, he changed a lot, but held to the faith. The second year he was removed a good distance from a warm church fellowship, and eventually stopped going anywhere to Christian gatherings.
>
> We learned about his discipline problems at the school where he taught, but also that the fact he was losing his faith almost drove him out of his mind. Now he has made a complete break from all church ties. He is not bitter—just says he cannot see any reality in the whole thing and feels he must follow a different pathway.

CAUSES OF BREAKDOWN

Hard teachings. In the portions of Scripture opening this chapter, the disciples are discomfited by one of Jesus' "hard sayings." Attracted to Him for superficial reasons, the commitment of some remained extremely loose in contrast to the Twelve. Somewhat similarly, a good number of adolescent MKs, faced with contrary winds, begin to flounder.

The questioning MK may reach a place where such doctrines as election, Satan, and hell become hard teachings. (The world and liberal Christians move along contentedly with a cosy, sanitized hell.) Evangelical emphasis on the supreme efficacy of the blood of Christ may likewise offend him. Perhaps the last bastion to be razed before the Gordian knot is cut leading to thoroughgoing skepticism is the deity of our Lord Jesus Christ. This truth stands as an absolute that perhaps only a minuscule number of MKs repudiate.

Many young MKs and PKs have read Isobel Kuhn's poignant autobiography *By Searching*, recounting experiences in her journey through doubt into faith. Diligently coached as a PK to refute Modernism, the writer later encountered unexpected assaults on her faith from various quarters. The book, an OMF offering, is published by Moody Press with this back-cover note:

> When Isobel Kuhn entered university, she was sure the Bible was true. But when a skeptical professor claimed that her beliefs were just a poor copy of her parents' faith, Isobel turned her back on Christianity.
> *By Searching* portrays Isobel Kuhn's determined journey from agnosticism to faith. A secret but shortlived engagement, suicidal intentions, financial crises, frustrating attempts to help an insane girl, missionary preparation—these played major roles in Isobel's search. . . . The incredible but true story of a doubt-controlled life. . . .[33]

Battle for the heart. Spiritual shipwreck doesn't present a black-and-white picture in regard to causal elements; pieces are often missing in the puzzle. A consensus of findings by several doctoral candidates writing on missionary children seems to identify deficient parental nurturance as the major cause of an adolescent's emotional and spiritual problems. Most missionary parents will be inclined to accept the verdict; they freely confess dereliction in important areas of child training.

While that's true, writers on the subject also recognize that abnormal factors of modern life in the West exert strongly adverse influences on the best-nurtured MKs. These young people respond differently to early home discipline, excellent as it has been, and sometimes walk an entirely different road than their parents. They choose different reading material, different friends, different goals in life. Our Lord's parable of the Sower and the Seed in Mark 4 and parallels illustrates the variant reactions of individuals to His teaching—the same good seed in each case—when confronted with pressures such as the activity of Satan, persecution, and "the desires for other things." Demas, we remember, left the Apostle in the lurch during a missionary journey because of an illicit love affair with the world (2 Timothy 4:10). The grass looks greener on the other side of the fence.

A prime cause, or causeway, of spiritual breakdown is the attacks of that virulent foe of young people—low self-esteem. The natural desire of the college-age MK for peer acceptance, when stymied by a sense of inferiority, can make him susceptible to discounting spiritual truths in favor of experimenting with sinful practices. And there's usually someone around primed to exploit such a situation.

Disaffection of this nature follows neglect of prayer and Bible reading as well as swerving from a biblically guided conscience. The MK's problems, ostensibly of the intellect, mainly stem from violating concepts he knows are right. Spiritual perplexities have primarily to do with the heart, the moral nucleus of man. ("My heart is at the secret source / Of every precious thing.") Surprisingly, quite often it's the top students in high school who defect from the faith, yet the principle still holds—it's heart trouble. A Christian leader, approached by a bright senior fearful of breaking rank with evangelical truth, answered, "You're not smart enough to lose your faith." Do we get the point?

Nursing a grievance at being shortchanged in regard to his rearing can make an MK vincible to the world's seductive voices that gradually chill his conscience, wangling him into unbelief and sin. Generally moral erosion follows unbelief. If at this stage we could present only one Scripture portion to a young person with a good testimony for Christ in the past, it would be Romans 6:11-14 (see also Colossians 3:1-17):

"Count yourselves dead to sin but alive to God in Christ Jesus. Therefore do not let sin reign in your mortal body so that you obey its evil desires. Do not offer the parts of your body to sin, as instruments of wickedness, but rather offer yourselves to God, as those who have been brought from death to life; and offer the parts of your body to him as instruments of righteousness. For sin shall not be your master, because you are not under law, but under grace."

CONSEQUENCES OF BREAKDOWN

Revamped lifestyle. Continuing to rationalize with one's noisy conscience leads to desensitization. When conscience is stilled, the individual is inoculated against receiving light and truth; the new wine is turned to vinegar. While the straying MK won't ordinarily go for the macho image, he may yield to practices formerly considered unprincipled. A rare MK may even fit into this Japanese saying:

"When a tame elephant becomes a wild elephant, it becomes worse than a wild elephant." A missionary mother states, "Our son's life is completely alien to everything we have taught him. It never ceases to shake us to see the things he does with no sense of wrong." Alexander Pope, in "An Essay on Man," describes the process:

> Vice is a monster of such frightful mien
> That to be hated needs but to be seen;
> But seen too oft, familiar with its face,
> We first abhor, then pity, then embrace.

To construct a God-honoring life requires years of assiduous care on the part of parents and child; much less time is needed to bring impairment to that same life. The threatening thing about all this is that a single young adult harboring unbelief can initiate a ripple effect, depriving not only his own offspring of a Christian testimony, and possibly a heritage, but also nieces and nephews and many others.

As to lifestyle, MKs manifest the impact of spiritual bankruptcy in various ways. They lose the sense of gratitude for the really good things of life. No doubt a few suffer from a low incidence of psychosomatic disorder. As adults they won't ordinarily be drawn into moral collapse, but their thought processes relating to moral issues in life are adversely affected. Friendship with an unblushing, unshockable culture could block any lingering desire for enduring life-values.

In this frame of mind and heart the MK lays himself open to falling into unchastity; exposure to trashy publications and advertising ploys enhances the inclination. (Joseph in Egypt reacted quickly when pressed to enter an illicit alliance: "How could I do such a wicked thing and sin against God?") The way would then be virtually closed to a marriage union of unconditional commitment, unless in the midst of such affinities God should pour upon the MK and his then-partner "a spirit of grace and supplication" (Zechariah 12:10).

Dark as this portrayal of the disaffected MK has been, there's another side to the lifestyle of this young adult. He doesn't flout his unbelief, sounding off at every opportunity. He's not a full-fledged cynic or avowed dissident skilled at fault-finding. Not strongly opinionated, he maintains a low-key manner of speaking; in fact it could be said there's no such thing as a fiercely partisan MK. Usually he's free of unkind criticism of religious systems; each has its good, honest people. By the same token, there are millions of nice people who aren't at all religious, while on the other hand there's a host of weird Christians who insist they have a corner on divine grace. All in all, this MK may feel he himself is on fairly good terms with God and understood in the heavenly realms.

If we can further generalize on such delicate characteristics, this MK is personable, courteous, and generous. He relates well to expatriates and incidence of racial prejudice is close to zero. He respects the forces of law and order, though on occasion he's not averse to cutting corners on financial transactions. Not addicted to drugs or alcohol (the latter, clearly, is also a drug) and considerably above average in terms of business integrity, his lifestyle strikes an agreeable note with non-Christian friends.

By the way, this well-traveled MK isn't one to be forever talking about his adventures overseas. Nor is he given to name-dropping, although ironically he's not given to lifting up the Name that is above every name. Yet in all likelihood, few MKs follow the crowd in taking the name of God carelessly; and we'd like to think that not a single MK invokes our Lord's name as an imprecation. Defecting daughters, it may be added, appear to use cosmetics temperately, so they're much less artificial-looking than the average non-Christian peer.

Clearly this MK is no hypocrite. In a day when it's fashionable to be marginally religious to keep up appearance, he doesn't polish up his act to maintain an outward profession. In turn he can spot unreality a mile off. Nevertheless he may scotch some who aren't culpable, like witnessing Christians. With parents he becomes techy at the mention of spiritual considerations that affect him. In the early years of "pilgrim's regress," Sunday can be a dreary day for rather obvious reasons.

Parental heart-searching. Protracted renunciation of the faith by a son or daughter calls for a full-scale adjustment in the parents' lives. In fact the crisis strikes at the very root of their commission and commitment. The young person won't normally be insensitive to the pain he has caused his folks; and he'll be aware of so much of their nurturing going down the drain. But he concludes that he must move independently for good or ill. Moreover, he may reason that plenty of parents of every religion grieve when their children forsake traditional values—in some instances to embrace the Christian gospel.

To put things mildly, it's distressing for those who have devoted their lives to sharing the Good News in the "regions beyond," and have seen lives transformed, to observe spiritual regression in their own offspring. Observing other MKs with a bright testimony accentuates the mood. Besides experiencing anxiety for the eternal welfare of a son or daughter, profound questions tumble over each other in reference to themselves and their ministry. But always the ultimate question emerges, "Will Glory be glory without our kids?"

Ordinarily Mom suffers deeper distress than Dad, though it may be only of a different character. Passing from hope to heartbreak, the ordeal whacks the tenderest springs of her being, especially if sexual sin is involved. She has cherished high aspirations for the child in terms of a happy and fruitful life as a man or woman of God; now such a prospect is endangered. Additionally, family relationships tend to crumble; still, though, most prodigal MKs, especially daughters, seem to maintain a good measure of communication with Mom and Dad.

The father may labor under concerns of a more practical nature. Sharp doubts arise in regard to his fitness for spiritual leadership in the House of God. Scripture teaches that the elder, or overseer, "must manage his own family well and see that his children obey him with proper respect" (1 Timothy 3:4). While this injunction can be understood to apply specifically to offspring before they attain independent status, Dad may sense he's violated its spirit in being largely responsible for what the home becomes. Thus he may be constrained to withdraw from any position of leadership in the church.

Moreover, a singular problem arises in the process of counseling enquirers. Both the advice and the adviser are to some extent suspect. The person being instructed may ask himself, "If this thing hasn't worked for his own kids, how can it do much for me?" The same response may emerge with reference to his teaching in gatherings of the local church.

That is not to say, however, that parents of prodigals need remain riddled with guilt because of real or imagined failures in early nurturing. Undeniably an experience of this sort tends to stifle one's incentive for wholehearted service—something that serious illness and other grim problems might not do. Yet for parents to continue in sackcloth and ashes—above all in the presence of the young person himself—is patently self-destructive; it's a dead-end street. The son or daughter will recoil rather than be aroused to repentance. When parents kneel together before the Lord and receive assurance of His understanding and forgiveness, this represents a blessed alternative to self-flagellation. Strength follows tears.

We who have emphasized to others the sufficiency of our Lord Jesus Christ to meet us in any and every circumstance of life should be able to appropriate for ourselves His restoring grace. Indeed, many missionary parents would testify that, having overcome "the fretting ghosts of vain regret," they've been deepened in spirit and able more effectively to empathize with others in their personal sorrows. ("If David's heart had not been wrung,/Then David's songs had not been sung.")

Throughout these experiences, parents can remain confident that the countless prayers offered by themselves and fellow believers will be honored in season. God puts our tears in His wineskin (Psalm 56:8, margin). The dozens of Bible promises received on behalf of a wayward son or daughter aren't God's teasers; they're as steadfast as His name.

Concluding this discussion, it may be noted that godly writers stress the dignity of personal choice as an indispensable component of an adolescent's growth. Parents must respect the personhood of their son or daughter and the right to choose. Wrong choices may result in irrecoverable loss since "a man reaps what he sows." God gives us freedom to mess up our lives.

Yet wise parents won't become accusatory, nor will they place their offspring in the hated captive-audience situation; such action impairs the prospect of open communication. Probably interaction of parent and young person should be more in the nature of loving friend to loving friend. This anonymous missionary mother reveals a becoming attitude with regard to an errant daughter (*Moody Monthly,* 12/76):

> My daughter is *not* in trouble. She is expecting a baby and she is not married, but she is not in trouble. I am not sticking my head in the sand. Neither am I defending a difficult situation. I am thanking the *Lord* for this love gift which He has used to bring my lovely daughter *out* of trouble. . . .
>
> We have come through this and have been surrounded by the love and understanding of our family and friends. The joy in my daughter's life has been a blessing to many people, most of all to her mother.

THE POTTER & THE CLAY

The potter at work. Jeremiah 18:1-5 records how the sensitive fingers of the potter reshape a marred vessel on his wheel, fashioning it "as seemed best to him." Because of some unyielding substance in the original clay, a painstaking process is required to make it pliable—all a sublime illustration of God's patient handiwork in reconstructing an impaired spiritual life so that it honors Him. A case in point:

> When the Korean War started in 1950, I welcomed the chance for active duty. . . . But my Christian faith and the principles of my youth gradually slipped away. . . . My wife and I were just back from a trip to Madagascar to visit some of the places where Dad and Mother had worked. . . . In 1978 I was sentenced to one year in prison for mail fraud. . . . As I sat in my isolation cell at Stillwater, the Holy Spirit began to speak to me

as never before. Totally humbled for the first time in many years, I knelt and prayed fervently. . . . God was working a real miracle. . . . He had to use drastic measures, but I thank and praise Him that He got my attention.[34]

It's impossible for us to pinpoint where God's sovereign working and man's response to His call mesh. But of one thing we can be sure: God is faithful; He is *for* the defecting son or daughter—neither is beyond the pale of His love and grace. "'I know the plans I have for you,' declares the Lord, 'plans to prosper you and not to harm you, plans to give you hope and a future'" (Jeremiah 29:11; see also Isaiah 49:14, 15).

What then is this MK's personal responsibility? If he desires solid answers to his deep-seated questions, is it too much to request him to humbly reread the New Testament? Or at least the Gospel of John and the Book of Acts? Though he feels he knows the Bible from cover to cover, the act of turning his face to the light could give him fresh assurance of its being God's message of forgiveness and restoration.

This MK's broader perspective of people and things gained along the way should enable him to approach Scripture with new interest and insight. Should he then sense a gentle stirring within to commit himself wholly to Christ, it may well be the divine Potter purposefully at work, to the end that "chords once broken may vibrate once more." Like the disciples in Luke 24:13-35, the humbled seeker, as he sees his Lord with enlightened eyes, may exchange his doubts for a blazing heart.

What is the alternative? Is it not to consort with those at the cross who sneeringly shouted, "He saved others; but he can't save himself"? Thus the great question facing the MK is this: "What will I do with the Lord Jesus Christ who gave Himself for me?"

Rebel reclaimed. Through the centuries Christians have found refreshment in reading Augustine's fascinating autobiography, *Confessions.* Born in the year 354 to a Roman official and a godly Christian mother who devoted her life to his upbringing, Augustine in late adolescence adopted the lifestyle of many university students of his day. Along with other practices he was drawn into an illicit union with a concubine and had a son by her.

On one occasion while reflecting on his wayward condition, he heard a voice next door, "Take up and read." Augustine opened his Bible almost randomly to Romans 13:13, 14. The reading brought such remorse to his conscience that he fell down before the Lord in abject confession of sin.

As the result of being delivered from a shattered past, and then the sanctifying of his unique mental and spiritual qualities, Augustine has since been acknowledged as the greatest of the Church Fathers. The first paragraph of *Confessions* has these immortal words: "Thou hast made us for Thyself, and our hearts are restless until they rest in Thee." No place like *Home!*

Sick of home, homesick, home. The Parable of the Prodigal Son in Luke 15 may more accurately typify an unsaved sinner than a backslider, but it has a message for both. The story is so well known that we'll pick it up where the son, enthused over the prospect of enjoying the good life—he had fallen for the glowing reports of the far country and had the wherewithal to realize his desires—leaves the strictures of home to live it up in "Las Vegas." He wasn't sticking around home at his age! A precursor of the present-day NOW generation, the son couldn't wait a few years for his full inheritance and its benefits.

However, he forgot one all-important principle: Sin makes one pay. After his sojourn with the pigs, he's thoroughly disillusioned with his chosen lifestyle. Having hit rock bottom but seeing a gleam of hope on the horizon, he turns his steps homeward with a well-rehearsed confession at the ready. But he wasn't prepared for his father's reaction (Luke 15:20-24):

> While he was still a long way off, his father saw him and was filled with compassion for him; he ran to his son, threw his arms around him and kissed him.
>
> The son said to him, "Father, I have sinned against heaven and against you. I am no longer worthy to be called your son."
>
> But the father said to his servants, "Quick! Bring the best robe and put it on him. Put a ring on his finger and sandals on his feet. Bring the fattened calf and kill it. Let's have a feast and celebrate. For this son of mine was dead and is alive again; he was lost and is found." So they began to celebrate.

God is like that! How wondrously our Lord Jesus reveals in the parable the heart of the eternal God! John Bunyan observes that God follows the prodigal with a pardon in His hands. In Luke 22:61, following Peter's betrayal, Jesus "turned and looked straight at Peter." This wasn't a look of condemnation but of unconditional love: "I forgive you. You turned your back on me, but we'll start all over again."

The family setting in the parable pictures life itself with all its potential bequeathed to each of us; in this case it was squandered. Despite a caring home, this young man insisted on tasting life to the full. In the far country, removed from godly restraints, he did exactly as he pleased with his fair-weather friends. In the course of time, however, he began to reap the fruitage of sin—and its thrill faded. (In the West nowadays, the "pigpens" are often elaborate and velvety)

Now the young man redefines the "good life"; it takes on an entirely new image. "I'm going home!" he determines, and immediately takes off in that direction. Soon we find him approaching the homestead. The father, who had never lost hope of his son's return, sees him in the distance and *runs* to meet him (the only instance in Scripture where God is depicted as being in a hurry). Embracing his son in smelly clothes redolent of the pigpen, he kisses him. The parable concludes with the young man sincerely repentant and completely reconciled. (Cf. Psalm 148:8, "Stormy winds that do His bidding.")

The *best robe* speaks of Christ's perfect righteousness replacing the shabby garments of self-righteousness. The *ring* is the symbol of sonship. The *sandals* suggest God's provision of grace and strength along the way of life and for cheerful service in His vineyard. The *celebration* signifies the joy of God's family at the restoration of the prodigal, and also, as verse 7 indicates, the joy of the angels in heaven.

To be sure, certain scars would remain in the restored prodigal's experience. He would suffer moments of remorse for so wantonly turning his back on such a father and such a home in favor of the cankered pleasures of self-gratification. Nevertheless the pervading note of his remaining years would be that of warm satisfaction and glad service. He would enter into the worth of God's promise in Joel 2:25: "I will repay you for the years the locusts have eaten."

A hymn that has meant much to our own family is Horatius Bonar's rendering of a repentant heart's prayer (*The Keswick Hymn-Book*). Two stanzas only:

> No, not despairingly,
>   Come I to Thee;
> No, not distrustingly,
>   Bend I the knee.
> Sin hath gone over me,
> Yet this is still my plea
>   Jesus hath died.
>
> .   .   .   .
>
> Then all is peace and light
>   This soul within;
> Thus shall I walk with Thee,
>   The loved Unseen—
> Leaning on thee, my God,
> Guided along the road
>   Nothing between.

14
VOCATIONAL INTERESTS
Goals & Shoals

---

*"The kingdom of heaven . . . will be like a man going
on a journey, who called his servants and entrusted
his property to them. To one he gave five talents of
money, to another two talents, and to another one
talent. . . . After a long time the master of those
servants returned and settled accounts with them"*
(Matthew 25:1, 14, 15, 19).

CHALLENGE & OPPORTUNITY

Approved or reproved? The above verses are part of three parables
our Lord gave to His disciples in order to illustrate the vital
importance of an earlier command, "Watch!" All to whom the
employer "entrusted his property" are instructed to seek every
possible avenue to realize a substantial profit on their original
capital. They would have been briefed on blue-chip stocks.

Finally comes the accounting. The first two servants receive
precisely the same commendation. Though the second would
normally draw a B for his lesser business acumen, he also gets an A
for incentive, for doing his level best. The one-talent servant, on the
other hand, ends up with an F and with it the master's stern rebuke.
Plainly he's unmasked, guilty as charged. Not only did he leave his
resources unused; he harbored bitter resentment toward the person
and practices of his master.

The figurative interpretation is quite clear. The master is God
Himself or the Lord Jesus. The servants represent those who profess
to follow Christ. The talents ("property") indicate the openings God
gives us to invest our energies in buying up opportunities to advance
His kingdom interests. The emphasis isn't primarily on ability but on
wisely directed ability, be it little or much. The accounting arrives
"after a long time," that is, when Christ returns from His "journey,"
thus ending the testing period. (Luke 19:13: " 'Put the money to
work,' he said, 'until I come back.' ")

Career horizons. From his preschool days, friends ply the
missionary child with the question, "What are you going to be when

you grow up?" Then, almost immediately, "Don't you want to be a missionary like your Dad and Mom?" At this stage, primed with missionary stories heard and read as well as seen exemplified in the home and community, a boy may propose the thrilling career of bush pilot while a girl opts for the more traditional but stirring role of nurse in a mission hospital—though in these days, not a stranger to derring-do, she may well become the bush pilot! One 10-year-old boy opines, "I would like to be a missionary preacher and preach all over Brazil, traveling by helicopter."

In such matters youngsters have as many phases as the moon, but at least the incentive is there. Older MKs, however, are often allergic to outside pressure. "People try to pour us into a mold," complains a teenager, "expecting us to become missionaries like our parents when God may lead us differently." A missionary mom makes this potent point: "All we have ever wanted for the children is for them to be in God's will. We'd be happy if they were ditchdiggers or bank presidents as long as they were in His will."

Many of these young people will indeed return to the foreign field in their own right, yet living overseas as teens needn't keep them from gaining some awareness of current job options in the family homeland. By the way, the privilege of moving without restraint to achieve one's vocational goals won't be lightly regarded by those sensible of restraints in many foreign lands. The future in the West isn't what it used to be, when young people could usually find work in their chosen field. But America is still a land of opportunity.

The libraries of the U.S. Information Service abroad are replete with material relating to career goals and opportunities, and the young person can generally procure sufficient pointers to keep up-to-date on things. By the time he reaches the mid-teens, therefore, the earnest MK should have taken a few simple steps toward deciding on a vocation in which he can honor the Lord. Whatever his inclination, he'll appraise his aptitudes and the degree of satisfaction a particular line of work should hold for him over the years. (It's estimated that only one out of six Americans is content in his job. So with the majority it's ballads on Friday, blues on Monday.) An MK speaks his mind:

> We are taught to separate ourselves from the world and are warned about the sin, materialism, and godlessness of that outside world. But often MKs are not taught the simple practical knowledge necessary to get along in that world. They need to gain a realistic understanding of what life is like beyond their own lives as independent adults.
>
> One thing is money. Many MKs feel the Lord has provided and will continue to provide. But out there in the ordinary

world one is expected to make a living. That means choosing a career realistically. And it also means having ability to assess different vocations and also oneself. Further it means choosing the right subjects in college. At that time they're praised by being knowledgeable about science and math, not only for getting good marks in Scripture and music.*

To the junior and senior high schooler the issue of a college major begins to take on weight. And rightly so, since the decision on this point reflects the goal, or one of the goals, in the young person's vocational vision. Several university theses report that at least in the past the majority of MKs not returning to the field choose service-oriented careers such as teachers, nurses, doctors, social workers, in which they can give themselves to people in need. Perhaps today this outlook is altering; for one thing, the richly talented seem to veer away from teaching.

Selection of a career ranks as the third most critical decision of a Christian's life, after personal commitment to Jesus Christ and the choice of a marriage partner. To be sure, a good number of MKs will later shift direction in vocation, but changing horses in the middle of a stream isn't necessarily a negative concept in business life today. Fluctuating conditions in the world and shifting patterns in the job market and in personal and family affairs may muddy the vocational waters at times. In a few instances the young person will have set his sights too high and later finds fulfillment down less-traveled roads; he may even hang out his own shingle. Remember the fable of the tortoise winning in low gear over the hare?

THE SECULAR DOMAIN

Entering the job jungle. Many MKs seek employment in Christian organizations, in keeping with their burden for gospel outreach. Yet if the young adult has adapted well to western culture, proving himself capable of standing firm in the fight against the evils of the day, he ought to find a congenial place in the secular business world. While there are plenty of business people with estimable attitudes that could well be cultivated by many of us Christians, this young man or woman will become keenly aware that industry is shot through and through with highly questionable policies. For example, take the sophisticated cutthroatism in competitive companies; also the "subterranean economy" whereby employers pay workers "under the table" in order to keep cash off the books and avoid certain taxes. In such circumstances the MK will experience a collision of conscience. He'll similarly be distressed by the foul language and sick humor bombarding him from all sides.

With regard to job prospects for the decade of the '80s, there's no clear consensus among economists; their pronouncements move from "bleak" to "tough but challenging." All seem to agree, nevertheless, that sweeping changes are in store; consequently the key to a satisfying career is *specialization*. In a competitive environment with such a flood of talent hitting the work force, the future belongs to the efficient.

Since several vocations or skills may overlap, however, experts advise prospective job-seekers to acquire some diversity of skills. An engineer may be more valuable if he's a good public speaker. Those enamored of English and writing should likewise develop a sideline, in case enthusiasm for aesthetics wanes when that particular brook dries up (1 Kings 17:7).

MKs at large colleges can take advantage of the placement bureau. Virtually all types of educational institutions report greatly increased difficulty placing graduates regardless of academic achievement, but assistance in career selection flows freely in placement offices in the form of personal counseling and listings of career opportunities. Actually as many as 80 percent of available positions aren't advertised; they're filled through a network of career centers which employers trust to recruit help.

At some period along the way the MK should arm himself with a carefully prepared resume—a summary of his personal, educational, and vocational qualifications, practical experience, and job objective. An applicant usually prepares several resumes, each with a slightly different slant in order to align a particular skill with an employer's need. Many good books offer sample resumes. Along with each post applied for, of course, a cover letter follows. Despite all this, at his first interview the young hopeful will probably suffer some degree of job-hunter's stomach and interview insomnia.

High-priority jobs. Presently there's a surge of student interest in business and engineering courses, career-centered. Plenty of good jobs are going to those with technological knowhow—ones at home in such areas as math, physics, and computer science. One of the major job opportunities in the future will undoubtedly be in the field of robotics. The micro-electronics revolution, the core of "high-tech," is upon us. A writer speaks of "high hopes for high-tech," the result of increase in semiconductor and computer manufacturing, telecommunications, robotics, aerospace, biotechnology, and suchlike. How long this high-tech surge will keep its competitive edge is open to question.

Economics classes in colleges and universities are swamped with students, most of whom won't become economists as such but will use their training in other business areas and the professions. One authority mentions the "mind-boggling" growth in economics jobs available.

One of the most valuable diplomas in the U.S. currently is a master's in business administration (the "golden passport," students call it). Burgeoning enrollment in business programs is straining the resources of many universities. Though most of the business graduates are going for the pot of gold, some of the better schools prefer students more idealistically inclined.

Business houses such as banks, insurance companies, and retailing firms, where interpersonal relations play an important role, highly rate liberal arts degrees, and of course these sheepskins are often essential for students looking toward law, medicine, and dentistry. Consequently, if the general education student carefully plans how his training can be not only stimulating but practically applied, he'll ordinarily find his skills "marketable," as they say, and his entire career enriched. The college graduate trained in business, engineering, or computer literacy has an initial advantage on entering the business world. In the long run, however, the advantage may well rest with the liberal arts graduate; he'll adapt more readily to new environments and think more critically and independently.

Opportunities in social work and public school teaching are becoming limited, but since many math and science teachers are being lured into industry, vacancies in that sector frequently occur in public schools. The increasing number of Christian primary and secondary schools throughout the U.S. and Canada opens up hundreds of teaching posts.

Young people gifted in art may find fulfillment in Christian publishing houses. Those completing graduate studies in university or seminary will find rewarding fields of service in Christian colleges, seminaries, and Bible colleges. The journalism field, both Christian and secular, is jampacked with talent, but there's always a niche for one endowed with extraspecial caliber. Or how about radio/television reporting or broadcasting?

Vocational schools. Young people by the thousands are beating a path to the doors of private and public two-year vocational schools. Scoffed at previously as fly-by-night operations, these schools are now geared to the real world of work. Federally approved and accredited, they achieve a high standard of instruction in course offerings. Upon graduation students enjoy good prospects of finding acceptable jobs. Experience gained in vocational schools and/or elsewhere is sometimes as good as a college degree when it's accompanied by incentive. Even MKs planning to proceed to undergraduate and then to graduate study could profit greatly from a year in a technical institute. That could lend a practical dimension to their lives and later enable them to work part of their way through college and beyond.

Several types of schools—community and junior colleges, technical institutes, trade and vocational schools—prepare students for almost every kind of employment. Here are a few occupational skills taught for which a demand exists in the job market of the '80s: computer programming (and nearly every other computer skill), electronics technicians, fuel science technicians (jobs in petroleum and applied products), respiratory therapists, paramedics, medical and mental lab technicians, physical therapy assistants, accountants, travel agents, aviation mechanics.

Two-year programs are available in the few Christian voc-ed schools. Public community colleges are the least expensive of the postsecondary schools, with tuition and fees currently averaging about $500 per year; boarding facilities are generally not provided. At private two-year institutions the costs come to about $2,000 a year, with tuition much higher for certain courses of study. However, these schools are normally more efficient and more in touch with what employers want; in fact some are backed by large industrial companies which enlist the pick of the litter. Most of the courses in the last-named schools can be applied toward a baccalaureate degree should the student decide to continue his education at a four-year college.

The above setting-forth of the various types of vocational schools will prove confusing to many MKs still overseas. It may be useful, then, to include names and addresses of bureaus from which information relating to courses offered by each type of postsecondary school can be obtained: American Association of Community and Junior Colleges, One Dupont Circle, N.W., Suite 410, Washington, D.C. 20036; National Association of Trade and Technical Schools, 202 L St., N.W., Washington, D.C. 20036. For a free directory of business courses and accredited schools, write: Association of Independent Colleges and Schools, 1730 M St., N.W., Washington, D.C. 20036. For courses in job skills offered by the 125 accredited home-study schools, write: National Home Study Council, 1601 18 St., N.W., Washington, D.C. 20009.

Success & failure. The true worth of an MK's nurturance, as well as his personal response to it, becomes evident in the manner he handles both success and failure—not in any sense a simple matter. Does he accept the thesis that it's all right to fail? (Even a monkey falls out of a tree once in a while, the Japanese say.) Many adolescents, some MKs included, daydream of what they'd like to be and do—to start with, moving right into Harvard—but have no concrete idea of what carrying out a responsible lifework entails.

Consequently some sample "the fine art of blowing it." The frank testimony of one such MK:

> While in college, the godly advice of my parents directed me into a major in business education. Three years of teaching in a Christian high school followed my graduation from university. During this first teaching experience I soon found that my B.S. degree did not guarantee spiritual reactions and attitudes in the face of failures and defeats. But God's Word *does* guarantee an overcoming victory. In spite of many discouragements and frustrations of a new teacher, the promise of 1 John 5:4 became very meaningful to me. I soon grew to love Christian school teaching. I now believe He is directing my steps into service for Him in foreign missions, and I rejoice in His leading (Psalm 31:19-21).*

While many of them consider it a privilege to have been a part of a missionary family in a developing country, MKs aren't normally given to credit-snatching and ego-tripping; opportunism isn't part of their makeup. But doubtless not a few are vulnerable to milder forms of this blight. In his small volume, Joseph L. Cannon lightheartedly illustrates a posture that MKs are exposed to (cf. 2 Corinthians 10:17):

> Most of us landed on the mission field just ordinary fellows, and from average to poor families at that. But all of a sudden we are now foreign dignitaries, ambassadors, rich capitalists. Wow! This is about all our poor humble heads can stand. We get looked at wherever we go; we are like movie stars; we are important; we are just discovering how wonderful we are![35]

Fame and fortune are highly esteemed commodities in the West. Achievement is becoming the venerated national God, generated naturally in a nation unexcelled among the nations for its wealth and opportunities for acquiring wealth. The victory cry of peak performers, particularly in athletics but also in industry, is "We're Number 1"—all of which acts as a goad and goal to millions of less prominent people. Media ads promote surefire get-rich-quick schemes, and autobiographies tell how celebrities made a big splash. Nowadays the lotteries, promising a rags-to-riches bonanza, attract multitudes of dream-builders.

The sensible, spiritually minded MK will pursue excellence and use all the help he can get to gain it, but he'll keep material acquisitions in balance. Should this MK eventually become chairman of the board, he'll remain intent on pleasing his divine Employer. Still, maintaining a lifestyle characterized by small kindnesses in Podunk Center could conceivably lend a more lasting influence for good than cutting a figure in New York.

We sometimes read that adult MKs rank high in the annals of Who's Who in America—a statement largely discredited though studies do indicate a high level of achievement and a few rather dazzling successes. In any event this saying is apropos, "You don't have to be in Who's Who to know what's what." And what about the Who's Who of Heaven (cf. Hebrews 12:22-24) that requires no revision? Let's note these superior words of the late C.C. Forbes, founder of *Forbes* Magazine:

> The money or place of fame that our endeavors may bring when crowned with so-called success will not yield all the joy we anticipated; such things may charm, may tickle our vanity, may effervesce a hectic sort of happiness for a little while, but we soon find our teeth grating at the core. The consciousness of the worthwhileness of the achievement itself can alone produce in us a state of happiness. Riches are mental, not material.[36]

MISSIONARY MANDATE

Viable investment. It may appear superfluous to introduce the issue of foreign missionary service in a study occupied with MKs and their families. Who among the world's Christians should be more awake to the need and qualifications of overseas workers? Indeed it's not easy to reconcile any MK's lack of interest in missions, whether or not he himself returns to the foreign field.

Acclimated to the environment and culture of at least one foreign country, knowledgeable concerning the major problems confronting a new worker, acquainted with one or two foreign languages, old pros in overseas travel—these factors give the MK a range of perception that might take a freshman missionary years to acquire. (As simple examples, he wouldn't use the expression "killing two birds with one stone" before a strict Hindu, or "bringing home the bacon" before a Muslim.)

The extent to which the MK identified with the local people in his earlier years and the attitude of his parents toward their ministry represent important elements bearing on his later initiative for foreign service. It's evident, however, that certain problems attend this area of missionary life. The ratio of MKs returning to the field is considerably below what one versed in missions would expect. For those who do return the attrition rate is remarkably below the average of all workers. We very much appreciate these comments by missionary leader Dr. H.S. Stam, passed on to us by his daughter, also a missionary:

While I have seen or heard of a few tragedies or catastrophes among missionary kids, I know of a large number of very happy and successful eventualities. In our own Africa Inland Mission there are some of the most wonderful leaders and bravest pioneers who grew up on the field. Their lives as children, close to native life and thus sharing in the prayer of their parents and of their fellow MKs at school, was of great value in preparing them for the work God had for them. . . .

There are hardships of course, and two of our children are buried in Africa. There is a simple standard of life which would be listed as on the poverty level in the USA. But as one daughter said, "Why, Mother, we weren't poor, except in money."

When MKs choose a nonmissionary career, their action needn't be assumed as indicating a low view of foreign missions. The disposition of many alumni of the missionary home presently engaged in other than vocational missionary service is undoubtedly reflected in these illuminating comments by MKs in missionary work or anticipating it:

It was while I was nursing in a Sudanese village clinic, with no doctor nearby, and I was living in a one-room hut, that I found I have a real fulfilled feeling. I suddenly realized that this is what I have been made for. I was a missionary kid; I could handle the heat and the dirt and the bugs.*

I don't think I would ever choose to live any other way than being an MK or in any other place than the foreign mission field. I was born on the mission field because my parents obeyed the voice of the Lord calling them to a lifetime of service in Central America. Mine was a happy childhood, full of the normal joys of play and friendships, of good schooling, and sprinkled with the excitement of travel in a foreign land. The Spanish learned as a child was a decided advantage when I returned as a missionary.*

I feel accountable for my exposure to the deaf Japanese and for the harvest I know needs to be reaped there.

My wife and I were both challenged for missions during our childhood years in Africa. Both of us came to the Lord while young and attended MK schools in Africa. I spent one year as a short-termer in Kenya, where I met my future wife who was visiting her parents. We plan to return to Kenya later this year under International Missions.*

It was not difficult to consider returning to Japan. It was home to me. I loved the people, the culture, and the food. There

I had experienced all the joy and pain of growing up as an MK, and the happy memories of childhood far outnumbered the not-so-happy ones. Christian friends thought it but natural that I should go to the field. But I began to have a negative reaction toward missionary work, yet I was open to whatever the Lord had for me. I rejoice in having been led back to the same language area in which my parents worked. It was a special joy to enter active ministry upon arrival, without problems of communication.*

My experience as a missionary's child has given me an insight into what I believe is the most purposeful and worthwhile occupation—that of giving my life wholly to God to be used where He sees fit. I have always felt there could be no more satisfying life than that of a missionary.*

It was during Spiritual Emphasis Week of my junior year in high school when I definitely sensed the Lord calling me to missionary service in Japan. No doubt there were several factors that made me receptive to the call, such as a first-hand view of the need and the example of my parents. From that time on I began planning and preparing in that direction. I don't recall my parents pressuring me. At our commissioning service, my wife and I were given a challenge to imitate Mother's faith (2 Timothy 1:5) and Dad's energetic service (2 Timothy 4:1-3). These have been difficult but worthy goals before us as we have worked together in Japan.*

Probably I am in missionary work today because of the intangibles my parents gave me as an MK. They communicated an awareness of urgent needs, established realistic programs to meet these needs, and executed the plans with genuine love. Since the family participated in these projects, our childhood experiences were practically the equivalent of a boot camp for Christian ministry.*

I am presently studying at Columbia Bible College, and feel very fortunate to have some members of the AEF family here. Right now I'm taking a variety of required Bible courses, but hope to enroll in the Christian Education program, as it offers practical training in working with a variety of age groups. In this program, all of which is in keeping with my interests, I am praying for the Lord's leading in the future, being open to whatever he has for me. Zambia and its people are very much on my heart, as well as the work my mother was doing. The ministry she has is often on my mind, as I remember her work with African choirs, women's groups, and young people. Her whole life was an example to me!*

Minding the Master's business. The highest motivating factor in the believer's life and vocation must always be the constraining love of Christ. This is true whether he's in a so-called secular job, in a Christian organization, in professional Christian service in the homeland, or in foreign missionary work. Moreover, the Lord Jesus is the model for our daily walk. (Philippians 2:4, 5: "Each of you should look not only to your own interests, but also to the interests of others. Your attitude should be the same as that of Christ Jesus.") In harmony with the thrust of the parable opening this chapter, the "multitalented" MK needs to be absorbed in prospering his Lord's affairs.

It's outside our province to judge the hearts of MKs with respect to putting their lives on the line for foreign service. Yet isn't it painfully significant that, as a missionary executive informs us, "the burden of evangelism and missions is being carried on largely by first-generation Christians?"

Assuredly the testimonies included in these pages reveal that many MKs are vitally concerned for the Master's interests worldwide. More than a few have been inspired by the indelible words of Jim Elliott, one of the five missionaries slain by Auca Indians: "He's no fool who gives what he cannot keep to gain what he cannot lose."

Since the rewards of faithfulness and incentive are so great—out of this world as inferred in our Lord's unqualified commendation in Matthew 25:21, 23—certainly each earnest MK will want to share in the inestimable joy of "harvest home" (Matthew 9:37, 38). A stanza of Charles Wesley's hymn, "A Charge to Keep I Have":

> To serve the present age,
>   My calling to fulfill—
> O may it all my powers engage
>   To do my Master's will.

15
LOVE & MARRIAGE
Continuous Commitment

---

*"Love is patient, love is kind. . . . It is not rude, it is
not self-seeking, it is not easily angered, it keeps no
record of wrongs" (1 Corinthians 13:4, 5).*

FORMULA FOR FULFILLMENT

Secular & sacred love. When the Apostle penned this hymn of love
to the Corinthian Christians, he was distressingly aware of their
deviant moral state. Their lives were being corroded as the result of
imitating the behavior of Corinth's populace—a way of life similar to
that which the MK encounters in the contemporary western world.
The knowledge and sophistication of that city, blended with carnal
glibness of tongue and ostentation, operated to blunt the edge of
spiritual values.

Accordingly Paul presents on order of things running utterly
counter to those practices. He spells out the preeminence, perfection,
and permanence of true Christian love—Christlike love. While this
type of love is impossible to define adequately, it's at least no easy,
sickly indulgence, no soft, cheap sentiment like Hollywood's tawdry
product. Nothing like that conceived Calvary. Tragically millions of
Americans haven't the foggiest idea of what true love is.

Among the wholesome forms of love at the human level is
brotherly love, illustrated by a young boy's rejoinder to a solicitous
questioner who observed him carrying a good-sized toddler: "He
ain't heavy; he's my brother." Again, a parent's enduring
commitment to offspring may approach the Apostle's lineaments of
love. It's no coincidence that patience ranks first in the listing of
love's characteristics in the Corinthians passage above.

Then there's that mysterious God-engineered attraction of man for
maiden and vice versa that causes sparks to fly. Concerning this boy-
girl relationship the adolescent MK normally has a few gray areas in
his thinking that he'd like to have cleared up. Since marriage ranks in
importance next only to the new birth in life's experiences, the
conscientious MK shows maturity when intent on becoming

marriageable—preparing himself to appear at the altar. But after all is said and read, subjection to Jesus Christ as Lord and the cultivating of New Testament love in daily contacts remain the key basis of conditioning for this most intimate of human affinities.

Marriage and the family are humanity's oldest institutions. God sovereignly ordained marriage, so it's here to stay despite the current mass-merchandising of sexual permissiveness. As far as missionary parents are concerned, marriage isn't an endangered species. And unquestionably a healthy majority of adult MKs have found or are seeking a fulfilling union entailing life commitment and fidelity.

Nevertheless a handful of other MKs entertain the notion that a legal nuptial document makes one feel trapped; they want the privileges of marriage without the restraints and responsibilities. So they arrange a trial run before making things legal. On that ground they enter a relationship variously called living together, live-ins, open marriage, trial marriage, and the like. Apparently taking each other for better or worse poses too great a hazard; instead of "until death do us part" it could be "equal playmates until something better turns up." Scripture has spoken regarding such practices, for instance Hebrews 13:4: "Marriage should be honored by all, and the marriage bed kept pure, for God will judge the adulterer and all the sexually immoral."

The issues of divorce and remarriage won't engage our attention in these pages. MKs have their share of domestic problems, though in the comparatively few instances when this distress expands to the point of divorce, it's usually of the "amicable" type. Suffice it to say, however, that when both partners are committed to the Lord and to one another, they'll close the door behind them, indisposed under any circumstances to join the blighted ranks of the "exes" and their children.

Single saints. How many MKs, whether by choice or course of things, continue unmarried into their thirties? Five or ten percent? For some, moved by the nesting instinct, Mr. or Miss Right has already appeared on the horizon, while for others it's a matter of single-but-looking.

In any event, a goodly number of single MKs gain fulfillment, self-respect, and social approval through commitment to worthy life goals. At a time of widespread sexual confusion and sounds of marital doom, and when chaste celibacy is considered an anomaly, these women and men have come to terms with their sexuality and rest quietly in God's will for them.

Doubtless some young MKs decline openings for marriage by reason of prior commitment to foreign missionary service. They're thus better able to reach out in ministry without the responsibility of a family (Matthew 19:12). Devotedness to the Lord and His interests helps to sublimate physical drives and also cut down on loneliness. When singles mix with marrieds and other singles of both sexes, satisfying friendships often follow.

While God designed marriage for most people, sin has wrecked the normal structure of one man for one woman. Nevertheless, though marriage is good, it isn't everything; the New Testament reserves a definite place for chaste celibacy (1 Corinthians 7:7). A British friend, John Kennedy, writes of alternatives to early marriage:

> I write from the point of view of that rarest of breeds, the missionary bachelor. . . . For a young Christian to consider marriage as a first priority is wrong. The first priority is the will of God, and the will of God allows for an alternative—remaining single. . . .
>
> The single man, or the man who would remain single in missionary service, faces his own problems, just as a single lady does, or a married couple for that matter. . . . Being single may restrict one's service in some directions, but it offers greater opportunities in others. It is not true to say that a person would be more effective in Christian service were he married or single per se. The decisive factor is the call of God. . . .
>
> With more than 30 years of missionary service behind me, I can testify to having fulfilled a ministry which would have been quite impossible had I been married. Not only has it been possible for me to continue for a long period (much longer than most missionary couples today feel they can give because of family reasons), but I have been free to travel and live for lengthy periods in conditions which a western couple or family would find extremely trying. . . .
>
> Young people, if you are serious about following the Lord, if you are serious about responding to the missionary call, marriage is *not* a first priority.[37]

A missionary lady in Pakistan declares, "I'm single by the grace of God!" Another: "I think it's easier to be single out here than at home. There are more of us." Two other missionaries share their sentiments:

> I don't think any normal woman wants to accept singleness. . . . But when a special opportunity for village work opens on our field, I'm available, on the spot, and able to be the contact person.
>
> In my youth I told the Lord I wanted to give my life entirely to His service, so I refused the offer of marriage. I supervised a

200-bed mission hospital and felt this would be my life's work. Later on, when a certain young man came by, my heart felt a twitter. I rebuked the feeling in the name of Jesus, as being from Satan! That's how strongly I felt. I was to find, however, that now the Lord's time had come for me to serve as a married woman, a helpmeet to a husband. I relinquished my independent role and became willing to add the responsibility of marriage to missionary service.

Miss Margaret Clarkson, author and hymnwriter, testifies how she remains fulfilled as a single woman:

> Through no fault or choice of my own I am unable to express my sexuality in the beauty and intimacy of Christian marriage, as God intended when he created me a sexual being in His own image. To seek to do this outside of marriage is, by the clear teaching of Scripture, to sin against God and against my own nature. As a committed Christian, then, I have no alternative but to live a life of voluntary celibacy. I must be chaste not only in body, but in mind and spirit as well. Since I am now in my 60s, I think that my experience of what this means is valid. I want to go on record as having proved that for those who are committed to do God's will, his commands are his ena- blings. . . . If we seek fulfillment in him, we shall find it. It may not be easy, but who ever said the Christian life was easy? The badge of Christ's discipleship is a cross.[38]

A CBFMS single in Pakistan suggests that the only remedy for vulnerability to stress in the unmarried state is "to reach out to God in commitment, to serve others, and to live positively with a spirit of adventure." Another single lady, returning from furlough to her work in Ramabai Mukti Mission, an orphanage for neglected children, writes in the Mission's news organ concerning her remedy for singles' main problem:

> I had just left my loved family and friends in Canada for my fifth term of service in India. There was no room in my heart for loneliness. The Lord in all His glory seemed so near. The love of a closely knit family is precious, but somehow being a part of the family of God with so many caring, praying loved ones I left behind with them, filled my heart with a special sense of peace and security.

DATING & MATING

"Just friends." The MK doesn't usually get wrapped up in a going-steady relationship during his secondary school years, whether he's

studying at home by correspondence, in a small-group setting, or in boarding. The often restrictive environment of the home community and school is probably the chief reason. That doesn't mean, of course, that these boys and girls remain indifferenct to the opposite sex or adhere only to platonic friendships.

On reaching the teens, as girls typically renounce their erstwhile aversion to boys and the latter follow suit somewhat later with reference to the fair sex, friendships are no longer limited to casual encounters. Instead, since misogynists and misanthropes are the rarest of species among maturing MKs, many manage to form supportive friendships marked by a degree of overt affection. (In the West the adolescent MK hears the lament of peers, "Where have all the nice girls gone?" One answer could be that there are plenty of them among MKs.)

From one viewpoint the situation in boarding school comes close to the ideal, to be preferred even to the western computer dating service. Students have plenty of scope for leisurely observing each other at their best and worst: in the classroom after one has received a poor grade or has studied most of the night for exams; in the dining room and in sports when the finer qualities are tested; and indeed in almost every other facet of school life. Thus a boy and girl can roughly tabulate a particular peer-student's pluses and minuses in regard to congeniality over a longer stretch. In this thrilling saga the grapevine—especially the female variety—though overworked, is never short-circuited.

In those school years a boy enjoyed a tactical advantage in being able to view a girl not artificially made up. On one of the occasional dates, of course, the dapper personality of the boy and the touched-up countenance of the girl took on a distinctive polish. (Incidentally, MKs are prime proof that being attractive needn't signify that a girl hasn't cultivated her brains.) The mere fact of such social contacts, regardless of the absence of dramatic converse, undoubtedly hastened maturation of both partners. Yet fifteen minutes after parting, each probably recalled a dozen witty trivia that would have enlivened the golden hours together.

Later in the family homeland conditions are changed. Social relationships are more transient and friendships may lack sufficient time to develop. Should the MK be enrolled in Bible school, however, he'll meet a situation similar to that in boarding. Rules for dating are specially restrictive for freshmen, considerably more so than in Christian colleges. In either school, nonetheless, dating will have both its sunny and sultry periods. Here's the first installment of an MK's stirring courtship in Bible college. The sequel follows shortly.

Soon after entering college I found myself asking the Lord to send me dates. That never happened. I prayed more and harder. In my sophomore year I grew very close to the Lord—so close that I took walks alone in the woods and felt His presence as I talked to Him. He was my constant companion. That year I had good times with two or three couples as a group, which made me feel I sort of fitted in. But I still prayed for some real dates.

Finally I reached a decision, after much struggle. I had just finished my quiet time with Psalm 37. I claimed verses 4 and 5, and told the Lord I trusted Him to find the right person for me, and if He didn't have somebody for me, well, I would accept that too. But I wasn't going to worry about guys or look for them anymore.

In my junior year I met Mark, a PK, but he was just an acquaintance. But through unusual circumstances we were thrown together, and then we studied and ate meals together. Mark asked me to go with him to the fall banquet. Before we knew it, our friendship was more than just a friendship.

More than "just friends." In the MK's late teens or early twenties, the plot thickens. He will have progressed beyond the mere thought of love to gearing up for the real thing. He may initiate an off-campus attachment with a girl he had a crush on in boarding school. Should this heart-throb of his dreams hail from Britain or Down Under, a fervent suitor won't be daunted by a mere ocean. Uncle Sam's postal system is ready at hand, and phone facilities come accommodatingly to his aid in extraspecial wooing sessions.

Be that as it may, many MKs find their bone-of-my-bone in a Bible college or in a Christian or secular college. We're all aware that Christian schools are good match factories, turning out A-1 products. There's much mixing and matching in Bible school. Some male students, it's true, intimate that most of the girls come to Bible school to obtain the "MRS" degree. Moreover, should a boy ask a girl out a few times, she and her friends consider that marriage is just around the corner. Appraised from the feminine angle, these impressions are totally unfounded. While remaining neutral in the controversy, we're constrained to relay two scraps of Buffam gossip:

Our younger daughter, on requesting literature from, as she thought, Columbia Bible College received material instead from Columbia College, a girl's school in the same city. Sharon, at first sight of the contents, exclaimed, "I'm not going to *that* school—there's no boys there!" For the record, Shari went to CBC and got her "boy."

A missionary prayer-meeting in Bible school may set the stage for something more than undergirding the work and workers overseas. In that identical room one's prayer-partner for life may be resting in league with the Lord for His choice for her. In precisely such a situation, in Moody Bible Institute 50 years ago, this writer got the first glimpse of his future wife. (Language school on the foreign field is another factory that produces matches par excellence—already conditioned for missionary life and service.)

DRAMA IN THREE ACTS

Act I—Going steady. Only rarely, of course, does a girl come into a boy's life with a glad upsetting rush and that's it, the first and only girlfriend.While a few of our missionary friends testify to such an experience, a whirlwind courtship obviously has definite demerits. (It was OK for Adam and Eve since God personally arranged things so nicely!) Infatuation leaps into bloom but love requires time to take root and grow. Dating a number of partners and thus checking the atmosphere before getting deeply involved is a sound principle, certainly for MKs who have a tendency to go along with the desires of the other person.

Love has been defined as "an inner inexpressibility of an outer alloverishness." But let's be content with a less sizzling description: a warming friendship that has caught fire. Yet young people going steady before discerning the dawn of love can drift with the tide into an unsuitable affinity—marriage without friendship. Worse, the temptation to introduce a degree of excitement through indelicate advances can open the door to tragedy.

The responsible MK and his girlfriend will spend sufficient time to see each other in the total person. Increasingly the starry-eyed couple experience harmony and delight over a wide range of issues. They enjoy being together, doing things together, and praying together. If steadies can't freely pray together, the relationship is ipso facto on shaky footing. They'll also go over things with both sets of parents at various times.

These young people won't limit their hours together to fellowship with the local church, important as that is. Indoor and outdoor games, reading and discussing good books (not always avoiding controversial portions that lead to "creative fighting"), having fun times with other couples and children in an assortment of interests, spending evenings with furloughing parents and older friends, shopping together and preparing meals in parental homes (and washing up afterwards), helping neighbors in one way or another— activities of this nature help to bring ease and fullness in communication; meanwhile the relationship strikes deeper levels. Each partner is also enabled to recognize the other's strengths and to bear gently with failings, or as a writer phrases it, to make them "beautifully blind to one another's faults."

Opposites attract, it's said. At least one example of this proposition is a long-time friend, s seminarian but still of a shy disposition. He acknowledges the blessing of having a self-confident spouse: "This has made marriage extremely rich in that I uniquely belong to/with my wife, who is also an MK." So here's the panacea for adolescent shyness: Seek out a warm, poised, identifying spouse, preferably an MK. But a unique problem arises on occasion, as this MK confesses: "I can never get organized, so I could never live with a perfectionist." Never?

The soothing sequel to the testimony begun a few pages back continues. The account won't represent a typical MK relationship but we think it's appealing. Sorry for the ellipses!

Mark and I wanted to take things very slowly, so that neither of us would get hurt or do things we'd regret later. I approached another MK and his special girlfriend (whom he later married), both of whom I admired very much. They guided me to some reading material that had helped them in their relationship. So Mark and I went through the articles and set some ground rules for our own relationship. We decided that all we could do was hold hands, and no more, until we both felt definitely sure we cared for each other in a very special way—then only would Mark kiss me. . . . We kept to our rules, and our first kiss came four months after we started to go together. . . . We were married a year later.

Act II—Engagement. Sociological studies make clear that couples who arrange for this interval enjoy happier married lives than those who dispense with it. One MK mentions that "following engagement we met every night and never parted before we had devotions together. This made our period of engagement a real prelude to marriage."

Between engagement and marriage the couple learn the reality and language of love. Every aspect of their future life together should be placed on the prayer docket. Fiance and fiancee deal in complete candor and honesty with regard to roles and goals—those having specifically to do with household responsibilities, employment, principles of decision-making, number of children anticipated, educational factors, and of course spiritual issues affecting themselves and their prospective family.

Family life counselors advise that, if the fiance plans to undertake postgraduate study, deferring marriage for a year or two makes good sense; academic pressures pose too severe a strain on marital obligations. Even if the young man isn't planning graduate study, a year of freedom following college will serve a sound purpose in gaining equilibrium and searching out vocational prospects. Particular considerations will require adjustments all along the line.

To address adequately the matter of *interracial relationships* nearing the engagement stage would be realistic, but we can merely touch on the subject. Attitudes toward interracial marriage have altered significantly in the last two decades—mixed marriages have tripled in number each year—yet many counselors in social matters continue to advise extreme caution on the part of persons considering this step, valid and comrade-like as such a relationship appears to friends. The majority of missionary parents may not strongly disapprove of a miscegenetic union, but they're apprehensive lest their son or daughter not be fully aware of the unique psychological and practical problems attending a bond of this nature.

Act III—Wedding bells. The much-awaited day draws near. Along with congratulations and exhaustion comes a tinge of reserve. Such a surpassing change in one's life, even with every promise of happiness, doesn't leave any of us undisturbed. It means giving up a considerable measure of freedom and autonomy. Yet both partners will appear at the altar smiling. (Somewhat curiously, Africans wonder why Americans smile so much when they don't really feel like doing so.)

The reflecting MK and his/her pledged life-partner, however, will come to the altar with confidence that God has drawn them together and they want to glorify Him in their united lives. They're committed to long-distance love, regardless of anything and everything. This young couple don't expect marriage to immediately iron out all their personal deficiencies, yet they're determined with the Lord's presence to guard their love for each other and increase in their practical consideration as well.

With regard to details of their wedding service, MKs will generate creative touches. Some of course prefer a black-tie affair; others settle for a semiformal pattern. Still others and their parents, reacting negatively to ornate weddings common overseas, opt for simplicity itself. If either the bride or groom has arrived recently in the family homeland, the couple may dispense entirely with an invitation list— at least the raised-print version—and invite all friends to share their joy. Should the ceremony be conducted in the local church auditorium, the congregation will appreciate an open invitation. In this way the Lord's people will be encouraged to follow the pair prayerfully in the years ahead.

Not infrequently nowadays the young couple prepares the order of service in concert with the officiating minister—appropriately the father of the bride or groom, on furlough, who will introduce affecting observations lending freshness to the function. By the same token, friends will relish personal testimonies by the twosome previous to the committal service. And the bride and groom may phrase the commitment in their own words. Here's one MK bride's declaration:

> "_____, I come this day to give my life into your care, lovingly submitting myself to you with joy as the Church is subject to Christ. I promise, as your helpmeet, to love you and our children, caring for your needs and our home as the Lord supplies strength. I love you and will care for you in sickness or health, in want or plenty, and will share your joys and trials.
>
> _____, I shall always cherish you as the Lord leads us through life together and until He takes us home."

A spirit of subdued rejoicing should characterize the proceedings—the singing, prayers, reading of Scripture, exchanging of vows and rings, even the charge to the bride and groom. God is honored by sincere, reverent joy expressed on behalf of the wedded pair in acknowledgement of His guidance and working in their lives.

When the deed is done, the nuptials duly recorded in the church annals, and the photos taken for posterity's sake, the greeting line forms. Happy tears and kisses blend unabashedly. Then the refreshments and the cutting of the cake. Finally the flushed couple gets off for parts unknown except to a select few—a matter which other friends won't enquire into too curiously.

CHRISTIAN MARRIAGE

Ecstasy & agony. Conceivably a few marrieds continue in a storybook fashion for years—connubial bliss with nary a blitz. Most of us, however, have found that well before the first year of wedlock passes, the exciting throb of romantic love moderates by reason of "the changes and chances of this mortal life," as the Book of Common Prayer terms the vagaries of life.

Recognizing that our mate isn't a finished product, we attempt to finish the job. A missionary wife, now enjoying a relationship on track, confesses, "I remember our honeymoon as a head-on collision between two radically different lifestyles. . . . Our early years could best be characterized as two people working frantically to change each other."

Marriage may be made in heaven, but it's worked out realistically here below. Significantly, sociologists appear to agree that marital problems principally stem from a sequence of trifling incidents. (The more we read and talk about difficulties in marriage, it seems, the more we look for them.) Lack of good communication between husband and wife accounts for much tit-for-tat verbal sniping.

On the other hand, a writer describes marriage as "a creative growing relationship requiring a long, complex process of mutual adjustment." It's how each partner handles times of thinness that determines the quality of the union. This aphorism from our vintage scrapbook sets forth an estimable principle in marriage: "High heaven rejects the lore / Of nicely calculated less or more."

An analogy has been drawn between married and missionary life. First of all there's the sparkle phase: Freshly arrived on foreign soil, we're delighted with everything about the country and people. But soon we begin to observe defects in both. At the same time we ourselves unwittingly commit one faux pas after another and offend national sensibilities. (We older workers marvel at the broad tolerance level of national friends in the thick of our mumblings and stumblings.) By God's grace things change for the better. After two or three years we and local friends learn to communicate within the bounds of saneness.

Married life is something like that. The countless minor and major adjustments that are part and parcel of family life can bring erosion in the husband-wife affinity. Yet if we're set to please our Lord Jesus Christ in all details of home life, we'll find that married life grows sweeter as the years go by.

Leaving, cleaving, weaving. The process of *leaving*, enjoined in Genesis 2:24 and New Testament parallels such as Mark 10:8, 9, is usually uncomplicated in the case of MKs—parents cut the authority strings by leaving the country! But whether they do this or don't, it's safe to say they'll practice hands-off in relation to the new family's private matters. From the young people's point of view, the door, figuratively speaking, is equipped to automatically swing open for Mom and Dad. (We may receive a bit of flak from some readers for this flowery statement!)

Ephesians 5:22-33 says it all apropos of *cleaving*—the line of action whereby the nuptial knot is further tightened through reciprocal support and companionship. Fortunately the idea of "the little woman following along submissively" is a thing of the past. Each partner's assurance of being loved and desired, with outward expressions of tenderness, goes a long way in bringing the sense of security. Also both will find exquisite healing power in confession and forgiveness.

The aspect of *weaving* (Mark 10:7-9) reveals itself in a blending of physical, emotional, moral, and spiritual qualities into "one flesh"—a comprehensive type of unity wherein two persons, still retaining the uniqueness of each, weave strands of different colors into a sacred whole. Physical intimacy in marriage specifically represents this bond, recognized and sanctioned by the Lord. The expression of true, exclusive intimacies in a trusting relationship assures a fulfilling union.

Scripture doesn't approve of asceticism as a normal feature of married life. In some areas of church fellowship, to avoid appearing prurient, teachers are reluctant to give God's answers to such essentials of the husband-wife relationship. Three passages in the New Testament present the primary instruction on weaving: Matthew 19:4-6; 1 Corinthians 6:15-18; 7:3-5.

Joyous espousal. Utterly basic to a compatible, fulfilling marriage is prior commitment to another Lover—an eternal, blood-sealed friendship shared by faith with our heavenly Bridegroom. To be alone with Him in loving converse fills a vacuum that no human relationship can effectively do. Lucy A. Bennett's hymn, of which we quote merely one stanza, catches something of the grandeur of this blessed union:

> I am the Lord's! It is the glad confession,
>   Wherewith the Bride recalls the happy day;
> When love's "I will" accepted Him forever,
>   "The Lord's," to love, to honor and obey.

16
PERSPECTIVE & PROSPECT
MK Report Card

"My times are in your hands. . . . He will be the sure foundation for your times, a rich store of salvation and wisdom and knowledge" (Psalm 31:15; Isaiah 33:6).

LOOKING BACK

Sunshine & shadow. We've come a long way since launching our MK on the sea of life. His uncommon voyage has revealed a personality being molded by two cultures—of his parents and the host country—and by a third if we include his composite expression of both. We've traveled with him in his growing years, observing him from infancy through the spirited years of childhood, the emergent experiences of adolescence, and the challenging period of early adult involvements. Now the MK has moved into the adult world where the pith of his moral and spiritual makeup is being challenged.

As for the MK's parents, we get the distinct impression that a substantial majority of them are committed to unconditional love of their children, sensitive to inward as well as outward needs. While parenting methods aren't always of the highest order, moms and dads seek to fill their children's lives with stimulating patterns designed to help them reach their potential as stable, well-rounded, productive Christians.

These parents' top priority is to provide an environment in which each child's hand is early placed in that of the Savior. All the while they're persuaded that an ounce of example is worth a pound of preaching. They appreciate their offspring for who they are as individuals and for what they're accomplishing day by day. Dad is becoming more approachable and more given to listening.

Bouquets for MKs? Generally speaking (as we do frequently in the study), we like most of what we see going on in the MK world. Forgive us if at times we espouse a somewhat romanticized version of these youngsters and adolescents while glossing over the warts. One reviewer of the manuscript, an MK and missionary, opines that the material "sounds too goody-goody, too sugary." She mentions that a non-MK reading the book might scoff, "Aw, c'mon, nobody's *that* good!"

Well, we must demur on the grounds that, though our reflections on missionary offspring do tend to be optimistic, we're hardly naive with respect to their realistic patterns of deportment. We're confident, too, that the variety of MK testimonies help us to walk in their shoes, to discover how they view and handle their often unique experiences. Some recall their upbringing with wry nostalgia, others with ill-humor ("God gave me a rotten deal in bringing about my birth into a missionary family").

We've avoided like the plague any stereotyping of MKs. And we haven't sought to unearth a heap of minute details of a negative nature in their early years that might later develop into serious problems. In a limited but definite sense the die isn't irrevocably cast in childhood; fifteen years down the road the young adult could learn to control certain unwanted trends in his makeup. This MK did just that:

> For a long time after returning to the States I groveled in self-pity. I regarded my background as a liability. After all, I hadn't been exposed to the countless advantages of American culture. The mission field was the only place I really felt at home. But now things have changed. With no bitterness and with progressively fewer regrets, I thank God for my parents, for their obedience to Him and for the variegated life that resulted for our family. I'm reaping what they sowed. I would be a reaper.*

Then there's this brief yet comprehensive and perceptive paragraph from one who has been evaluating things from various angles:

> I never felt like a "deprived MK." I doubt that any of us do in any overall sense. Some kids have had really rough experiences, but what normal child growing up in a Stateside home doesn't have problems too, however ideal his family life is. So I think even those MKs, when they have enough maturity, look back with appreciation of the fact that the pluses far, far outweigh the minuses.*

Undeniably, however, problems in the social sphere represent the MK's feet of clay. A sagging self-image and sense of rootlessness may loom large in adolescent years. Consequently more than a few of these young people experience a measure of cultural disorientation on entering the western scene. Significantly then, a paradox exists in their lifestyles. On the one hand their generous, open, non-opinionated nature generates a manner of life highly respected by discerning people. On the other hand, these features aren't always complemented by caution in conducting social relationships. The desire for peer acceptance leaves them vulnerable to emulating practices of today's permissive youth culture.

Yet by and large the testimonies of MKs reveal respect for parents and appreciation of clearcut benefits in their background. Most alumni of the missionary home appear to be satisfied with who they are, feeling that the years overseas prepared them conspicuously for responsible adulthood. Following are affirmations of MKs in different stages of life:

By seeing other countries, I gained real appreciation for the freedom of the U.S. I feel I can be a better citizen.*

Growing up as an international citizen, we get another perspective of life and values. I've come to appreciate a simple and sane lifestyle.*

I see that for me to identify with Christ demands that I be willing to be sent. I want a heart that seeks God, and one that in compassion brings His invitation to others. I never want to block out His voice.*

Thus far I have followed Him—with some straining at the bit—through numerous jobs and the necessary training for a music degree. Now I feel the Lord is channeling this knowledge into an avenue which will give Him honor.*

Having grown up in a godly home, my years as an MK represent the outstanding blessing of my life. Since I have seen something of the world at large, I know the best and the worst the world offers. To be wealthy isn't a big deal.*

I have an unsurpassed Christian background and been an integral part of my parents' ministry. I'm thankful to have had some orientation for missionary work.*

My primary goal in life is to know God personally in a more dynamic and vital way. Then I want to build men.*

In the West the very word "missionary" brings negative reaction. But if you've grown up where stones were thrown at you, you can take the lumps of life. Many MKs have the ability to bounce back, landing on their feet when they're tossed into the air.

Being an MK enriches a person. There's an understanding of human pain and suffering and an awareness of true human and spiritual values.

The very Puritan, conservative upbringing of my type of MK was a good but straining precursor to real life. New situations are still hard. . . . Despite all the difficulties—all youth has its trials—I see being an MK as a rich heritage. Through travel I know the varieties of life to be found in other parts of the world. I have had the privilege of learning other cultures firsthand. So, in a sense, I view being reared as an MK a unique initiation to life.

Life after 40. Quite obviously this hasn't been a full-circle journal of the MK from cradle to hoar hairs. The young person is left focusing on vocational and marital issues. 'Twould be inviting to follow him through his thirties as he moves into broader fields of life and service, establishing his place in the world of people. Oftentimes, of course, this stage can be fraught with uncertainties in family matters, vocation, and health, but the disciplined MK, with the Lord's help, will stay the course and exhibit the bloom of gracious middle age.

No bell rings at this juncture to signify the arrival of senility. In the ebb and flow of daily responsibilities the MK of 40-odd years undoubtedly has his priorities straightened out and his life invested for solid gains—not keeping his eyes glued on the biological clock. Still, he'll be prompted on occasion to stop and take stock of his quality of life and possibly plug a few cracks in the dike. In this connection an older writer, Clare by name, expresses his wistful aspiration: "If life had a second edition, how I would correct the proofs!" The middle-age MK has time left for some editing.

Without access to relevant statistics, we dare to suggest that most of these older MKs are known to their business associates as men and women of integrity. The distilled experiences of the past continue to promote in them an attractive personality and a less-than-average complexity of life, whether they rise to prominence in the affairs of men or fulfillment down simpler paths. Many will be content with more or less in regard to perquisites of industry. Should there be one MK participating in a strike, go mark him well!

Finally, what about those glory-bound alumni who have eased into their sunset years? It's nice to think of them, not as stodgy, irascible oldsters fizzling out and headed for the tranquil pastures where they can nap to their heart's content, but as those with expansive minds still learning and engrossed in the King's business. As Psalm 92:14 predicts, "They will still bear fruit in old age, they will stay fresh and green." Certainly old age has its conflicts, but grace comes with the wrinkles. A dear old missionary friend, when informed by doctors of a variety of serious stomach maladies, exclaimed, "Bless the Lord, O my soul, and *all that is within me!*" These "septo/octogeraniums" may not retain 20/20 vision but they're fully satisfied with John 20/20 vision, "The disciples were overjoyed when they saw the Lord." A stanza from W.T. Matson's hymn (*Keswick Hymn-Book*):

> O blessed Life, the soul that soars,
> When sense of mortal sight is dim,
> Beyond the sense, beyond to Him
> Whose love unlocks the heavenly doors.

LOOKING AHEAD—*Change & challenge*

Signs of the times. As satanic forces intensify their struggle for compliance of the masses, currents of change are underway in the things Westerners consider important. Millions of men and women, drifting relentlessly into the tentacles of secular humanism, won't be content with anything less than outright hedonism. Having crowded God out of their thinking, they're attempting to find happiness and peace of mind in pleasures, possessions, and power.

Meanwhile we Christians are falling down on the job. "In the midst of a generation where the world is screaming for answers," says a Dallas Seminary prof, "Christians are stuttering." Nevertheless God continues to draw out from many nations a bride for His beloved Son. It's heartening to learn that throngs of young people, disenchanted with parroting the jokes and songs of lewd celebrities, are earnestly seeking a better way of life. Thousands of Bible study groups are springing up here and there across America. Indeed these are exciting days for committed believers to be alive.

Along with other Christians characterized by conviction and caring, many MKs are bearing a good testimony for the Lord Jesus. Like a tiller of a small field, each is determined to greet Him sooner or later with the produce of a creditable life's work (Luke 12:35-38).

An MK of his times. The changing focus in missionary enterprise is introducing a different brand of missionary children. While the present type isn't a vanishing breed, the repressive posture of many governments in refusing visas for new and returning missionaries— thus cutting down on the number of MKs born abroad—is bringing into being a host of non-Waspy (see Index) missionary children. Thus in a sense today's MK is passing the baton to his counterpart of another nation. An African MK writes in the AIM magazine:

In the year 1950 the AIM founded a church in Kenya that
proved mature enough to send a missionary to work among the
Massai near the border of Tanzania. My father was the first
Kenya citizen missionary to go to the Massai. So I am an MK. I
call the AIM missionaries my grandparents. Now I am a third
year student at the Moffat College of Bible at Kijabe.

My heart is full of Massai ministry. My target is to serve with
this tribe the rest of my life. I feel I will fit in well in this
missionary field where my father has worked for so many years.

Thus foreign missions is no longer only the "white man's burden."
Already God has raised up more than 10,000 Third World
missionaries engaged in evangelism and church-planting. Black,
brown, and yellow workers, sponsored by national churches and
missionary societies (though some western missions recruit foreign
nationals on a par with other members), are moving into *their*
Jerusalem, Judea, Samaria, and remote areas. "The Lord has done
this, and it is marvelous in our eyes" (Matthew 21:42).

Acknowledging oneness and interdependence of all members of
Christ's body, Word-minded nationals welcome the fellowship and
gifted ministry of western missionaries whenever available.
Moreover, many countries keep their doors open to western workers.
Veritably then, fair-skinned MKs will brighten the foreign scene for a
long time to come. In this respect, two testimonies evince unusual
sidelights:

As an MK, I want my children to be MKs. I want them to
have all the joys, privileges and opportunities I had. And, yes,
to learn through such hardships as I had.*

There's nothing I would exchange for the privilege of being
an MK. It isn't a burden or drudgery. Recently someone else
expressed my feeling about being an MK: "If I ever needed an
ulterior motive for becoming a missionary, it would be to give
my children the opportunity of being MKs."*

Epilogue. More than ever before, it's precarious to theorize as to
what the next decade holds for any of us in regard to world
conditions. Yet it's a blessed privilege to be related to Him "who
works out everything in conformity with the purpose of his will"
(Ephesians 1:11). The measure in which the MK becomes "fuel
efficient" makes an immense difference in his quality of life and
productiveness as a child of God. Being conscious of being linked,
even in a minimal sense, with God's eternal purpose in Christ will
constrain him to live and move "for the praise of his glory" (v. 12).

Our sovereign God isn't passive with respect to the purpose of the ages; He is working ceaselessly and meaningfully toward having His beloved Son "vindicated and enthroned unto earth's remotest end, glorified, adored and owned" (as Frances Havergal's hymn has it).

MKs will have had a glimpse of the outworking of God's earthly plan—to reach all classes of people in hundreds of countries and thousands of languages with his message of redeeming grace in Christ, whereby increasing millions of renewed sinners ascribe praise to the Savior. Who then should be more responsive to God's revealed purposes than one reared in a missionary home—when he's conscious of who he is and whose he is.

Let us conclude our study of the MK and his times with a Bible passage which sets before each of us a becoming lifestyle in these last portentous years of the twentieth century:

> For the grace of God that brings salvation has appeared to all men. It teaches us to say "No" to ungodliness and worldly passions, and to live self-controlled, upright and godly lives in this present age, while we wait for the blessed hope—the glorious appearing of our great God and Savior, Jesus Christ, who gave himself for us to redeem us from all wickedness and to purify for himself a people that are his very own, eager to do what is good. (Titus 2:11-14).

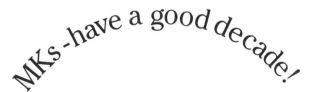

Appendix

In November, 1984, over 400 missionary leaders and educators convened in Manila, The Philippines, for the International Conference on MKs. Following the conference a Continuing Committee was organized to develop a network of research and information on the subject of Missionary Children. Plans are underway by the committee (chaired by Dave Pollock of Interaction, Inc.) to develop and publish a Compendium of the conference papers as well as a regular newsletter and/or a quarterly journal. For more information, and to "plug in" to the resources that will be available through the committee write:

Dave Pollock, Chairman
International Committee on MKs
c/o Interaction, Inc.
P.O. Box 2177
West Brattleboro, VT 05301

Other Resources

COLLEGE SHOCK Series
Grace P. Barnes and Raymond P. Rood, faculty members of Azusa Pacific University, California, have developed and are publishing a very helpful series of booklets titled COLLEGE SHOCK. The series addresses life's most significant transition time—the move from adolescence to adulthood generally framed by the college or university experience. The authors also conduct COLLEGE SHOCK seminars and workshops and will be glad to make arrangements when contacted. For more information write:

COLLEGE SHOCK
P.O. Box 1239
Glendora, California 91740

A WORKING "MK" BIBLIOGRAPHY, Steven Van Rooy, Dan Bowell, and David Hoffer, editors, EMIS. Lists books and materials published between 1908 and 1981. Available for $2.00 each.To order write to:

Evangelical Missions Information Service
P.O. Box 794
Wheaton, Illinois 60189

LINK CARE MISSIONS

Link Care is a support group organization dedicated to providing services to all Christians, but with a special emphasis on full-time Christian workers and missionaries. Included in their programs are a Candidate Assessment Program, a month-long Missions Insitute, Off-site Consultation, a Furlough Evaluation Program, a Re-Entry Program, *and* a M.K. program. The M.K. Program is based on the assumption that missionary kids are a vital part of effective missions and as a part of the healthy family unit they too must be prepared for effective cross-cultural living. An M.K. pre-field orientaton is designed to introduce children to the dynamics of leaving America and entry/living in a foreign culture. For more information about the complete Link Care Program write:

Link Care Missions
1734 W. Shaw Avenue
Fresno, CA 93711

NOTES

1. Lockerbie, D. Bruce. *Education of Missionaries' Children: The Neglected Dimension of World Mission.* Pasadena, CA: William Carey Library, 1977. In a personal letter, Mr. Lockerbie, headmaster of Stony Brook School, Stony Brook, New York, explains his position:

I'm sure that the difference in response between what I encountered regarding the term MK and what you have found may well lie in several overlapping factors, including such matters as *age/maturity* (I enquired only of teenagers still in their parents' homes or in mission schools; your enquiries appear to have been mostly conducted with older, college graduates); *self image/respect for parents' vocation* (many of the young people we encountered ten years ago seemed troubled by their parents' participation in alleged "colonization," and were therefore troubled by their own presence as seeming "imperialist" intruders, rather than seeing their parents as called by God to minister); and, finally, *the personal spiritual condition of the responding teenagers* (to an alarming degree, ten years ago, we found young people in stages of spiritual malaise at some schools, in outright rebellion at others).

Remember that I speak as someone who has worked with teenagers in a school for 27 years, and so I do not judge flippantly. The higher view of Scripture the teenager held, the greater his respect for his parents' work; the lower his view of the Bible's uniqueness, the greater his concern about the equal merits of Hindu or Muslim or Buddhist or pagan religion and the greater his disaffection for Christian missions.

2. *The New York Times,* February 21, 1981. Reprinted by permission.

3. Lockerbie, *Ibid.*

4. Stafford, Tim, *Leadership,* Winter, 1980. Used by permission.

5. MacDonald, Gordon. *The Effective Father.* Wheaton: Tyndale House Publishers, 1977. Used by permission.

6. *Moody Monthly,* October, 1977. Used by permission.
7. Hunt, Gladys, *Honey for a Child's Heart.* Grand Rapids: Zondervan Publishing Co., 1969. Used by permission.
8. "Who Dares Handle a Rebellious Child?" *Thrust,* June 1979. Used by permission of Worldwide Evangelization Crusade.
9. Schaeffer, Edith. *What Is a Family?* Old Tappan, NJ: Fleming F. Revell Co., 1975. Used by permission.
10. Used by permission of Radio Bible Class, Grand Rapids, Michigan.
11. Used by permission of Health-Tex Inc.
12. White, John. *Eros Defiled: The Christian & Sexual Sin.* Downers Grove, IL: InterVarsity Press, 1977. Used by permission.
13. Brashler, Peter J. *Change: My Thirty-five Years in Africa.* Wheaton: Tyndale House Publishers, 1978. Used by permission.
14. Cannon, Joseph L., *For Missionaries Only.* Grand Rapids: Baker Book House, 1969. Used by permission.
15. "Who Makes the Decisions in the Education of Missionary Children?" Used by permission of Wycliffe Bible Translators.
16. *In Other Words,* December, 1983. Wycliffe Bible Translators. Used by permission.
17. *SIM Now,* March/April, 1983. SIM International, Scarborough, Ontario, Canada. Used by permission.
18. *Evangelical Missions Quarterly,* April 1974. Used by permission.
19. Anderson, Ken. *Himalayan Heartbeat: A Biography of Dr. Geoffrey D. Lehmann.* Waco: Word Books, 1965. Used by permission.
20. *The Alliance Witness,* January, 1974. Used by permission.
21. Gordon-Smith, Mrs. E.L., *In His Time.* OMF Books, 1981. Used by permission.
22. *Pigtails, Petticoats and the Old School Tie,* OMF Books, 1981.
23. Drake, Julia M., *Christian Teacher,* September/October, 1976.
24. Lockerbie, *op. cit.* (Note 1).
25. *CAM Bulletin,* January, 1967. Used by permission of Central American Mission.
26. *Hymns II,* InterVarsity Christian Fellowship, USA, 1976. Used by permission.
27. Kriegbaum, Ward, in *Alumni* Magazine, Wheaton College, September/October, 1981. Used by permission.
28. *Christianity Today,* November 2, 1978. Used by permission.
29. *Moody Monthly,* March, 1974. Used by permission.
30. Used by permission of Wycliffe Bible Translators, Inc.
31. Guinness, Os, *In Two Minds.* Downers Grove, IL: InterVarsity Press, 1976. Used by permission.

32. *Moody Monthly,* June, 1976. Used by permission.
33. Kuhn, Isobel. *By Searching.* Chicago: Moody Press. Used by permission.
34. *The Alliance Witness,* January 21, 1981. Used by permission.
35. Cannon, Joseph L., *op. cit.* (Note 14).
36. Used by permission of Forbes, Inc., New York.
37. Excerpts from *Thrust,* January 1, 1983. Used by permission of Worldwide Evangelization Crusade.
38. *Christianity Today,* February 16, 1979. Used by permission.

Index of Abbreviations & Mission Periodicals Used in Study

AEF—Africa Evangelical Fellowship—*African Evangel, Pioneer*

AIM—Africa Inland Mission—*Inland Africa, AIM International*

BMMF—Bible and Medical Missionary Fellowship—*Link, Goal*

CAM—Central American Mission International—*CAM Bulletin*

C&MA—Christian and Missionary Alliance International—*The Alliance Witness*

CBFMS—Conservative Baptist Foreign Mission Society—*Impact*

IM—International Missions—*Eastern Challenge*

LAM—Latin America Mission—*Latin America Evangelist*

MAF—Missionary Aviation Fellowship—*Mission Aviation*

OMF—Overseas Missionary Fellowship—*East Asia Millions*

PK—Preacher's (Pastor's) Kid

RBMU—Regions Beyond Missionary Union—*Regions Beyond*

SAT—Scholastic Aptitude Test

SIM—Sudan Interior Mission—*SIM Now*

TEAM—The Evangelical Alliance Mission—*Horizons*

UFM International—*Lifeline*

WASP—White Anglo-Saxon Protestant

WBT—Wycliffe Bible Translators—*In Other Words*

WEC—Worldwide Evangelization Crusade International—*Worldwide Thrust*